SO-AEW-626

bare

bare

The Naked Truth about Stripping

Elisabeth Eaves

Seal Press

BARE: THE NAKED TRUTH ABOUT STRIPPING

Copyright © 2002, 2004 by Elisabeth Eaves

Published by
Seal Press
A member of the Perseus Books Group
1700 Fourth Street
Berkeley, CA 94710

First published by Alfred A. Knopf, a division of Random House, in 2002.

All rights reserved. No part of this book may be reproduced or transmitted in any form without written permission from the publisher, except by reviewers who may quote brief excerpts in connection with a review.

Cataloging-in-publication data has been applied for.

ISBN-10: 1-58005-121-9
ISBN-13: 978-1-58005-121-7

9 8 7 6 5

Cover Designed by Stewart Williams
Interior Designed by Justin Marler
Printed in the United States of America by Malloy
Distributed by Publishers Group West

Contents

A Note from the Author

To preserve anonymity, some names and identifying details have been changed.

*You must really begin to harden yourself
to the idea of being worth looking at.*

—Edmund to Fanny in *Mansfield Park*, by Jane Austen

I was naked.

I looked at my reflection in the dressing room mirror. At five minutes to the hour, I noticed faint sweat beads on my forehead. At four minutes to, I patted my face with beige powder. With three minutes to go, I remembered that I was supposed to punch in. I slipped my time card into the clock, which gripped it for a second, made a loud clunk, and let it go. At two minutes to the hour, I brushed my hair for the fifth time and stepped back into the black shoes that I had kicked aside.

When the clock ticked over to seven P.M., I was supposed to climb the three steps through the narrow bottleneck between the dressing room and the stage. I hesitated, and April, who had been having a smoke down the hall, materialized in the dressing room, liberated herself from a sarong and jean jacket, then strode past me and up the stairs without so much as a glance in the mirror. Venus came the other way, out of the bottleneck, and paused on the landing to punch out. *Clunk!* Even in my apprehension I admired the efficiency. Then Georgia came down the steps, a leggy brunette in a pearl necklace. She didn't punch out; it was her turn to take a break.

The clock was "on the zero," as the managers said, so with one last breath I mounted the stairs and entered a dazzling scarlet and silver womb. The stage was a rectangular room about the size and shape of a hallway in a modest suburban home. The floor was carpeted with red velvet, and every other surface, including the ceiling, was mirrored. The space was lit by hot theatrical lights covered with pink and red gels, giving the three women who were already in it a rosy glow. I joined them with the sense that I was stepping into a well-oiled machine.

Onstage were Sasha, a creamy-skinned redhead in black gloves and thigh-high boots; Satin, a tall, caramel-colored woman in a curly bobbed wig; and April, whose wavy blond hair cascaded to her thighs. And then there was me, Leila, five feet seven inches tall, in black knee-high stockings, my lips painted "plum wine" according to the label on the tube, my body pale, my blond hair shiny from multiple brushings. I was surprised to realize that I didn't look out of place. From a quick, sidelong glance at the mirror I could barely pick myself out of the group. I was just one of the naked women, and the anonymity was reassuring.

While the stage had only one entrance and exit, which I had just come through, it had twelve windows. Each window was covered with a mirrored screen when it was not in use. I heard the clink of coins hitting coins and then the low whirring sound of a lifting screen. I turned my head to where the sound was coming from and saw a man appearing on the other side of a pane of glass. First his waist, then his chest, and finally his face appeared as the mirror lifted away. He was white and middle-aged and wore a beige jacket. If he had disappeared a second later, I wouldn't have recalled a single detail of his appearance. He stared at me expectantly. I glanced around at the other dancers for guidance, but they were all looking elsewhere, so I approached the man, trying to exude confidence that I didn't feel.

I needn't have worried. I watched his eyes follow my different body parts as he decided where he wanted to settle them. He seemed to be a breast man. Closer to the window now, I looked down as he undid his pants. I danced for about two minutes, he came, the screen went down over the glass. *Whirrr.*

That was how my hours on the red stage began. It wasn't my very first time onstage; I had danced for about eight minutes during my audition. The only difference now was that I would do this for the next three hours. The strangest thing about it was that it wasn't very strange. I had never done this work before, but it felt like a fragment of a dream coming back to me. There was the music, and I was dancing to it; that wasn't new. There were the mirrored walls, much like a dance studio or a health club. And there were men watching me.

Always, it seemed, men had been watching me, assessing, surmising, deciding. Even the masturbating strangers weren't without precedent— I had run across public masturbators before. Once a taxi driver had done it in front of a friend and me, and we had yelled at him and made him stop. I felt onstage as though a combination of different experiences had been scrambled in a machine and come out as something familiar but new. My only fear was that three hours of this would make my legs ache.

Half of the windows were two-ways, through which I could see the customer on the other side. The rest, the one-ways, reflected my own image. The one-ways were easy, like dancing in front of a mirror at home. The two-ways were harder to get used to. I watched the men behind them watch me, and sometimes one of them looked up at my face, even up beyond my mouth, and made eye contact, and it was hard to say who was more disconcerted, him or me.

Through the two-ways I saw their heads bob and swivel, their attention flicker around the stage before alighting on a particular body. Most of them smiled, and some even tried to talk, but I couldn't hear them well and didn't much want to anyway. Some tried to communicate with facial and hand gestures, only some of which I could decipher. One made frantic licking motions, another did a miniature breaststroke intended to convey "spread your pussy."

"Just tell him you don't want to go swimming," called Georgia from across the stage. She was back from her ten-minute break, and now Satin had disappeared.

One guy pointed his finger in the air and circled his forearm, possibly asking me to turn around. My first instinct was to comply—I was in the habit of being accommodating when I was in a new job— but then I remembered that I didn't have to, and stopped midturn.

"You think you get to tell a naked lady what to do for a quarter?" Georgia asked a man in the corner booth.

The company of the other dancers, and Georgia's levity, put me at ease. For a while I became so absorbed in watching the other women that the men seemed incidental. I watched Sasha kiss a customer through the window, both of them touching the cold glass with their lips in a bizarre facsimile of affection. That proximity looked perilously intimate to me, even across the glass. It was like approaching a tethered pit bull: intimidating even if you knew it couldn't escape.

Even so, it wasn't until the first break in the music that I was hit with a vertiginous jolt. A silence of several seconds filled the stage, during which time we had to keep moving. When the quiet hit, I suddenly felt exposed. The comforting veil of sound had been ripped away and with it my pretense of dance. It was all I could do not to freeze. I felt ludicrous, but everyone else seemed indifferent. The customers continued their movements, supplicating with pursed lips and squinting eyes. The women kept dancing, their mirrored reflections tangling with my own, until, after an eternity, the next song came on. Before the end of my shift I had learned the trick of keeping a rhythm, any rhythm, playing inside my head.

My coworkers were politely friendly, neither gushing nor taciturn. They didn't talk much; the managers discouraged excessive talking onstage. Having worried that I might, somehow, have been different from these other women, I was relieved that they seemed to accept me right away. But I was also disappointed. I wanted acknowledgment, maybe even congratulations, for getting myself to this glass-walled room. When I told them it was my first day, I expected more of a response than I got, like maybe a knowing roll of the eyes, or a recollection of someone else's first time. But I was just another new girl in a profoundly egalitarian trade. The only reaction came from Sasha, who, leaning her upper body back against the mirrored wall, rolling her delicate white hips, and keeping her eyes leveled on the window in front of her, said softly, "Welcome to the fishbowl."

Almost a year after my first day at the Lusty Lady, a Seattle peep show, I left my job, my boyfriend of four years, and the city where I had lived on and off for seven years. I moved from Seattle to New York, went back to school, and later got a job as a reporter.

At first, after leaving, I talked about my short career as a stripper with a few carefully chosen acquaintances. Sometimes I enjoyed the unsettling effect the subject had, and sometimes I was eager to share a glimpse of what it was like. But I soon stopped mentioning it at all. It was an unnecessarily hazardous topic, likely to cause confusion or unwanted titillation. It was one of those things that others either got or didn't. There was a certain kind of woman, the kind I gravitated to, who would say, "Of course you did. I always wanted to myself." But I discovered that most people didn't understand, and that I was incapable of explaining. For many, it didn't seem to fit in with the more palatable pieces of history that I put on display, like a fortunate childhood or a college degree.

I have always been terrible at revealing anything of myself. I think I was drawn to journalism because I was shy about expressing myself and it offered a sort of refuge. I wanted to ask other people prying questions and then tell their tales. I might splay my name promiscuously across the top of a story, but it exposed others, not me. Journalism never called for me to say, "Here's what I think"; the most impassioned words I wrote always came out of the mouths of others. Somewhere behind my desire to be both a reporter and a stripper lay an impulse to conceal. Stripping—in competition with acting and espionage—is the ultimate job for someone who's instinct is to present different façades of who she might be. There is nothing more illusory than a woman pretending to be a sexual fantasy for money.

But though I went silent about my one-time job, stripping didn't go away. Certain things continued to vex me. One was the collection of facile stereotypes persistently applied to strippers. These ideas seemed so hackneyed as to be barely worth my irritation. Yet they did irritate me, always surprising me out of my wishful thinking when they turned out to be widely and deeply held. To name a few: Strippers are dumb. Abused. Desperate. Amoral. Sexually available. And one stereotype especially bothered me. A professor remarked to me that I had "gotten out" of stripping, while others had not. I had never considered it a job to escape. I thought it shouldn't be assumed that strippers lacked free will, or that they were trapped. I hadn't felt that way. Part of me even thought I might someday go back.

I also began to see echoes of stripping in my personal life. After quitting the Lusty Lady, I entered and then left relationships, all the while slightly bewildered at my own behavior. It had become a strange mix of submissiveness and aggression, and I often felt that I was watching myself play a role. It was a feeling I had often had as a dancer.

And three years after I left the Lusty Lady a question still hounded me. Why did I do it? It was an aggravating, unjust question. When it was put to me by others, I wanted to reply: "Why not? You tell me why you didn't, and I'll you why I did. You might as well ask me why I am the way I am. No one torments insurance salesmen or surgeons or data-entry clerks with questions of why, though I could think of a few I would like to ask: 'How can you telephone strangers all day? How do you stomach being up to your elbows in blood and guts? How do you keep from getting bored? How do you live with a job that gives you no passion, satisfies no curiosity, gives you no sense of higher purpose?'"

But there I was again, deflecting attention from myself. I had always preferred to shine a light anywhere but on me. But now I really wanted to know: Why had I felt driven to do it? How had it affected me? And what did the existence of strippers say about sexuality and society? Was stripping as seductive a dead end for the dancer as looking at her was for the viewer? Could it be said to be right or wrong?

With these questions in mind, I quit my job and went back to Seattle. I worked again as a naked girl. I looked up the women I had known from the Lusty Lady and put questions to them that others had put to me, far more comfortable pressing them for answers than dredging up any answers of my own. Eventually, though, with their help, I did.

I learned that no one is neutral about female bodies. If they aren't sex objects used to sell every conceivable good, they are political objects, causing bitter debate on how to manage their fecundity. And where not sexual or political, they are imbued with society's ideals and fears, turned into Miss Liberties, Virgin Marys, and Wicked Witches.

Everyone has an opinion on what to do about female bodies, and sometimes it feels as if the only people who get in trouble for holding such opinions are young women themselves.

Some of us, though, have to live in them, and we each get by in our own way.

Leila—Part I

Most plain girls are virtuous because of the scarcity of opportunity to be otherwise.

—Maya Angelou, *I Know Why the Caged Bird Sings*

I had a deep distaste for clothing as a child. The cloth always seemed to bunch up and constrain me, and I would shuck my garments at the slightest provocation. My favorite clothes were leotards, tights, and bathing suits, but if I could I'd wear nothing. My parents have a photo of me at six that they point to as an example of early exhibitionist tendencies. In it I'm seated at a piano, back to the camera, in my short boy's haircut and not a stitch of clothing. They say I jumped out of my bath and made straight for the piano, sat down, and started practicing my scales. They also tell me that when I came home from preschool and kindergarten in midwinter, I would change into a bathing suit for playtime. When we went to Europe when I was nine, I was delighted that all the girls my age still went topless on the beach, and I enthusiastically joined them. There is another photo of me standing next to my shell collection, wearing only a bikini bottom, at age ten or so, utterly flat-chested. When I showed the photo to a friend a few years later, she was shocked at my toplessness; and I thought to myself, What a prude.

At around the time of the shell photograph, my breasts began to make themselves known. They were introduced to me as a medical problem. A tiny lump appeared on my chest near my left nipple, and when I told my parents, they were alarmed and took me to the doctor. "Mammaries," he told us, laughing, and since then I've often wondered what he thought of us. Did other families take their daughters to see doctors because they were growing breasts, or was it just mine? Another lump soon appeared, but they were both so small, and grew so slowly, that we weren't forced to think about them again for a long time.

My parents didn't consider being pretty any kind of goal or virtue, and encouraged me neither to aspire to it nor to think that I was. Education was the thing, brains and hard work the path to whatever I might desire. Though for a while I coveted one, my mother banned Barbie dolls lest they give me ideas about what women were supposed to look like. Nevertheless, from somewhere I developed a strong wish to be pretty, a sharp awareness of people looking at me, and a deep curiosity about what they might think. I pleaded with my mother until, when I was thirteen, she bought me my first cosmetics and let me buy a fashion magazine for teenagers. I read the magazine word for word, taking to heart every article on what to wear on face and body. It and subsequent magazines presented both a challenge and a promise: If you execute all your grooming and shopping correctly, you will look good, and if you look good, others will think highly of you. For several years of high school, I took an average of two hours to get ready every morning, during which I painstakingly showered, washed, combed, dried, sprayed and painted, and usually tried on several outfits in front of the mirror. Only after this donning of armor did I feel I could be looked at without embarrassment.

Those were the eighties, the years of mesh, fluorescent ankle socks, and plastic shoes, and I followed every trend assiduously. This didn't make me fit in, since Moscrop Junior Secondary, in a suburb of Vancouver, was a mostly jeans-wearing school. I was surprised when I learned that kids my age smoked cigarettes, and that some girls got beat up by other girls in the nearby woods. These were kids with bigger things to worry about than clothes. But I loved my outfits, and in addition to the few new items my mother would spring for each season, I bought stacks of secondhand clothing to add to the mix. When I entered the tenth grade, my best friend, Kristin, and I started a competition to see who could go the longest without wearing the same exact outfit twice. Nonrepetition seemed a great virtue to me, more important than the quality of the outfits themselves. We both made it nearly two months, but I won.

I was much relieved when I successfully petitioned for contact lenses to replace my glasses. When I had to wear a metal retainer that protruded from my mouth and was held in place behind my neck, I was so mortified that I felt nauseated. I always removed it as soon as I arrived at school and was pained even by the risk of being seen in it between parental vehicle and school door. I strategized against every hazard to my appearance. Braces: I would keep my mouth shut. Zits: I would attack with chemicals. Straight hair: I would get a perm.

My mother had a mantra about looks that she repeated to me with increasing frequency as I became an adolescent. Cheekbones, lips, breasts, and thighs were all "accidents of nature" or "of bone structure." I was slim, long-legged, and, except during the permanent waves, had slippery blond hair. I had full lips and green eyes, and I grew to be five feet seven inches tall. My mother drove home the fact that I had done nothing to merit my looks. I think because she was a psychologist who worked with disabled children, she was acutely attuned to the spectrum of genetic accidents.

My parents expected excellent grades from my younger brother and me and punished mediocre ones. My father, a math professor, enforced a near-total ban on television for years—certain documentaries were allowed to slip through—but I could read anything I wanted to, and I checked out a stack of books every couple of weeks from the library. My life was a triangle of school, library, and extracurricular classes. Our parents lavished us with so many classes that I was sometimes busy every night of the week. Of choir, gymnastics, swimming, ice-skating, and ballet, the last became my favorite. I spent entire summers in mirrored ballet studios, hair pulled severely back, amid rows of girls in identical leotards. We studied our bodies in minute detail, comparing and disciplining, questing for perfection.

When I was thirteen or so, just before I plunged into full-blown self-consciousness, occasionally strangers started to talk to me for no reason that I could discern. This usually happened on buses or at bus stops, the only places where I was alone in public for any length of time, and my usual reaction was embarrassment for having drawn attention and annoyance that my daydreaming or reading had been interrupted. The first time a man tried to start a conversation with me at a bus stop, I was so abashed and disbelieving that at first I looked away and ignored him, as though he were an apparition I had created and could make disappear. When he didn't, I spoke to him haltingly, like trying to talk in a dream. He often took my bus, was only nineteen or twenty himself, and spoke about music and the car he planned to buy. Some months later a man with the lined face of an adult approached me on the bus. Though at first I thought, What a nuisance, I had no training in being rude and no cause to think it might be called for, so I talked with him. I told him I had a dance recital at a community center the next day, and he showed up. When I told my mother about the weird man, she questioned me with tense, controlled interest, and I said something like, "I don't know, he just started talking to me on the bus." I didn't understand his attention. I still thought of myself as invisible to the world of strangers and adults. But those safe walls were crumbling.

If my parents were overly worried about my body when I was ten, they seemed oblivious when I was fourteen, on a family trip to Turkey, at which time I wore braces and my breasts had come into their own. I was repeatedly pinched and groped by strange men. I was angry, mortified, and, on one occasion, very frightened, but if my parents were aware, they didn't let on. I wondered later how it couldn't have been obvious to them, but reasoned that no one wants to see their child as a sex object.

Within a year or so of that trip I started to put things together, beginning on a warm evening when I went to my school alone, by bus, for a rehearsal. The buses ran sporadically, so I had taken one that dropped me off about a mile away, at a station on a new suburban road surrounded by trees. The sun was starting to set, and there was no one at the stop. As the bus pulled away I broke into a jog because I was running late and wanted to get up to the school where my friends would be.

A carful of boys suddenly came careening around the bend, its revving engine and hollering occupants bursting into the dusk. As it passed a young man with shaggy hair bellowed out the window: "Fabulous set of tah-tahs, baby!"

I heard the crunch of a can hitting the ground, then the car was out of sight and the evening quiet again. I slowed to a walk and looked behind me, trying to fathom whom he was talking to, but there was no one else around. I realized, slowly, that it must have been me. I kept walking up toward the school, thinking about what he had said. I had never heard the term "tah-tahs" before. It sounded like a stupid, babyish word. I wished that he had used something more sophisticated, or at least more recognizable. But I knew instinctively what he was talking about. It struck me right away as ironic because that particular night, until the car went by, was one of the few occasions—perhaps because it was evening, or because I was only seeing a few friends—when I had not given a second thought to my looks.

Before then I had thought that effort or at least some sort of consciousness on my part might lead to sexual attention. Now I realized that I—my head, that is, my brain, my thoughts—had nothing to do with it. I looked down at my white turtleneck and pink jeans and saw my body in a new light. It was an object of interest to others that was entirely independent from who I was. And now my body became a new kind of object of interest to me. I had done nothing to achieve it. I couldn't escape it. Yet it had quite clearly made those boys—or were they grown men?—behave the way they had. I felt like a child who had been handed a heavy sword and told to learn how to use it before she cut off her foot. Some time after the car had gone by, once I had put this all together, I laughed with a mixture of flattered pride and disbelief.

The incident at the bus stop united my internal and external sexual worlds. I was familiar, after all, with sex, in the sense that you can be familiar with anything you read about in a book. I checked out the seamiest romance I could find at the library, and I had an illustrated tome called *The Facts of Love* that my parents had handed me with little comment. I thought about sex frequently, running through various things I had read and embellishing them with my own detail, and I masturbated often. But up until that day at the bus stop I had not connected what went on in my head with tangible experience. Having sex was a goal, but in the abstract, in the same way I thought I might someday be a lawyer. I had assumed there were many hurdles between me and it. I had not yet discerned the link between my private thoughts and the way others saw me. And then suddenly it became clear that there were no hurdles at all. Sex was there for the taking. It was up to me.

It was a revelation. I understood that boys were now sexually available to me. But just as this world of possibility opened up, other forces rushed in to shut it down. I started to become dimly aware of an unwritten sexual rule book. I was stunned when I discovered that boys and girls were expected to behave differently. It violated my sense of fair play.

In my tenth grade science class I had what I considered the misfortune of sitting near Tommy, a boy I had known since we were six years old. We had always gone to the same schools, and we had been actively cantankerous toward each other, on and off, for years. Now our large science tables, big enough for messy dissections, sat at right angles to each other. Back at our junior high school I had ignored him as one of the crowd that enjoyed role-playing games, but I no longer had that luxury. At our new high school he was one of the few students I knew. It was in science class, before our white-haired teacher shuffled in, that he first told me I was a slut.

"A what?" I asked. I had never heard the word. I asked him to explain.

"It's a girl who sleeps around," he said in an insinuating whine, realizing that his words would be ineffective if I didn't know what they meant.

I wasn't sure how I was supposed to take this. I looked around to see if anyone had heard him, but no one reacted. Tommy's voice was malicious, so clearly he meant to insult me. But I hadn't even had sex with one person. And beyond the fact that he was mistaken was a larger, more confusing issue: What would it matter to him if I had?

I puzzled over it that night and came up with what I thought was a good comeback, which I deployed the following day.

"You're the male equivalent of a slut," I told him. Equivalent. Hah.

"Yeah, well you *are* a slut," he replied.

I hadn't seen that coming. That day I asked around but couldn't find a comparable tag for boys.

Our classroom exchanges on sluttiness got progressively more heated. I was frustrated because the whole thing seemed so unprovoked. One day this nerdy kid was, if not my friend, at least a passive ally, and the next day I was under attack. My rage grew until one morning I took a swipe at his face. He shouted in pain, clutched both hands over his eye, and sat hunched over until our teacher doddered in in his lab coat. I had left two neat red scratches on Tommy's eyeball. He stopped calling me names.

I promised myself on my fifteenth birthday that I would have sex before the next one came around. I was curious and horny, but I also had a kind of grim determination about it. I had a growing sense that my virginity was best done away with. Tommy helped forge this view. So did my favorite novels, where I learned that some societies, past and present, had raised female virginity, terrifyingly, to a hallowed ideal. This was the bogeyman lurking under my bed when I was twelve, thirteen, fourteen: That I could have, might have, lived in a time when women were trapped by draconian expectation. I had a feeling that if I kept my virginity, it would become an awful responsibility. It would become *other people's business*. Being other people's business was my worst nightmare. If I got rid of it, on the other hand, it would be nobody's business but my own.

I succeeded, with my boyfriend at the time, a not-very-bright policeman's son who was handsome enough to resemble a certain movie star, which had seemed like as good a reason as any to go out with him. We did it at his parents' house while skipping a class. It was excruciatingly painful, which did nothing to dampen my resolve. I wanted the initiation chapter over and done with so that I could get on with the rest, whatever it turned out to be. When I got back to school that afternoon I told my best friend, Kristin, who had recently accomplished the same herself, and we hugged and jumped up and down in the hallway while students swarmed around us and lockers slammed. In the following years, when I met nineteen, twenty, and twenty-one-year-olds agonizing over first-time sex, I would congratulate myself again and again for having gotten it out of the way.

As sex improved with each episode I wanted to carve my initials on my boyfriend's torso in exultation. It became both a pleasure and a pastime, and I found it cleared my head of everything else for as long as it lasted. I could forget that I still had undone chemistry homework or a midnight curfew. And the boys—there were three more before I graduated from high school—were attentive and generous. They fascinated me with their mysterious bodies and behaviors. I felt, finally, that I was learning things about life that no book could tell me.

Sex also mitigated an asphyxiating boredom. I lived on a dead-end street on a hillside, where every house sat in the middle of its own private patch of green, with views of the water and the mountains. The street was surrounded for miles by detached houses and an occasional park or school. It took about an hour on city buses to get downtown, and I had no car. People in the neighborhood sometimes went out on foot to exercise or walk their dogs, but no one ever walked to an actual destination because there was nowhere to go. It was beautiful, peaceful, and the urban equivalent of a sensory deprivation chamber. School I had mastered; my family was predictable; and movies and malls, the main cultural attractions in our suburb, failed to entertain. Boys, though, were a world to be discovered. While I waited for my life to begin, I had sex.

In the eleventh grade Tommy and I had a biology class with the same bespectacled, late-arriving instructor from the year before. Now we shared a desk, but we had made peace and could look back on our tenth grade antics and laugh. We were older and wiser. I had a new boyfriend, and Tommy had mellowed with the discovery of alcohol. He queried me. "So have you, ah, sullied your cloak?" he asked with mock delicacy. We both laughed, and I didn't try to scratch his eyes out.

Tommy was just one of dozens of boys and girls in my high school who called a girl a slut, I noticed, when they wanted to drag her down. Like Dean, who telephoned me regularly. Our respective groups of friends didn't hang out together, and there seemed to be no real possibility of our actually dating, but our conversations were frequent and flirtatious. Then, like a punch in the gut, he called my house one day and said things about me to my parents. Sexual things. My parents wouldn't tell me exactly what, but they warned me to watch my behavior. I was outraged both with Dean, for getting me in trouble, and them, for concluding that I was the problem. What was I supposed to do, never talk to anyone? I stalked into my bedroom, slammed the door, and fumed. It wasn't only students anymore; even my parents had gone berserk. Aside from the Dean episode, their strictures on what I could wear had started to pile up: no tank tops, even though, as I often pointed out, other girls wore them all the time. No miniskirts. My father, confusingly, had told me I wasn't allowed to wear yellow nail polish. When the men's wear look—baggy pants, shirts, and neckties—was in fashion, when I was about fourteen, my father had banned that, too. He didn't like to see girls in boys' clothing, my mother explained. When it came to the miniskirts and tank tops, I always nodded and said all right, and sometimes I changed in a toilet stall when I got to school. My mother caught me coming home from school in a tank top one day and yelled at me about deceit.

In my mind my parents confirmed their status as insane on the day they thought I might have had sex in the house. My bedroom was directly under theirs, with a window at ground level. They woke me up early on a weekend morning by knocking loudly on my door and then marching in, both yelling at me before I was fully awake. They were in rages the likes of which I had never seen before, and it was a few minutes before I could make sense of what they were saying.

I put together what had happened after begging them to explain and making distraught phone calls to friends. A boy—I think my ex-boyfriend, the policeman's son, though I would never know for sure—had tried unsuccessfully to get my attention in the middle of the night by knocking on my window. My father had been awake and had seen him leave. My parents threatened to ground me. It was almost summertime, and I thought I would choke. I can't claim that I had been planning to tell my parents about my sex life, but, if I had been, their reaction to the boy at the window would have convinced me not to. I had to live with them for another year and thought I would surely suffocate if I got on their bad side. My plan was to lie low, get into a distant college, and escape.

The lessons of the window were clear: What you do with your body matters to us and everyone else. Appearances count just as much as actions, and we won't necessarily take you at your word. I felt as though they saw me as a shape-shifter. One minute I was a normal kid, the next a sexual monstrosity. All my parents' distrust of me seemed bound up in sex. My tits, my body, my lust seemed to throw up monumental barriers to their approval. I began to wear the loosest, grubbiest clothes I owned around the house, an effort at camouflage. I stopped showing any affection toward members of my family, or in front of my family—I was furious when a boyfriend gave me a big hug and kiss right in front of my mom. But these habits of dress and behavior, which persisted well into adulthood, were all I could do. I could no more eradicate my sexuality than cut off an arm. So I attempted just to keep it out of sight.

No one explained why my sex life mattered so much. My parents never addressed sex directly. In areas that they made clear were important to them—mainly good grades—I proved myself. Had I not felt I had much to lose by bringing up the subject, I would have said to them: "I'm not hurting anyone. I'm the last teenager in the world who would get knocked up or tied down." I was scrupulous about birth control—pills, foams, condoms, sponges, I dealt with them all. Kristin and I made regular, surreptitious visits to the local Planned Parenthood clinic, often in the company of our boyfriends, where the kind female doctors seemed to trust us. In exchange for whatever contraceptives we wanted, they demanded only that we submit to medical exams.

Sex became my single rebellion. I didn't want to smoke, and I rarely saw drugs. I came across alcohol sometimes but was left only with the impression that too much made people throw up. Failing at school was out of the question; it would just ruin my only chance to get away. But I wasn't seeking attention with my rebellion: I wanted the opposite, to hide. Somewhere between childhood and adolescence I had begun to wish fervently for more siblings so as to escape parental scrutiny, and this desire grew stronger with age. Sex was my precious private world, the one thing that I felt should have been mine and mine alone. When my right to it seemed under threat, I wanted more. It became fused in my head with notions of freedom.

My obsession with freedom meant it was easy not to get too wrapped up in any one boy. Attachment looked to me as though it led mainly to chores, as in the case of the cat I had wanted for my eleventh birthday. I fed her and emptied the kitty litter for the next seven years; she drooled and shed on my bed. The rewards were slim. Throughout high school I cleaned our house once a week to earn my allowance, swearing through every second of mopping and toilet scrubbing that I would hire someone to do my cleaning the instant I could afford it. Caring for something led to mess and blame; attachment, I was sure, led in a long but direct line to vacuuming. Feeding, cleaning, and responsibility were what went on in households, and I wanted to run as far from them as possible.

I strove for independence. Though my ambitions varied daily, they always included great success in whatever career I chose, and I was positive that they would take me away from Vancouver. Getting attached, I was sure, would only hold me back. This may have been why, with every boy I dated for any length of time, no matter how sweet he was, no matter how kind or fascinating, at some point I felt as if a time bomb went off inside of me. When it did, I had to end the relationship right then and there. The need was absolute.

I had this notion until my teens that my body was my own. How to clothe it, how to gratify it, whether to impregnate it—I had believed these to be matters of personal choice. And I had a notion that the rules of society should be applied fairly to all. With the discovery of a sexual morality especially for girls, equality suddenly seemed to have been an idea meant to go the way of Santa Claus. My shock and anger would have been difficult to overstate.

Chapter 2

The power was exhilarating.

Being young, female, and attractive was one long bout of intoxication, with all the dizzy pleasure and vulnerability the word implies. In the careening, can't-get-off, sex-saturated roller-coaster from puberty to adulthood, I discovered I could hold sway over boys and men. They did things for me. It started small, in high school. They drove me around in their cars, bought little things like flowers and meals, and went out of their way for me. In college came more of the same, with the amount of time and money spent gradually increasing. Their gifts and their flattery became a desirability score card, and a constant stroking of my ego.

I tested the limits of my power, seeing how much I could get for how little attention returned. How many times would he call before giving up? How many times could I piss him off and still have him come back? I lined up three dates in an evening, just because I could. I walked out of restaurants on a whim, just because I could. When I was in need of a ride, I had boys drive me to other cities, just because they would. I was never surprised when other young women toyed with exploiting this power; I was surprised when they didn't. It was an irresistible muscle flexing.

I was always a little disappointed when my expectations were confirmed. I was disappointed when the boy telling me tearfully about his faraway girlfriend tried to touch my breasts. I was disappointed when a professor took a more-than-academic interest, and when someone said "just friends" but meant something else. I was disappointed because I held out a small hope that men would turn out to be more complex, that there was something more complicated and interesting about them than what appeared to be a simple penis-to-behavior equation. But my disappointment was mild compared to the satisfaction I took in having my worldview confirmed. I took comfort in the knowledge that while I may have been out a friend, or a respectable older acquaintance, at least I was in control.

When I became bored with men seeking my attention, I tried asking other men out, and the subsequent rebuffs I took gave me a new respect for them. They were stuck doing so much of the chasing and taking so much rejection; it had to be difficult. But if one man turned me down, I bolstered my confidence with another. And when my advances worked, they worked too well. There was no chase. Men were too easy. They were a foregone conclusion. For a while it seemed as though an entire half of the world could be gotten at sexually. It was a heady feeling.

Few of these hovering males actually knew me very well. They may have known a few choice pieces of information that I had chosen to dispense, but for the most part they understood nothing about me. Therefore, I could only trace their eagerness to my body. However much they might come to learn about me, whatever qualities they might imagine I had, I thought it was all extrapolated from the starting point of my looks.

Being a young woman induces such a high because of the sheer absurdity of reaction to oneself. Men's responses struck me as absurd because, even as I thrived on them, I never completely escaped the knowledge that my body was ordinary. It was that accident of nature my mother had talked about. It was one of some three billion female bodies in the world, an eating, sleeping, mundane bunch of cells. It was hard to constantly regard it as a big deal, and the only reason it was one, the only reason it was anything other than the comfortable thing that I lived in, was because of the way people looked at it. I imagined a world with no clothing, mirrors, or photographs, and I wondered if my body would be such a big deal then.

In a sense I had two bodies. There was the one that I lived with, that had senses, hungers, and a connection to my brain. Then there was another entity, separate from myself, that I could look at as the object others held it to be. This disassociation was essential, because the meanings ascribed to my body were simply too arbitrary, and had too little to do with me, to be taken seriously. That people might think they knew something about me because of the color of my hair, the size of my chest, or the length of my legs was ridiculous, yet they did it all the time. And it wasn't even as though my body told everyone the same thing. It might cause one person to think I was stupid, another to think I was sexually available, and another to go all gooey and worshipful. It was a blank slate for the projections of others.

Somewhere between the ages of fifteen and twenty-five I developed a split personality, fashion-wise. I had no style of my own but was dependent on my environment. Sometimes I wore outlandish things—up to here and down to there, tight and bright—but my sense of propriety could be acute. At office jobs, or faced with anyone I hoped would take me seriously, I erred on the conservative side, always adding layers to obscure my contours. If I was traveling, especially alone, I draped myself in fabric. Invisibility was a relief. I developed an affinity for overalls and silent, uncommunicative black. Through clothing I achieved some control over when and how people looked at me.

As well as connecting sexuality with power, because it made men do things for me, I learned to associate it with fear. At first this came from my parents, with admonitions not to walk under a certain bridge, or not to wait at a particular bus stop after dark. My father gave me an infuriating piece of advice that I didn't follow: It wasn't safe for me to bounce from place to place, on buses and trains, alone. And then there were the men themselves, the ones I was supposed to fear. The first time I had been catcalled from the veering car I had been flattered after my initial shock. As I continued to get that kind of attention I began to feel vaguely threatened. Sometimes the comments seemed designed to scare—"Wanna fuck?" growled from behind a Dumpster, or a driver slowing his car and asking me if I wanted a ride. And sometimes I doubted they were meant to scare. They were just men, I told myself, trying to make themselves known. But still, every time I heard one, I did a quick mental check. Were there people around? How far was I from home? How far from a telephone? In general, I believed that whatever strangers said, they wouldn't actually *do* anything. Occasionally, though, some small incident would shake my confidence. A man followed me out of a restaurant and down an empty street, and he kept turning, when I did, until I entered a hotel. Another time a man mumbling obscenities in an elevator lunged and grabbed me—fortunately just before the doors opened. In general, though, I was more annoyed than frightened by commenting men. I developed an ability to tune them out. I learned not to turn when I heard a honk, a whistle, or the "ts-ts-ts" noise that some of them made. Walking most places alone meant putting on a sort of mental armor. I learned to behave: I never wandered too slowly looking lost, even if I was, because it drew attention and invited conversation. I walked purposefully. I kept my gaze straight ahead and slightly down so as not to make eye contact. And above all, I tried not to hear what they said.

I was slow to lose my belief in the infallibility of grown-ups. Fooling around with other kids felt like a natural course of events. But I was surprised when older, married men began to make passes at me, breaking a code of seriousness I still expected from adults. I met the first one at the stock brokerage firm where I worked the summer before starting college, when I was seventeen. At the end of an office party he tried to kiss me repeatedly while his pregnant wife waited for him not twenty feet away. He deliberately got my lipstick on his collar and complained loudly about it, satisfying some marital dynamic I couldn't understand. A year later at my next summer job, when I was a nanny, there hovered a man old enough to be my grandfather, a friend of the family I worked for. He followed me into the water from a crowded beach, grabbed me, and tried to feel me up behind an anchored rowboat with all the finesse of a horny fourteen-year-old. I laughed—at him, at the absurdity—and swam away.

There were others, and their sagging flesh and settled ways didn't interest me the way smooth-chested boys did. But they stoked my view that sexual morality was a giant hypocrisy, as I marveled at the gap between what they said and did. Marriage was a sham, I concluded, and making women responsible for chastity was clearly some kind of hoax. It was a joke, and someone was going to deliver the punch line soon. Weren't they?

I waited.

But it wasn't just men buying into the scam. I arrived at the University of Washington, a three-hour drive from Vancouver, and moved into a sorority house. The mansions of the Greek system filled a network of leafy blocks just north of campus. My mother was disappointed to learn that sororities didn't have curfews anymore like they did when she was in college. But she shouldn't have worried, because they had subtler ways of keeping us in line.

Girls walking home in the morning were said to be making "the walk of shame," a term used readily, to my horror, by the girls themselves. Shame, I thought, as it related to sex, was nothing more than a transference of responsibility. It was childish excuse-making. Boys and girls, I wanted to say, have sex if you want to and don't if you don't, but then don't whine about doing it and wishing you hadn't.

Fraternities permitted the consumption of alcohol, whereas sororities did not. Guys could have girls over to fraternity houses any time of the day or night, but girls could have guys over only under heavy restrictions. In my sorority we could invite boys to our rooms only on Tuesday evenings from seven to ten, and most girls had three or four roommates. The upshot was that boys never made the walk of shame. The rules of the Greek system upheld an intricate web of double standards. Sororities had to have a resident "house mother," a supervising adult; the fraternities had no equivalent. When I asked other sorority girls about this rule, they told me that a house mother was required to get around an old law that classified a group of women living together as a brothel.

If I thought I couldn't have been more disgusted, I was soon to be proven wrong. Sandra, a senior at the university and a sorority officer, lectured us one night in a chapter meeting to be "aware of our reputations." She mentioned seeing certain sisters (she didn't want to name names) entering the house at dawn, their hair disheveled. It was one of those subjects about which people were never very specific yet everyone was expected to know what they meant. And I did, of course, even though I didn't want to. Be "aware of your reputation" meant stop having sex, stop failing to be ashamed, or at the very least, please lie. A few nights later I bumped into Sandra in the stairwell after midnight, minding her reputation while she furtively escorted out a boy. I ranted about the double standard to my freshman roommate. Why did Sandra say one thing and do the other? Why did she have to go through this charade when fraternity boys, her equals in age and education, did not? My roommate agreed that it was unfair but told me I wasn't properly socialized. She was right. How had this happened? What was wrong with me that I should have developed such a sense of entitlement?

My failure to be properly socialized, I think, started young. When I was six years old, my grandmother gave me a children's Bible, which my father read to me every night until we had finished it several times over. He began: "God saw that it was good and she separated the light from the darkness." Right through, he replaced "he" with "she," and this all-powerful creature became entrenched in my mind as a woman. Other adults disabused me of this notion, of course, but maybe it was never really pried loose.

I moved out of my sorority in the middle of my sophomore year.

I had steady boyfriends. I dated one of them faithfully for the entire twelfth grade, a lifetime in high school years. But it wasn't until Alex that I fell in love, and then only years after we first met. When I was sixteen and he was seventeen, Alex and I had met on an airplane. We were on separate trips with our respective schools, and after flirting at the back of the plane for an hour, we didn't see each other until he called me after my return. He took me to his senior prom and then, shortly after graduating, went away to travel. He sent me letters on ultralight paper with no return address, mailed from somewhere different each time. When I was a freshman in college, he returned to Vancouver with longer hair and darker skin, as though now visibly marked older and wiser. I visited him there, and he visited me in

Seattle. He told me about his year of backpacking and odd jobs, and we talked together wildly about all the places we wanted to go. In some ways my surprising, unprecedented feelings for him changed everything. I didn't want to play with him to see how he reacted, I didn't want to manipulate him, and it was important to me not to hurt him. I did want to have sex with him, and he made me wait a long time. When we finally did, he always insisted that we both be entirely naked, as though this were somehow more honest. I was ever so slightly disappointed by this. I was turned on by the slow removal of layers of clothing, or by sometimes leaving a skirt or a bra in place. I resigned myself—I was in love. We had all-nude sex.

My feelings for him had little effect on the rest of my life, because I went away the next summer, and after I came back he left again, and it went on that way. While we were apart I continued as I had before, sometimes remaining celibate for a few months but often seeing different men. I tended not to have one-night stands but to date one person for at least a month or two. Alex mailed me pebbles from a Mediterranean beach and told me to put them in water so that they would look like they had when he found them. I brought him mementos from wherever I went. While we were thinking of each other and writing to each other, I didn't expect him to be sexually faithful either. It was as though we had silently agreed that we had no right to make that sort of claim on each other. I never questioned this at the time. When we finally moved within closer range of each other—about a four-hour drive apart—we became monogamous, also without discussion. It was as though the subject were taboo.

We had little in common other than a restless love of travel. He wanted to work in outdoor seasonal jobs; I wanted to finish university and maybe live in a big city. He liked dangerous sports; I liked to read. It became a struggle to find things to say to each other, but when he eventually told me that he had fallen out of love, I crumpled with the pain. By rights my heart should have broken, but I was so stubborn that it seemed to flatten instead. While I reeled, I met Erik.

I had gone to a party of ten or so people in a cozy living room strewn with mattresses, where we all took Ecstasy. It was my second time on the drug. A friend introduced me to Erik, and with our psyches well lubed by the E, he and I spent the night talking and staring at each other in platonic admiration. His girlfriend moved out of their house-boat the next day. He cajoled my phone number out of a mutual friend and called me a week later, and we talked for hours. On our first date, I looked at him across the table and wanted desperately to be high with him again, to experience a repeat of that illusory euphoria.

He was six foot four, with broad shoulders and cheekbones. His hair was like Alex's, only wilder, a tangled blond mane like a force of nature, unruly even when he tried to tie it back. He worked with his huge hands, moving from one building job to another, becoming deeply attached to each house. He had been a varsity rower at the University of Washington, where he studied architecture and engineering before dropping out. Some of his friends called him the sun god—he was huge, haloed, and gave one an impression of invincibility.

One of the first things Erik told me about himself was that he had an addictive personality; a second thing was that he was manic-depressive but would never take drugs for it. I wasn't sure what manic-depressive was and thought maybe he was just giving moodiness a clinical-sounding name. We spent night after night talking and sleep-ing on the floor of his old houseboat. We burned things—wood in his heating stove, candles, incense. He came down with a fever and soaked everything with sweat, and I continued to sleep beside him. Without planning to, we waited to have sex—not years, as had passed with Alex, but months. It was the spring of my senior year, and I was headed to Pakistan that summer for a foreign service internship. As easily as some men decide to go buy cigarettes, Erik decided to visit me in Karachi. We returned to Seattle together at the end of the sum-mer, and he stayed with my housemates and me. We said it was just while he looked for a place to live, but he didn't look much, and I didn't push him, and we decided we would live together for real. We bought a house and said we would get married. We fought, had sex, bought groceries.

I struggled with the idea of monogamy. I knew that it was required of me now, but I didn't know if I was up to it. Kristin and I had always said to each other, as though joking boastfully, that we could never be sexually faithful. But these conversations always had a worried, serious undertone. What if we really were incapable of it? What would it mean for our futures? I told myself that Erik might be the last man I ever slept with. The idea overwhelmed me, as though I were a recovering alcoholic telling myself that I would never, ever have another drink. It wasn't that I found it difficult to be faithful day to day. But I was tormented by the idea of losing an essential part of myself, my sexual freedom.

There was one thing, though, that I liked about monogamy. It was liberating in that it freed me from all the other men I might be with. I missed the excitement of always having someone new, but I felt calmer and more able to devote my attention to other things. And I was freed, most of the time, from being commented on in the street. Strangers only rarely whistled or said "ts-ts-ts" or tried to start conversations with women who were accompanied by men. I hated to admit that I was more relaxed beside a man—it violated my independent self image. But I was. I didn't have to wear the armor. I didn't have to concentrate on looking purposeful and pretending not to hear. I could wander aimlessly or loiter on street corners. I could even wear skimpy clothes to walk down the street. It took one man to make me feel safe from the others. Knowing this made me angry with myself for being weak, and angry with Erik because I felt dependent on him.

I was split. I found it hard to imagine life without Erik, but at the same time I felt trapped. I had once had the exhilarating sense that I could go anywhere and be anything, and now my horizons had narrowed to a pinpoint: Seattle. Erik. Our house. After graduating I had taken an office job with a shipping company, and as my salary slowly filled my bank account, I mentally divided the balance into travel expenses—so much for a plane ticket, so much to live on for X number of months. Almost two years after moving in with Erik, the part of me that had never fully acquiesced to the plan, that had hoarded ambitions and dreams against an onslaught of domestic bliss, rebelled. I quit my job and left the country. I called and said that I wasn't coming home and no longer wished to marry. The morning after I made the call I felt the beginning of an exquisite and long-lasting rush. The pinpoint my life had become expanded back out to a panorama.

But Erik's life and mine were messily intertwined. We jointly owned a house and had a mountain of debt. And he wanted very much to get me back. Some six months after the phone call we reunited in New Zealand, where we got jobs and a basement flat. I felt like a kite that had been reeled back in. Erik and I made peace, but it was different than before. Then, it seemed, I had opened my entire soul to him and lost myself. I had needed him so much that every small insult or argument had felt like an overwhelming threat. This time I guarded my secret urges in a small, hard core. They weren't sexual—after our hiatus, during which we dated other people, we went back to monogamy. My dreams, again, were about escape.

Chapter 3

In 1996 Erik and I arrived back in Seattle with no money or jobs. We both talked about big plans. Erik's involved single-handedly turning our old, charmless house into a thing of beauty. Mine involved graduate school and a departure from Seattle. At first we talked vaguely about a future together, and sometimes we spoke as though he would follow me when I moved away. We no longer talked about marriage. I told him that the delicate heirloom he had given me as an engagement ring was too fragile to wear, and I stored it in a cupboard. The days got wetter and shorter, and winter loomed ahead.

Erik and I were both legally responsible for the money we had borrowed to buy the house. Neither of us was willing or able to pay the mortgage on our own, neither of us could buy out the other, and any failure to pay would result in a permanently ruined credit rating for both of us. It was frightening to think that I could have destroyed my financial prospects by the age of twenty-five. We were forced to cooperate, because the only person who had the power to release either of us from the obligation was the other.

My mistakes had now forced me to wear a mask. For the sake of my future I had to keep the peace, even though I was furious inside at my situation. It would have been impossible for us to buy the house without money my parents had contributed, and for this I harbored a secret, unreasonable anger toward them, too. They had wanted me to settle near home and get married, I told myself. I toyed with the absurd notion that they and Erik had conspired.

Erik and I got along. We still cared for each other; we were still affectionate. But we never talked about the glaring fact that we would not have been back in each other's arms if it weren't for our debt. For the first time in my life I had let myself be bought. Now I had to live behind a façade. I had to pretend, at least at first, that there was a possibility I would stay. If I was extremely careful, watching everything I said and did, I thought I could gently pry myself out of the situation and part with Erik as friends. But any premature move, any storming out in a rage, and I risked either hurting or angering him enough that he would make a resolution impossible.

I didn't apply for permanent jobs because to do so would have been to admit to myself that I might stay. I signed up with a temp agency for office jobs that paid a high hourly wage without long commitments. I wrote away for brochures from the schools I wanted to attend. And I started working, part-time and for free, in an internship. This particular one was for a nonprofit organization called the Global Affairs Council; I hoped that my job there, which consisted mainly of stuffing envelopes and making name tags, would help me get into graduate school.

My temp jobs paid ten or twelve dollars an hour and were uniformly undemanding. In the worst jobs I had to keep up the pretense of looking busy when there was virtually nothing to do. In one typical job, I was required to sit at the reception desk of a silent, carpeted, twenty-fifth-floor holding company that had only seven or eight employees, who would pass me on their way in and then disappear into vast offices with tall windows. My job was to answer the phone and greet visitors, but the phone barely rang and there were no visitors; on one occasion someone had me type a letter. The man who appeared to be in charge praised me for my skills. In another job, for a windowless actuarial firm, I kept a copy of a book about climbing Mount Everest in my desk drawer, and I read for long stretches between tasks. Nothing, though, was worse than filing, which I did for a construction company in a Bellevue office park. I filed in a small, pale-walled box of a room lined with metal cabinets, sometimes for an hour or more at a stretch, placing manila folders between more manila folders like a robot. Without stimuli my thoughts turned inward, and I wondered if I could actually feel my brain atrophying. I marveled at all the time I had spent in my life cramming facts into my head, and I thought that if I filed for very long all that would have gone to waste. I thought about which directions the freeways went that led away from the office park and wondered how long I could stand working there.

I worked half days at the construction company starting every morning at eight A.M., and I joined a gym near the office. The gym saved me from spending the entire day sitting still, in my car and at desks. If I rose at five-thirty, I could beat bumper-to-bumper bridge traffic, work out, and arrive at the office just in time, at daybreak. At midday, three days a week, I drove back across the bridge to the Global Affairs Council office, downtown, where I spent the afternoon. In the afternoons I had off I studied for the Graduate Record Exam, the standardized test most schools required. Erik spent his days sketching drawings of our future home, or pacing off the property, lost in thought, smoking cigarettes and joints. On weekends I helped him tear into the house. We emptied the basement of the ancient furniture the previous owners had left. I attacked walls with a crowbar, watching with satisfaction as rotting two-by-fours whined and broke and Sheetrock crumbled under my blows. Wearing thick canvas gloves, I piled Erik's pickup truck high with load after load of wreckage and drove it to the dump. It was satisfying work. We left the upstairs, where we lived, mostly untouched, though in a fit of visualization Erik ripped out the wall between the kitchen and living room. He left its guts of insulation and wiring hanging in the air.

The construction company offered me a permanent job, which I declined. By that time I had found another source of income that would pay me more and bore me less. Though in the end it just came down to answering an ad in the newspaper; my interest in stripping was nothing new.

My natural inclination had been to wear sex on my sleeve. To an extent, through high school and college, I did—I had sex, talked about sex, sometimes wore sexy clothes, and tried to seduce people I didn't even want to have sex with, just to see if I could. But I was always aware of the stifling pressure to conform that I had felt from my parents, my peers, and my sorority's rules. The only women who seemed to be free of the rules were prostitutes and strippers, which I think is why they fascinated me. In high school Kristin and I sometimes cruised the downtown streets where the hookers worked. When we spotted them, we checked out their bright outfits, decided whether they were male or female under their tight skirts, and drove on by, sometimes returning to make another pass. When we were about eighteen, the same curiosity drove us to visit the Marble Arch, a Vancouver strip club, with our dubious boyfriends in tow.

When I saw the first woman descend the staircase from the ceiling to the stage and, under a spotlight, piece by piece, shed her glittering clothes while the audience clapped and cheered, I was spellbound. Strippers were free of the straitjacket. They were not only permitted to be ostentatiously sexual, they were celebrated for it. No one, I was sure, told them that their skirts were too short or that they should be aware of their reputations. They weren't insulted for being sensual and lascivious. Instead they were applauded, glorified—even paid, which seemed, with all the other pluses, almost incidental.

By the time the dancer climbed back up the stairs, now wearing only her heels, trailing her sparkling dress in one hand, the ancient-sounding phrase "women's liberation" had started to mean something to me. It had never resonated in terms of the laws I lived under or the careers I might choose, because I took that kind of freedom for granted. It was only in terms of sexual expectation that I sometimes felt smothered. And the glowing, strutting women in front of me, I thought, were free.

That weekend I was home from university visiting my parents. The next day I had just set the table for supper, and I was leaning against the white-tiled counter while my mom cooked. Our dog buried his head in his dish, heat radiated from the stove top, and my dad poured drinks. My brother, who was in the ninth grade, was in his bedroom studying. None of us were used to the fact of my living away. I savored my newfound freedom even more here at home than I did away at school, like an ex-convict dancing in front of the jailhouse. My parents had suggested a midnight curfew during my visits home, and I no longer even minded their rules. Now that I had escaped, what had once seemed oppressive struck me as quaint. I felt exuberant and untouchable.

"I'm thinking about becoming a stripper," I said. My parents didn't react for a couple of seconds.

"You're not," my mother said, stirring vigorously.

"Yes, I am," I said. Still no answer. "What's so wrong?"

My dad inhaled and exhaled through his nose like he wasn't sure whether to laugh or be angry. He decided to laugh. "Ten years of ballet for this?" he asked.

He concluded that I couldn't be serious, but my mom decided to address the subject. She told me it was dangerous, that I would have to associate with drug dealers and other criminals and cross dark parking lots late at night. She noted that several strippers and prostitutes had been murdered recently in Vancouver.

"She's just trying to get a reaction," my dad told my mom. He was only half right. I was trying to get a reaction. But I also genuinely wanted to hear arguments against stripping, because I had forgotten what they were. "Go get your brother," my dad said, closing the subject. I called him, and we ate dinner.

The summer after my sophomore year of college I came home to save money to go to Egypt, where I was going to spend my junior year. My parents and I agreed that I should contribute as much money as I could. I hated looking for summer jobs, but with Egypt beckoning, I threw myself into the process. I scanned help-wanted ads, filled out applications, and continuously came up underqualified. I had been a salesgirl in a clothing store one summer during high school and had disliked it intensely. I hated selling, hated pushing miniskirts and leather jackets on uncertain buyers, hated the sterile shopping mall. I had stood around in the store all day, legs aching, never pouncing on the customers like I was supposed to to earn my commission. I preferred to tag clothing or vacuum.

I crossed sales off my list of potential summer jobs, but unfortunately I didn't have any other skills that paid. I didn't know how to waitress, tend bar, or make espresso. I applied anywhere that would let me fill out a form, including a gas station. I lied to employers and told them I would be around for longer than just the summer. In the end I landed three jobs: as a rental clerk in a video store, as a waitress in an Irish pub, and as a nude model for art classes.

The art classes paid the most, at ten dollars an hour. I worked for a pleasant couple who had just opened an airy studio in cobblestoned Gas Town, where they taught drawing and painting. Their students were all polite, sketching quietly while I watched drawing after drawing appear in broad strokes. These takes on my body seemed to have little to do with me. I was just a starting point, a tool like their easels and paints. Between sessions I put on a satin bathrobe and ate tea and biscuits. Despite the air of civility, I was nervous about telling my parents. I mentioned it to them in the kitchen one night before dinner.

"Art modeling?" my mother asked. "Is it nude?"

I paused.

"Uh, yes."

"Oh."

They were unruffled. They asked questions about the artists and the owners.

"Do you remember that photo we have of her at the piano bench?" my dad asked.

That summer, while I wasn't working at one of my three jobs, commuting, or reading about Egypt, I sewed myself two long, loose cotton dresses to wear when I got there. I bought long skirts, big shirts, and baggy trousers, all in pursuit of appropriate modesty, and I saved just enough money to cover my airfare.

At the beginning of my senior year of college, back from Egypt, I moved into a loft on Pioneer Square in Seattle with two former sorority sisters. After we moved in and I settled into my classes, I scanned newspaper ads for a part-time job. A chain of clubs was recruiting dancers—topless, it said—through an ad in the student newspaper. I called and made an appointment. I told myself I didn't have to go through with it if I didn't like it. I would just check it out.

I went to an office billing itself as a modeling agency, where I was interviewed by a fortyish woman with brittle platinum hair and pink lipstick, who told me she had always wanted to be a dancer when she was growing up. She said she started her girls at Razzmatazz, a club near the Seattle Center, which was popular after sporting events. After they gained experience she moved her girls to the Déjà Vu clubs, of which there were several around the city. At Razzmatazz, she told me, dancers performed topless.

A club manager came in to look me over. I said to him, "So it's topless, right?"

"Oh no. You're completely naked in there," he said. I looked back at the woman. She flushed and stumbled over her words.

"Why, I spend so much time in those places I don't even notice what they're wearing anymore."

She explained that, as a dancer, I would be an independent contractor and would pay rent, or a "house fee," of seventy dollars for each shift that I worked. I would work it off by getting customers to buy five-dollar soft drinks—alcohol is illegal in strip clubs in Washington—and by selling table dances for ten dollars a dance. After the first seventy dollars, the money I earned would be mine, except that I was expected to tip the disc jockey and the bartenders. I couldn't get a fix on how much I was actually likely to make. She said it would be about forty dollars an hour.

My interest was already waning when she started explaining to me that they could help arrange a place for me to live, and that the rent would be taken directly out of my pay.

"What?" I asked, snapping to attention.

Two young women arrived, whom she introduced as her "girls." Though she had insisted on seeing my proof of age, these two didn't look a day over fifteen. They were both pale, blond, and slightly built. They wore clumsily applied blue and purple eye shadow. I was reminded of myself playing dress up as a little girl.

I suddenly imagined young girls being conscripted from Interstate 5 farm towns, lured to the city with promises of big money, housed in shabby apartments, gouged on rent, lied to, and made to hustle for table dances. I couldn't hawk dances. I wasn't cut out for sales. I said I would have to think about it, left, and never called back.

I enjoyed dancing, being sexy was already something of a hobby, and I certainly wanted cash, mainly to finance future plane tickets. It seemed like such an easy equation on the surface. But this stiff woman and her waifish protégés struck me as sinister, and I was forced to admit to myself that my fascination was just that and nothing more. I was kidding myself if I thought I was going to work as a stripper. I was dipping my toe in the deep end when I knew I was afraid to jump. I had been intrigued, I had investigated, and I was done.

Erik and I had been living together for over a year when I suggested on Valentine's Day that we go to a strip club. I had been to one other since the Marble Arch, again with Kristin, driven by the same curiosity that had impelled me the first time. Erik had never been to one, and he found the notion bizarre but came along to humor me. We went to one of the Déjà Vu chain, downtown on First and Pike. We paid the ten-dollar cover charge and five dollars each for soft drinks. We sat against the back wall in an upholstered booth, where I felt as if I could watch without being seen. A dancer appeared onstage in high heels and a pink bikini bathing suit. The disembodied voice of the disc jockey introduced her and she danced, first removing her top, then bottom. After two songs, she put her bikini back on and circulated through the sparse audience while another dancer took her place onstage.

Four dancers were working in all, rotating in turn from stage to audience. One was obese, one young and blond, one an athletic brunette with well-honed back muscles. The fourth was called Obsidian and played up a Native American theme with a costume of leather fringe and beads. The disc jockey announced in a velvety voice that we could pay for table dances with Visa or MasterCard.

I watched the athletic brunette do a private dance for a customer. Straddling his lap, she shimmied up and down, closer and closer, then ground her pelvis into his. I winced. He put his hand on her thigh, and she briskly picked it up and put it back on the seat. He put it on her thigh again, she removed it again, and they repeated the game a couple more times before he stopped. Obsidian retreated to a dark corner with a customer. I tried to follow them with my eyes, but they were lost behind a pillar. If I had needed more confirmation that this occupation was not for me, I now had it. These women had to sit on laps, slap away hands, go behind pillars.

We watched from our padded bench, curious but unaroused, commenting to each other about the women's looks. I wasn't as taken as I had been on my visit to the Marble Arch, maybe because the audience was so small, or because of the groping customer. But I was still transfixed while I watched Obsidian and the brunette, both skilled dancers, perform onstage. I still had the sense that they were free of something I was stuck with. Despite my visit to the "modeling" agency, I hadn't shaken the idea that maybe I could be one of them. I could cross from my daily life and become the unabashedly sexual girl in the spotlight.

They all offered us private dances but we left without buying any. It started to snow while we walked to the truck, and it was sticking to the ground by the time we got home.

A short time after the Valentine's Day when we went to Déjà Vu, I stood in our living room shaking with nervousness.

"Just sit. Just sit on the sofa. Give me a minute," I told Erik. I closed the blinds on the window that faced the dark street. Then I bent over the stereo, still wearing a ragged sweat suit. None of the music seemed right. "Relax," he told me. He thought my jangled nerves were funny. This had been my idea, but I had insisted that he tell me, convincingly, that he wanted me to do it. I found a disc that seemed danceable.

"Okay, okay, give me a minute. I just need a minute," I said, but I was talking more to myself. He was calm on the sofa, drinking a beer, watching me. My armpits were damp. I felt I might be about to do something ridiculous. I was going to feel terribly self-conscious if this didn't turn either of us on.

In our bedroom I took off my outer layer of clothing. Underneath I already wore a black push-up bra, a thong, my only garter belt, and stockings. I had had the garter belt for so long that I couldn't remember buying it. The stockings had a few snags. No shoes seemed right so I didn't wear any.

"Press play," I yelled to him. I crossed the kitchen and crept around the corner into the living room, swallowing my embarrassment through sheer willpower. He was smiling on the sofa, legs wide, arms behind his head, his relaxed mood the opposite of mine. I began to dance. I had practiced a little, but most of it was ad lib. I twisted my hips a lot and knelt on the floor. I removed my bra, breathing hard. To my relief, I saw that I had his interest. His lips were parted, and he stared intently. When the second song began, I removed my panties. Sometimes it wasn't easy to arouse Erik, but this seemed to be working. To my pleasant surprise I was also arousing myself. I turned the music down and crawled over to him, then stood up, my thighs inches from his face. I bent to help him undo his paint-crusted jeans. His thin white boxer shorts sprang up at me. He was ready. I danced a little more.

Though afterward we agreed that it had been fun, we didn't repeat the experiment. It was an oasis of pleasure in an increasingly strained relationship, because I, by then, was already planning to go away. I left in May, and we didn't see each other until we met six months later in New Zealand; seven months after that we were back in the house.

I saw the Lusty Lady's employment ad in the back of a weekly newspaper. It wasn't the first time I had seen it—they ran ads regularly—but this time I circled it and underlined the phone number. It said, "dancers wanted," "full nudity," "no contact"—the last of which got my attention. Applicants had to be at least eighteen years old, with healthy hair of chin length or longer, and have no body piercings or tattoos. I let the circled ad sit on my desk for a couple of days. I was apprehensive. I said things to convince myself: "If you never try you'll never know," and "It's now or never." In a couple of years I thought I might have precluding responsibilities, or even a serious job. My body was still young, taut, and therefore marketable. What if I looked back when I was eighty, wishing I had tried? I might always wonder if I could have played that role. I might wonder if those women had found a sort of freedom that I had not.

On an overcast November afternoon I found myself in the Lusty Lady's small, dim foyer, concentrating on remaining calm and avoiding eye contact with the customers. I felt them look at me as they went in and out. I focused on the paintings of naked men and women along one wall, some of them showing close-ups of genitalia. I stared down at the dark, mottled carpet, then shifted my gaze to a bright display of dancers' photographs. Behind the front desk I could make out a set of black-and-white video monitors. One showed a lingerie-clad woman lying on her side, moving slowly, projected from some far corner of the premises.

I had an appointment with Catharine, a "show director," as her business card read. On the phone, she had said, "It's very important that you arrive on time. We will take punctuality into account in our decision to hire you." Obviously, I thought. Did people really need to be told?

Now she appeared, extending her hand to shake mine. I was surprised by her appearance. She was young, with smooth skin, short mousy brown hair, and an earnest gaze from behind wire-rimmed glasses. Her baggy orange pullover gave her an androgynous look. Looking me in the eye, she told me that first we would watch the show from one of the customer booths so that I would know what I was getting into. The Lusty Lady wasn't a club with a conventional stage and seating area, like ones I had visited before. It was a peep show. Customers stepped into private booths and watched women from behind glass windows.

Opening a black door, we squeezed into a dark compartment designed for one person. I heard a clinking sound as Catharine deposited quarters into a slot, then a mechanical hum as a screen rose to reveal a long rectangle of a stage stretching out in front of us. Its mirrored walls and bright red velvet carpet dazzled me after the darkness of our closet-size space.

Three mostly naked women occupied the stage. A tall brunette turned and walked slowly toward us, swaying her hips. She appeared to be focused on a point just above our heads. Gradually I realized she couldn't see us through the one-way window. With the floor of the stage at the height of our chests, the dancer's statuesque figure loomed above us as she got closer. Long, glossy hair fell to the middle of her back. She wore only knee-high white patent leather boots.

"That's Korina," Catharine said. Then, after a pause, she added, "She's doing a good job."

Korina undulated to the music, moving nearer, then farther, then kneeling in front of us and leaning so close I felt sure she could see us. Then, standing up, she turned her back to us, spread her legs, and bent over. I was startled and tried not to flinch. Korina turned and backed away from the window again, allowing us to see her whole curvaceous body.

By the time the window closed after a couple of minutes, leaving us in darkness, I was mesmerized—even more so than I had been at the Marble Arch. I felt something similar to desire, but it wasn't that I wanted Korina. I wanted to *be* Korina. We stepped out into the hallway. "Do you think you can do that?" Catharine asked.

I made an appointment to audition. As I left she told me to think about a stage name.

Erik, who had once told me I didn't have a romantic bone in my body, suggested the stage name Ice. "Oh, thanks," I said sarcastically, though actually it appealed to me. I wanted to be unthawable. When I proposed the name Ice to Catharine, though, she rejected it. She said they had recently had another blonde named Ice, who had been widely disliked and left under "difficult circumstances." She thought a new Ice would create tension. I didn't mind, though, because I already had another name in mind.

Leila, L-E-I-L-A. When I told Catharine, she thought I meant L-A-Y-L-A, as in the song by Eric Clapton. The spelling wouldn't matter much to customers but it did to me, and Catharine had to have something to write on the schedule. Once I started, dancers would always mention the Clapton song when I told them my name. One of them, Carmela, took to belting out "Layla, you've got me on my knees" whenever she saw me. But I hadn't had the song in mind at all.

Leila was a common Arabic name that was close to "leil," the word for night. I had studied Arabic in university, and I often used the name Leila when I was traveling around Egypt and the Middle East. At the time, I had said I did this because the people I met couldn't pronounce "Elisabeth," which was sometimes true. But calling myself Leila had also felt like an extra layer of defense against the overly curious. It made me untraceable. So I took my old play name and applied it to my new secret life, scripting a private joke for an audience of one. I enjoyed imposing this line of continuity from past to present, as though I could turn my life into a story that made sense.

Strip clubs, as it turned out, were full of double-L names. Lilies, Lulus, Lolas. At the Lusty Lady I would meet a Lola, a Lolita, and a Delilah. The two Ls made the person saying the name flick the tongue up and down in a licking motion. As well as having two Ls, Leila was simple and easy to remember, and I knew I didn't want a complicated name. Turning randomly selected syllables into a stage name, as some dancers seemed to do, made them easily forgotten. To dancers with names like Dajah, Tasia, and Anondii, the customers were bound to continually ask, "What's your name again?"

Conventional club wisdom held that girl-next-door names like Jenny, Crystal, and Heather worked best. Fantastical names like Fantasia and Stardust worked against strip-club psychology, which was about suspension of disbelief. Customers wanted the fantasy of a real woman, much easier to provide as an Ana than as an Octopussy. But even with a relatively normal stage name, the men would still ask "Yeah, but what's your real name?" Each guy liked to think he was unique: clever enough to ask and special enough for her to tell him, as if he was not one of ten men on a given night to ask her the same thing. Every dancer had her own policy on this. Some told, some didn't, some told just a few regulars, and some made up new fake names to pass off with coy reluctance as their own.

Not everyone believed in the girl-next-door theory. Jewel names were popular. I would meet a tiny Jade, an awkward Ruby, a baby-oil-wearing Diamond, and a heroin-addicted Sapphire. In precious metals, the Lusty Lady had a Gold who had golden hair and studied geophysics, and I once met a club dancer named Silver. Food names were also widespread. Cherry, Candy, and Cinnamon were the most common, but I would also come across an Apple Jack, a Peanut, a Spice, and a Sauce. Mythology and religion were well mined at the Lusty Lady, which had an Athena (goddess of wisdom and warfare), Atlantis (lost city), Avalon (Celtic paradise), Cassandra (prophetess, doomed never to be believed), Jezebel (heretic queen), Kali (Hindu destroyer), and Lilith (Adam's first wife, noted for opposing the missionary position).

The purplish end of the color spectrum featured strongly among dancer names, as in Blue, Indigo, and Violet. I would also meet a Tawny and several Ambers. I never met a Red but could picture her perfectly: voluptuous in cowboy boots and a mane of red hair. Clubs were full of Kitties and Cats, and I would also meet a Krickette, a Raven, and a Hawk. Flames and Fires were rampant, and Summers, Autumns, and Winters numerous. One Autumn said that she chose her name because at twenty-nine she was in the autumn of her career.

Some dancers at the Lusty Lady carried on two separate stage personas, distinguished by name, look, and, if they took it seriously, character traits. In some cases they did it because they thought having two different looks would get them more shifts. Others believed a new look would freshen up waning customer interest. And some did it for their own amusement, to play with hairstyles, lipstick, and costumes. Thus wild-haired, nipple-ringed Lucia became Kitten, with a slick ponytail and a pink negligee. Demure Sheeba, who wore pastels and had silky bronze hair, could also be Ilianna, in black hair and aggressive red fingernails.

At most clubs, when a new dancer started, the manager asked for her stage name and expected a quick answer. Names were vetoed only if there was already one of her on the schedule. The Lusty Lady, though, took naming seriously, and when the occasional new hire wanted to use her real name, they forbade it—hence Abby, who always used her real name when she worked bachelor parties, had to go by Delilah at the peep show. Catharine had said to me when I left: "Think carefully about it. It's a chance to try on another identity."

Was a name an identity? I didn't take this too seriously. I would never feel that Leila was a completely different person from Elisabeth. On the other hand, it gave me a small thrill to be called something new. While away from Seattle and Erik, I had spent several months in Australia, where I was called Beth. I had never used the nickname before and hadn't planned to, but most people I met tried to shorten Elisabeth. I didn't like other variations and so quickly became Beth. I felt a flush of pleasure every time I heard someone call my new name, as though I were wearing a successful disguise. The fact that I could so easily shed my old name reminded me that I could always become something new. When I had a short, intense affair with a man in Australia, I came to think of the name Beth as belonging exclusively to him. Beth was what I left with him—she was me, for him, and would remain so even after I went away.

But if I didn't take the business of names too seriously, others did. I would meet a number of strippers—at least six—who had permanently, and in some cases even legally, changed their real names. With the exception of most married women, I had never met anyone else who had done this, and the dancers weren't doing it to declare themselves tied to a man. One of them told me she just wanted to try being someone new; another hinted at wanting to mark a psychological shift. I understood the desire to self-invent, but I thought permanently changing one's name was drastic. While I might like to call myself Beth in one place or Leila in another, I didn't see them as different people. They were more like different roles to play. I would always go back to being the same actor.

Chapter 4

My stomach had been fluttering with a sense of foreboding all afternoon, as though I had to write an exam I wasn't prepared for. I felt I had no choice but to go through with it, and I just wanted to get the event over and done with. My fear was vague, though, with nothing exact to fix on. I had only one concrete anxiety, which was that I might see a customer I knew. I reasoned that if I did, he should be at least as embarrassed as me. We were on opposite sides of the same equation, and if one was socially unacceptable, the other had to be, too. Other than this one possibility, I didn't know exactly what it was I was going to find difficult. I compulsively ran through the upcoming events, as Catharine had explained them, trying to smooth them out and identify any potential unpleasantness. By the time I arrived I had thought dozens of times about where I would park, how I would announce myself at the front desk, how Catharine would take me to the dressing room, and how I would take off my clothes. But after undressing my enumeration of events hit a blank spot, and my imagination failed. While I knew theoretically that at some point I would go onstage, I couldn't conjure up any idea of what it would be like. I resigned myself to not knowing what was in store.

In the show directors' office, Catharine asked me to strip naked so that she could examine my body. There was no point in auditioning if I had some physical characteristic that would prevent me from working. Her main concern was to make sure I had no tattoos or body piercings.

I turned slowly around while she inspected me. For a moment I imagined myself for sale on an auction block, and I felt an anticipatory thrill of pleasure in knowing that Catharine would say yes, my unpierced, unmarked body would do nicely.

"You look great," she said finally. I put on my costume that made me barely more than nude: Black knee-high stockings, low black heels, and a gold choker necklace. Later I would think back and realize how amateurish I had looked in my scuffed shoes and flat hair, like a girl pretending to be a stripper for a night, but I didn't know this at the time and no one mentioned it. Catharine walked me through the dressing room to the edge of the stage. We had to squeeze around a tall black dancer in a satin push-up bra standing in the dressing room's narrow corridor, talking loudly into the telephone. "We've got to figure out how we're going to market these," she was saying into the phone. The words lodged in my head, and though I was too nervous to give it much thought, I wondered for a long time afterward what she was trying to sell.

I stood at the edge of the stage and steeled myself.

"Whenever you're ready. Take some deep breaths," Catharine said. Then she announced to the four dancers: "Ladies, we have an audition. This is Leila."

I entered at the opposite end of the stage from the window where I had watched the week before. It looked much brighter now that I was actually in it. I was immediately surrounded by reflections of naked women, including my own. In that rectangular, mirror-walled room, it was impossible not to see your own image unless you closed your eyes or looked straight at the floor. Ten windows lined one long wall, with two more on the short wall opposite the dressing room entrance. The bright red carpet and multicolored lights combined with the mirrors for a dazzling, garish effect. A floor-to-ceiling transparent pole stood toward one end of the rectangle, and transparent bars affixed to the walls framed the windows, all acting as prisms for the light. The windows, set in the mirrored wall, were covered with mirrored screens. A quarter raised the screen and kept it open for fifteen seconds. Catharine was going to watch me from a one-way window, but I didn't know which one. She said she would wait one song before she started, which was supposed to give me a chance to get comfortable. As I entered the stage each woman gave me a soft and subdued hello, as though to calm the lurching I felt inside.

My first few minutes passed in a daze. I wasn't the sort of creature to freeze in headlights, and most feelings didn't write themselves on my face. I could go through motions convincingly even when I felt unbalanced. And when I heard music I didn't have to think about dancing, I just did. So I performed adequately while I waited for my mind to thaw out. All my past recitals and school plays came back to me, distilled into one cardinal rule: Remember to smile. The normal process of observing, absorbing, and reacting slowed to a glacial pace, as though my brain was assimilating so much information it needed to shut down for a few moments while it got back up to speed. After a few minutes it did, and then, playing catch-up, my mind started to race.

I was breathing fast and sweating lightly, conscious of my heart pulsing, blood racing, and a flush rising to the surface of my skin. Any of these symptoms could have signified exertion, nervous excitement, or arousal, and I couldn't at that moment tell one from another.

The stage was small and warm, enclosing me, and started to have a calming effect. I looked at the other dancers and could tell that I was doing roughly what I was supposed to. I realized that in violation of all expectation and common sense, this felt natural to me. It felt so natural that I tried to remember when I had done it before, but of course there was nothing in my memory bank. My mind was playing a trick on me. I was quite sure I had never danced naked for strangers in a red glass box.

With a happy frozen face I circled my hips and ran my hands over my body in a parody of sex. When a window opened, I flirted with the customer in it, dancing farther away, then closer, then right in his face, always turning and moving. I gripped the bars framing the window and leaned back, lifting a leg to rest it on the bar below the window like I watched the others do. When the screen closed, I moved to another window. I tried a few one-ways at first and then moved on to a two-way. Was this all there was to it?

It wasn't. Most of the customers I could see, and presumably the ones I couldn't, were masturbating. Catharine had warned me. She had asked me if I had a problem with this, and I had said no. In the smaller windows, if I looked at them straight on, only their trembling chests and puckered faces tipped me off. If I looked down, though, I could see their penises, wrapped in sliding hands. The two large corner windows displayed the men behind them from the groin up, framed like paintings.

The masturbators unnerved me, but I didn't let myself react outwardly. The phrase "keep smiling" played over and over in my head. Showmanship meant that the show went on even if the theater collapsed around you, so surely I could handle a few men with their pants down. But they were a reminder of what, exactly, we did in here, which had been easy to lose track of through the interviews and introductions. We were paid to help men jerk off.

I favored the one-ways at first. If you got close enough to a one-way, blocking the light from the stage and looking down at exactly the right angle, you could sometimes make out fragmentary body parts, but you could never see their faces. I felt I could make a career out of one-ways, just dancing for my own image. But why were they so much easier, I wondered, when I knew that the men behind them were doing the same things as the two-way men? It was that the two-ways forced an acknowledgment from me. When I saw them I couldn't pretend I wasn't assenting.

My aversion wasn't visceral. Rather, I felt a fear of getting caught. I wasn't opposed to being viewed, I was opposed to others knowing that I allowed it, which showed an immature submission to received morality. So most of my discomfort came from worry over what others would think, and it was my willingness to join in what the men were doing that I knew would be looked at askance. There was very little stigma attached to being a passive sex object. Images of the legs, breasts, and lips of strangers suffused my life thoroughly, from billboards to magazines to television. Far from shaming the bodies' owners, society made them starlets, supermodels, and video queens, glorifying them with money and fame. Yet to actively pursue sex-object status—to say, "Okay, I agree, please look at me"—in this I felt as if there was reproach. The difference between a stripper and a woman modeling bathing suits was that the stripper acknowledged her intention to arouse, whereas the model could pretend ignorance. I felt uneasy at the sight of all these men because I had crossed the line from passivity to engagement.

While these thoughts crashed through my head, I was also thrilled. I had taken up a glove that had been thrown down by the first stranger to shout at me out of the window of his car. These men couldn't get me. I was safe and in control. I felt none of the vague alarm that accompanied stares and comments in the streets. I was taking back what should have been my own, freedom from a sense of menace. I was even feeling vengeful, glorying in the fact that they were down there, trapped in their little boxes, and I was above them in every way. They were a substitute for every man who had caused me fear.

But despite feeling aggressive, I saw almost right away that this wasn't the us-versus-them, black-and-white situation I had braced myself for. The men looked benign. Of the ones I could see, all but one smiled and made eye contact. Only one hung back in his booth with a surly frown. They looked eager and weak, with their puckered faces and intent, needy eyes. I remained wary, but I softened to them.

I was surprised when Catharine called "Leila" from the stage entrance after four songs, snapping me out of my tumbling thoughts. She asked all the dancers to clap for a great audition, which they did. As I came down to the dressing room, which felt noticeably cooler, she handed me a cup, and I poured cold water for myself. I realized I was exhausted and dripping with sweat. I wondered how I would be able to do what I had just done for three hours at a stretch in four-inch heels. My muscles were tense, and I shook as though I had just been on a roller-coaster ride. I felt weak and exhilarated, and my body seemed to buzz. I was pink all over. I guzzled water, splashed my face, and got dressed. It was over.

Sitting in the office next to a video monitor of the stage, Catharine told me that I was good but that I could slow down a little. That was a relief. She said it would give the customers more time to appreciate what they were looking at. I had worn my hair up, and she suggested

I wear it down. "Try curling it. Try some different styles," she said. I didn't tell her that my hair was determined to be straight. She asked me how I felt about performing, and I told her what was foremost in my mind, which was that I might exhaust myself well before the end of a three-hour shift. I also told her, more tentatively, that I found the one-ways easier. They were like dancing in front of a mirror. She said it was all right if I favored them at first but that I shouldn't make a habit of it.

Catharine handed me a thick package of company policies and proceeded to go through them at length. They ranged from the specific and obvious, like showing up for work on time, to the vague and utopian, like the requirement to "be supportive" of other dancers and staff. We were required to follow certain dress requirements: Clothing had to decorate, not cover. No more than one dancer at a time could wear all black. Private parts had to be exposed: bras nippleless, tights crotchless; any skirts or shirts had to be brief and arranged to expose breasts and vaginas. Other rules included the break rotation—exactly ten minutes in length, one girl at a time—and the exhortation to never, ever, agree to meet a customer outside of work, or even appear to suggest to do so. It took her about a half hour to go through all the stage rules, and then she mentioned something called the private pleasures booth. It was basically a one-on-one stage, down the hall and around the corner from the dressing room, where dancer and customer spoke via an intercom. "Most dancers wait before giving it a try," she told me. I said I would wait, too.

Chapter 5

Below the hovering firefly lights of the shipping in the sound were other lights that raced and flashed on trip circuits—lights of pleasure and temptation. Down on First Avenue, the Midtown Theater was showing Depraved Innocent *and* Interlude of Lust. *The Champ Arcade ("The Adult Superstore") advertised LIVE GIRLS—50 BEAUTIFUL GIRLS—& 3 UGLY ONES! Another sign alerted one to the fact that Nina Deponca, the XXX STAR, was playing Seattle LIVE IN PERSON!. . .*

This was, after all, the city from which the phrase "skid row" had made it into the American language.

—Jonathan Raban, *Hunting Mister Heartbreak*

Throughout the late 1990s the Lusty Lady became progressively better known to people outside the sex industry. When they heard it mentioned, many Seattle residents would remark that it was owned and run by women, though this was only approximately true. The family that owned it included at least one woman, but June, the general manager when I began, was replaced by a man in 1997. The show directors, though, who had the most contact with dancers, were women.

The Lusty kept appearing in the news for reasons good and bad. The photographer Erika Langley published a book called *The Lusty Lady*, a collection of her black-and-white photos of dancers, and she exhibited her work in local galleries. The Lusty was also briefly in the spotlight when workers at its same-named sister outfit in San Francisco became the first strippers, nationwide, to launch a union, which they did between 1996 and 1998. Unionization never took hold at the northern branch, but the subject received attention again when the movie *Live Nude Girls Unite!,* which documented the San Francisco unionization drive, came out in 2000. And for a while the Lusty was in the crosshairs of city council member Jane Noland, who launched an indiscriminate drive to have the doors removed from customer booths in all adult businesses with private stalls. She declared the stalls a public health hazard on the grounds that gay men used them for anonymous, unprotected sex. It's plausible they did that in some establishments, though not at the Lusty.

Much of the Lusty's growing prominence, though, came simply from its location and its marquee. Though First Avenue was known after World War II as Flesh Avenue, in the '90s the peep show gradually became an anachronism in a rising tide of boutiques and condominiums. The new home of the Seattle Art Museum opened on First Avenue in 1991 and became an anchor for a brighter, less smutty downtown. The Lusty Lady, dubbed the city's "aristocratic filth-art gallery" by one local journalist, was directly across the street. (On one occasion the filth actually crossed the street, when Langley showed her work at the museum.) In the plaza in front of its new glass-and-concrete building, on the corner of First and University, the museum installed *Hammering Man*, a gargantuan, perpetually moving metal sculpture. He was a forty-eight-foot-tall, thirty-inch-thick man in profile, made of black-painted steel. Like a giant metronome, the arm that held the hammer moved slowly up and down at the shoulder joint, and he pounded relentlessly from 1991 on.

With the arrival of *Hammering Man* and the elegant museum, the pawnshops started closing and boarded-up buildings came back to life. Next door to the Lusty Lady the Harbor Steps materialized, a complex of apartments, fountains, and shops that included a celebrity-chef restaurant, the Wolfgang Puck Café. The apartments were quickly occupied, even the penthouse suites that rented for more than four thousand dollars a month. As money flowed into downtown, city officials tried to ease out the sex trade. Seattle had passed its first ordinance regulating adult businesses in 1988, sponsored by the crusading Jane Noland. A decade later the city imposed a moratorium on opening new sex businesses, which was extended in 1999. The Déjà Vu on Pike and the Champ Arcade peep show on First closed in 1997, and in 1998 Seattle's new symphony hall opened on Second. Seattle became a technology boom town, and visitors swarmed in. To get from one of the city's most-promoted tourist attractions, the Pike Place Market, to another, Pioneer Square, they had to walk right by the Lusty Lady. That meant that the tourists, along with all the shoppers, gallerygoers and classical music fans, could catch a glimpse of its pink, white, and black marquee.

The marquee deserved landmark status. Surrounded by flashing white lightbulbs, it displayed two catchy, lewd slogans at all times, one facing up the street and the other facing down. The slogans were often tied to local news or sports events. When the World Trade Organization met in Seattle in November 1999 and was greeted with violent demonstrations, the marquee read, "W T Ohhhh" and "Nude World Order." After the earthquake in February 2001 it read, "Come Feel the Earth Move"; and during the controversial ballot counting after the 2000 presidential election, it read, "Electile Dysfunction?" Around Christmas it always said, "Merry XXX-mas." The maxims were changed every week without fail. Just below the phrase of the week, permanent smaller black letters read, "Have an Erotic Day!"

The marquee guided me like a lighthouse as I drove down First Avenue. The road was slick and shiny with rain. It was already dark at six o'clock in the evening on a Thursday, and the streets were busy with commuters trying to get out of downtown. At ten o'clock, when I finished my shift, the streets would be quieter, so I wanted to park nearby.

I passed the Lusty Lady on my right and took a left at *Hammering Man*, then cursed when I realized Second Avenue ran one way. I was already nervous about my first shift, and the excruciatingly slow traffic made me more tense. I circled until I found a spot two blocks away. I grabbed the bag I had packed, which contained the same black stockings and scuffed shoes I had used for my audition, and a zippered toilet kit that held hair accessories, jewelry, and crumbling pans of makeup. I figured I would wait to see if I was actually going to stick with the job before investing in new gear.

At the front desk I introduced myself as Leila, as I had been instructed. The guy at the desk picked up a clipboard, scanned the weekly schedule, and checked off my name.

"First shift?" he asked. I said yes.

"Welcome. I'm Jeff."

I walked down a long dark hallway past the customers' booths to the dressing room. Jeff watched the dressing room door on one of his video monitors, and he unlocked it with a buzz just as I appeared on his screen.

I entered the brightly lit room that I had now visited twice, on the day of my first appointment with Catharine, and on the day she auditioned and hired me. She had given me a tour, pointing out the time clock, the coatrack, the music-request box, the complaints-and-suggestions box, the watercooler, the refrigerator, the microwave, the free snacks—usually instant noodles and popcorn—and the "free box" full of old clothes, where dancers could discard or acquire what they liked.

I looked into the show directors' office, which adjoined the dressing room. Catharine was absent, but Debra, the other show director, sat at her desk. I hadn't met her before.

"Hi, I'm Leila," I said.

She looked at me blankly for a moment, then said, "Oh hi. This is your first shift, isn't it?" I nodded. She was what I had expected a strip-club manager to look like before I met Catharine: permed brown hair pulled up in a girlish style and a weary face. I missed Catharine's hand-holding presence already.

"Let me know if you have any questions," Debra said, and turned back to the spreadsheet on her computer screen. Above one of the office's two desks was a black-and-white video monitor of the stage, with a slim, pale body moving silently across it.

The dressing room was shaped roughly like the letter C, with the toilet, shower, and sink off of the short passage that formed the middle stretch. My assigned locker was at ground level in that stretch. It wasn't a great location because it was narrow and heavily trafficked, lying as it did in the path from the stage to the telephone, toilet, or managers' office. But it could have been worse. Dancers assigned lockers next to the hallway door got a whole locker to themselves to compensate for the inconvenience of having the door open onto them, sometimes flung wide.

Two computer-printed signs were taped to my locker door, reading "Leila" and "Sarah." "You'll like Sarah as a locker mate," Catharine had told me. "She only works once a week." Our locker was plain compared to all the others. Except where there were mirrors and makeup counters, much of the available wall space was taken up by lockers. Dancers had decorated them with exuberant self-definition, as ardently as high schoolers though with a more sexual tone. Favorite movie stars, favorite porn stars, photos of themselves nude, themselves with boyfriends, themselves as children, catchy photos ripped from fashion magazines, comic book drawings of fantastical sexual acts—all this and more papered both the outside and inside of the locker doors. A few lockers above mine, one with the name tag "Marilyn," had photos of Marilyn Monroe on it.

I read the combination off the slip of paper Catharine had given me and opened the wooden door. The locker was almost empty. It contained a snapshot of a brown-haired toddler—Sarah's perhaps?— and an orange vibrator. Never having actually seen one up close, I picked it up warily and turned the dial at one end. The batteries were dead. It was months before I actually met Sarah and found out that neither of the items belonged to her.

I took a seat on a stool in front of the dressing room mirror, which was surrounded with lightbulbs, and started to apply my makeup. It reminded me of getting ready for dance competitions as a preteen, when putting on stage makeup had seemed dramatic and grown-up. It no longer seemed quite so exciting, but watching my face transform still fascinated me. "We like a glamorous look," Catharine had told me, though she noted that some dancers simply had a "look"—a wholesome or girlish look, I took her to mean—that didn't require makeup. But she wanted me to aim for glamour.

Once you learn how to apply makeup you never forget. I painted my eyes and lips with delicate, steady movements. Wearing cosmetics had once been a daily addiction for me, until sometime in college when I decided it was a monumental inconvenience. I still regarded it as addictionlike, in the sense that a little makeup always led to more. I could continue a streak of abstinence for a long time. But if I started, with, say, some mascara and foundation one day, maybe some lip gloss the next, I was always tempted to go for more. I became seduced by the idea that I could crank up the drama and polish of my face, and I was loath to go in the other direction, toward the horror of plainness. Before I knew it I would be wearing more makeup, spending more money on it, and feeling hooked. In order to avoid getting trapped in this vicious circle, I tried, for the most part, to abstain, but like addiction it was a touchy, one-day-at-a-time business. Now, though, I had an excuse. It was part of my job.

Makeup made women prettier in the most conventional way, I thought as I outlined my lips. It made skin a little smoother, lips a little fuller, eyes a little bigger. I wondered why more women didn't regard it as an expensive trap. I hoped that someday it would go the way of corsets and foot binding, but I saw no movement in that direction. Cosmetics companies continued to profit. A woman wasn't considered "professional"-looking without makeup. And as if makeup weren't enough, women in their twenties—bankers and lawyers as well as strippers—had plastic surgery, adding pain and danger to expense and inconvenience. Prettiness was as strong an imperative as ever in the lives of women, which was why I admired those who swore off cosmetics completely. I thought they had sprung themselves from vanity, whereas I sometimes had to concentrate just to keep from looking at myself in a shop window. Maybe stripping would get the fixation out of my system. I noticed that many dancers weren't wearing any makeup when they arrived in the dressing room. It was as though they went so over the top with clichéd femininity at work, gorging themselves on false eyelashes, wigs, and shimmery face powders, that they no longer needed to wear it anyplace else.

I had not come up with any new styles for my hair, as Catharine had suggested. I thought about back combing it now to make it look bigger, but that could veer into messiness, and Catharine had warned against mess. I put on a black headband to hold it away from my face, thinking that maybe I needed to get it cut or lightened. Another job-related investment to add to shoes and makeup.

I began to peel my clothes off, feeling the oddness of the context. It wasn't like home, even a home where my lover was so used to my body that he barely noticed. It wasn't like a gym locker room, either, because in those most women were furtive in their nudity, dressing and undressing with quick utilitarian movements and not a hint of pride. It was rare that I had seen a naked woman in a locker room looking casual or relaxed. Far more often I had seen women swathe themselves in towels and try to change awkwardly underneath, or simply duck into toilet stalls.

The Lusty Lady dressing room was an altogether different scene and one that I felt much more at home in. Around me women read, ate, fixed their makeup, and chatted, all nude. Taking my clothes off always made me feel pleasantly unfettered, and here it did so even more because no one thought it was strange. I felt almost eager to get my clothes off, wanting to assure the women around me that I was one of them. I stuffed my clothes in my locker and put on my black, just-over-the-knee stockings and pumps. I cleaned the soles with alcohol and paper towels, because we were not supposed to wear street shoes on the velvet-carpeted stage, which we crawled around on. I added the gold choker and a bracelet and appraised myself in the mirror. Technically, I supposed, we couldn't be called strippers because we didn't take anything off. We started out naked.

It was only twenty to seven by the time I was completely ready. I was so afraid of being late that I had arrived too early. I took my shoes back off and stood in my stockings, my hands clasped behind my back, looking at the walls. A bulletin board was cluttered with notes: notices from the show directors like "Paychecks are not available until five P.M. on Thursdays," phone messages, requests to trade shifts, and postcards from dancers who were on holiday or had moved away. The schedules for the current and following weeks were posted, covered with corrections in ballpoint ink.

I sat down to wait. A dancer came offstage, introduced herself as Venus, and laid a piece of paper towel on the red easy chair before sitting down. I realized I had forgotten this courtesy, which Catharine had told me about. I was sitting with my bare ass on the wooden stool. I jumped up and looked at the bulletin board some more.

A woman with wavy, nearly thigh-length blond hair arrayed around a slim body came offstage, causing me to check my hair in the mirror. She introduced herself as April, then threw herself on a chair.

"These things are fucking killing me!" she burst out.

She unzipped her boots, but they were so tight she couldn't yank them off. A friend had just given them to her, she explained, and she had thought at first that they fit. She couldn't go back onstage in them; she could barely walk. She asked me to help get them off.

I knelt down in front of her and gripped her calf with both hands, pulling on the boot, and I was struck with a sudden and overwhelming sense of the surreal. I had arrived where I had set out for: completely unknown territory. A pornographic movie of myself played in my head: me kneeling in front of April, straining against her boot, both of us naked. I had been here for only a half hour. What would I be doing next?

Another dancer, Georgia, came off the stage to quickly brush her hair.

"Whoa, what's going on here, ladies?" she asked.

"My boots are stuck!" April said.

The boot eased, and I fell backward. The other one came off more easily.

"Friends for life!" April said, thanking me. She changed briskly into a different pair of black boots, covered herself with a sarong and jean jacket, and took a cigarette from her purse. She was headed for the smoking room down the hall, with five minutes before she had to be back onstage.

Clara Bo, a brunette with curly hair and rosebud lips, returned to the dressing room in giddy spirits from the private pleasures booth, also down the hall.

Smack-smack-smack! She spanked Venus with a multicolored rubber dildo.

"What are you doing? What's gotten into you?" asked Venus, laughing and making no move to get away. Clara Bo giggled and threw the dildo into her locker.

A tall, gangly brunette entered from the hallway, wearing jeans and a rain-spattered Gore-Tex jacket, carrying a bicycle helmet. It took me several minutes to figure out why she looked familiar. It was Korina, the same dancer I had watched perform the first time I came to interview. The Slavic features I had thought were so beautiful now looked flat and square. The figure I thought was statuesque looked awkward as she shed her not-quite-long-enough jeans. Zits crowded a corner of her chin. I stared, looked away, stared again.

"Is it still raining?" asked Clara Bo, pulling on jeans.

Korina said it was.

"I guess I'm taking the bus then."

"Do you want a transfer?" asked Korina, producing one from the pocket of her jeans, which now lay on the floor. Girls taped bus transfers to the mirror, I had noticed, so that others could use them.

The conversations around me provided a much-needed distraction from the fact that I would be walking onstage with April at seven P.M. exactly, on the zero. A digital clock near the stage entrance displayed 6:54 in large, red numbers. I looked at my reflection in the dressing room mirror. I dusted my face with powder, punched in, and stepped back into my shoes. When the clock ticked over, and April brushed past me, I climbed the steps and entered the dazzling red-and-silver room.

Tight rules and a well-established hierarchy kept the Lusty running smoothly. At the top of the pyramid was June, the general manager, whom few dancers had much to do with. Below her were the Seattle and San Francisco branches, with two show directors each, who were chosen from the ranks of dancers. As well as Catharine, Seattle had Debra, who had a timeless air about her. Over several years, Catharine was replaced by Simone, and Simone by Dorthea, but Debra remained; the two positions gradually evolved so that Debra remained the senior show director and the other woman her junior. If a dancer was interested—because, for example, she was pregnant—and the show directors needed help, they might hire her to do office work, though for much less than her stage wage. Debra and her sister Candy had both at one time been show directors, but Candy had gone back to working onstage and later, when she retired from the stage, took a job at the front desk. Debra's daughter, a single mother in her twenties, also came to work at the Lusty, after working as a club dancer at Déjà Vu.

Under the show directors the hierarchy split into two branches: support staff and dancers. The support staffers were mostly men in their twenties. They included Jeff, the guy who had checked me in on my first day. I had formed an impression of him as sweet-natured because of his polite voice. Before being hired at the Lusty Lady Jeff had worked in the restaurants of five-star hotels. At the last one all the waiters had been men, and he had found the milieu overwhelmingly straight and obnoxiously macho—every time a pretty woman walked by someone said what he would do to her that night if he could. Jeff quit and applied to the Lusty Lady, where he knew a couple of dancers. After one interview, during which Debra had asked him if he understood what went on there—"Basically a lot of masturbation," he had replied—she had offered him the job.

Like most support staffers he did both janitorial and cashiering shifts. On his morning janitorial shifts he started by cleaning the dressing room and stage, making sure it looked good and was stocked with essentials like baby wipes, aspirin, and tampons. The rest of the time he spent touring, going from booth to booth, sweeping up Kleenex and mopping. If there were two customers in a booth, he asked one to leave. Occasionally someone tried to smoke crack or shoot up in one of the booths, and he threw him out. He kept a close eye on things. Customers sometimes gave him a hard time, calling him a jizz-mopper, which he had found difficult at first. But he came to look at his task as one of simple sanitation, and he compared himself to a nurse, since they had to deal with bodily fluids all the time. He always used rubber gloves and never touched anything with his bare hands. One time on a weekend night, a guy he took to be a frat boy, trying to show off to his friends, asked Jeff what his gloves were for. "The gloves are so that when I fist fuck you I won't get my hands dirty," Jeff had replied, which almost got his face punched in. But Jeff had been defensive back then. Now he ignored rowdies.

On the cashiering shifts he saw himself as a communicator. He took phone calls from customers asking about the show, screened calls to the show directors, and made sure the girls showed up ten minutes before their shifts. If they needed something in the dressing room, he dispatched a janitor to get it. He watched the video monitors and kept an eye out for unruly men. On his favorite shift, the day shift, he knew many of the customers by name. He became close friends with a few dancers, and he felt protective toward them all. The Lusty gave him raises, medical benefits, and paid vacation, and he never had to pretend he wasn't gay. Once he'd even come to work in drag, which everyone had thought was great. Where else could you do that? Jeff thought the Lusty was a class act.

Regulations existed to encompass nearly every aspect of dancer behavior. The main instrument of implementation was the weekly schedule, and producing it was one of the show directors' most important tasks. Using a spreadsheet program, they organized as many as seventy dancers into shifts of two to five hours, filling the sixteen to eighteen hours the stage was open every day of the week. Each dancer had a permanent schedule request on file, specifying her hours of availability and number of shifts desired. Dancers could also make special schedule requests on a weekly basis, provided they met the deadline.

Once the schedule was made, every dancer received a copy for the upcoming week enclosed with her paycheck from the week before. The back of the schedule listed dancers' phone numbers, show directors' hours, instructions for replacing shifts, and other important information, like the dates of upcoming staff meetings and the names of new dancers. The week I started it said "Welcome Leila!" in the bottom right-hand corner. The phone list, which ran the length of the legal-size sheet, had an alphabetical column for stage names and a column specifying what name to ask for, stage or real, when telephoning the dancer's home. The letters "PP" next to a dancer's name indicated that she did shifts in the private pleasures booth. Asterisks next to her name told the caller to be discreet and not to mention work to whoever answered the phone. We were instructed to keep the schedules to ourselves and tear them up as soon as we had been paid for the week so that the phone list didn't fall into the hands of crank callers.

As well as accommodating schedule requests, Catharine and Debra tried to make up what they called a "diverse stage," which meant mixing hair colors, skin tones, and breast sizes. "Leila" was underlined on the back of the phone list, indicating that I was busty. If I traded or gave away a shift, I was only allowed to replace myself with another busty, so the underlines told me whom I could call. Dancers made a flurry of changes every week after the schedule came out, wreaking havoc on the show directors' carefully planned shifts. To try to keep the stage something like they had planned, we were required to look for someone who resembled us as closely as possible when trading. A list of dancer descriptions hung by the telephone in the dressing room to help. It began:

> ACEE—Busty, curvaceous, brunette
> AMBER—Busty, sensuous, red hair
> APPLE JACK—Busty, tall, curly red hair
> APRIL—Slim, petite, blond
> ATLANTIS—Tanned, athletic, brunette

We were also required to consider the overall makeup of the stage when trading shifts. Blond busties had an advantage in getting scheduled, but it was harder for us to give shifts away. Of the four to six dancers working at any given time, they always tried to include at least one blond busty. If I was the only one scheduled, I could only switch with another one. But if there were already two of us scheduled, I had more leeway. There was a system to trading shifts. Keeping in mind the rules on appearance, I first had to call dancers until I found someone who agreed. Then each of us had to call the show director on duty and inform her. Then I had to write in the change on the dressing room master schedule and inform the front desk.

Once at work, the system of breaks was similarly precise. We took ten-minute breaks in rotation, which came after no more than fifty and no fewer than thirty minutes onstage, depending on how many of us were working. Remembering the order of the breaks, Catharine had warned, could be difficult. She said she had been terrible at it when she danced. On my first day, my break followed April's because she had returned from hers when my shift began. But the order changed as dancers started and ended shifts every half hour. Sometimes dancers traded breaks, jumbling the sequence even more.

We had code words to communicate with each other onstage. If someone said she was "getting a perm," it meant her shift was over. We were not allowed to announce the end of our shift in any other way in case the customers overheard us. This was partly for our own safety but also for legal reasons. Telling a customer I was getting off work, even unintentionally, could be construed as soliciting. If a dancer said she was "getting lucky," it meant that her break fell right before the end of her shift, allowing her to leave ten minutes early. And if she said "Gordon" it was short for "Flash Gordon," meaning she had seen a camera flash go off behind one of the one-way windows. If that happened, one person was supposed to continue dancing for the window so that the culprit wouldn't leave, while someone else called the front desk to have the customer ejected and his film destroyed.

There was a system for the music, too. The sound system played a set of a hundred songs, changed weekly. A dancer named Cinnamon was responsible for putting the music list together. To make her job easier and to add variety, dancers were encouraged to put together lists of fifty songs from the Lusty Lady's collection and submit them to

Cinnamon, who would then add the other fifty. Dancers could also make specific song requests. The result was a mix of everything: top-forty pop, obscure local bands, old jazz singers, world music, everything.

My hourly wage increased according to schedule. When I started, I earned ten dollars an hour, about the same as I had made temping. Provided I showed up on time and didn't break any rules, it was slated to rise by a dollar an hour every month for my first six. After that raises were granted based on performance, and most dancers who stuck around reached twenty-four dollars an hour, the top rate of pay, within a couple of years. (By 2001 the ceiling had increased to twenty-seven an hour.) I moved up to eleven an hour, then twelve, thirteen, and fourteen as the months rolled by. Some dancers complained about not getting enough shifts, but I had no trouble. For one thing I didn't want to work as much as some—three shifts a week were often enough for me. I could easily get that, partly because of the blond busty rule and partly because as a new performer I was still relatively cheap to have onstage. Blond, busty, and cheap. Except for the fact that I didn't do the private pleasures booth, in management's eyes I was perfect.

Chapter 6

The dressing room was warm and collegial. We had talkers, readers and studiers, snackers, a knitter, and women who fussed with their makeup and hair. I often brought news magazines but rarely read much, since our breaks were short and the distractions many. The strangeness of meeting people for the first time while naked vanished quickly. One woman introduced herself to me by saying, "You have beautiful breasts." She was matter-of-fact, as though complimenting me on a dress. New faces always introduced themselves, with everyone observing the rule that we use only stage names. Despite or perhaps because of this anonymity, along with the fact that most conversations were easily overheard, openness reigned. Boy problems, girl problems, home, health, school, and aspirations were all up for discussion. This may have been fostered by the fact that, for many of us, the one thing we might have kept secret from others was already known and considered unremarkable.

The stage, smaller than the dressing room, hung off of it like a bright Christmas stocking. The managers discouraged talking out there because the customers could overhear. My dancing settled into a routine: Window opens. Start three feet away. Turn, twist, bend. High kick. Sink to floor. Approach window on knees. Stand up. Raise foot to bar, show pussy. Crouch down, show face, lips, tongue. Stand up, turn, bend over. Sometimes they were done in one minute, sometimes it took half an hour. I could do this consciously, which I often did at the very beginning of a shift, or right after a break, or if the customer piqued my interest. But I often did it mindlessly. The stage could be relentlessly monotonous.

My routine varied depending on the size and location of the window, the customer's preference, and my mood. Sometimes the sameness sparked bursts of creativity. If I was near the floor-to-ceiling pole, I used it. The corner windows were larger and flush with the floor, so in front of them I did more floor work. If I liked another dancer's step, I would copy it, practicing over and over until it was polished to perfection. I could see exactly how I looked at all times. I could fine-tune moves, making quarter-of-an-inch adjustments to hip or shoulder or chin. What was sexier, leg forward or back? Right side or left? Flat foot or tiptoe? I had hours to contemplate these questions. I noticed minute changes in my body. I saw it swell with salt and water every month, then recede. I came to understand high heels. They made my legs and ass rise up, taut and tight. I watched muscles appear on my thighs. Between customers I stretched my legs and ankles, flexing my feet to counter the effects of my shoes. As the weather became warmer and dryer I started cycling to work, parking at the well-used bicycle rack under the marquee. I felt fit.

There were ways to break the monotony. I could ponder the customers who stood out through strange behavior—or, rather, behavior I would have called strange until I worked there but that now seemed commonplace. Men pulled down their pants to reveal all sorts of things—silky panties and garter belts, cock rings, various piercings, balls tied up in string. They brought talismans with them. One had a patch of rabbit fur; another, notoriously, a Barbie doll. Some brought their own lubricants and handkerchiefs.

The foot fetishists were a revelation to me. They wanted to stare at pretty feet while they jerked off. They wore hangdog expressions and licked frantically toward a dancers' shoes. They followed feet with their eyes, never distracted by other body parts. All a dancer had to do, really, was hold her foot up to the window at a variety of angles and occasionally stare sternly at him if he dared to look up. Some of them were hand-and-feet men, just as excited to see a hand as a foot. I did a slow, deformed march for them: right foot, left foot, right hand, left hand. For certain men, if I was in an obliging mood,

I might take off a shoe or even a stocking, unbuckling and rolling down the nylon with seductive slowness.

At first I didn't think I had the feet for it. My feet had become callused and twisted when I was in my teens and going to ballet class four days a week. I had bound them with tape and lamb's wool, stuffed them into pointe shoes, and tried to carry the entire weight of my body on the tips of my toes. They hadn't improved since then. Sometimes in the summer I tried to toughen them up by walking barefoot on sand and pavement, and the rest of the time I ignored them. My pinky nails had split and grown awry, the backs of my heels had become gnarled, and my soles were rough. I had never given much thought to my feet, except to note if they were in pain. So it was startling to learn that they had sex appeal. The foot men invented my feet as sexy things. I suddenly saw them through the men's eyes, as though discovering a new part of my body. The feet had escaped my knowledge of myself as a sex object; now they had been roped in, too.

I suddenly became self-conscious about my feet. I compared them to the other women's smooth, pink things, with their eye-catching nails, and mine didn't measure up. This was a new sensation for me entirely. Though I had always been very conscious of being looked at, and of my body, I had never doubted that it was just right. I didn't dwell on it being perfect either—I just had never thought that it should be any other way. To feel that blasé had been a kind of innocence, I now realized. It was an innocence I threw out with abandon as I headed for the drugstore and bought nail strengthener, nail files, nail scissors, cuticle sticks, a pumice stone, cuticle-removal cream, and clear and colored nail polish. I hadn't known some of these things existed. There was a whole industry out there just waiting to help.

Always on my mind with the fetishists, foot and otherwise, was the question of how they got that way. How did a fetish become so distilled that a man found himself ducking into a closet three times a week; making the conditions just so with his handkerchief, talisman, or bottle of lube; and staring at precisely the right part of a woman's body until he came? There had to be a line that led back from the closet to something in his past, and I was often curious to know what it was. But maybe there was no specific event, no big fetish bang. Maybe once upon a time a foot fetishist had just had a mild impulse to submit, but it had become so stylized over the years that now he had to get below the lowest part of a woman's body.

There was one foot man we saw all the time. I had held my feet—right, left, right-left-right—to the window for him dozens of times. He was always a perfect picture of pleading submission. The skin under his eyes sagged, his jowls drooped, and the corners of his mouth, even as his tongue darted in and out, hung down. His shoulders hunched a little, and his irises rolled up periodically to stare, fearfully, at the woman above the foot. He was the embodiment of pathos.

And then one day as I walked down First Avenue on my way to work, I saw someone familiar-looking coming toward me. He was fair-haired and fiftyish, wearing a leather bomber jacket and carrying a motorcycle helmet. His lined face was handsome for his age, and on the whole he cut a distinguished figure. I was so astonished I almost broke my stride. He saw me coming, too, and I don't know what he made of me in jeans and a sweater, but he caught my eye. We gave each other the quick, polite nod of busy colleagues passing in an office hall—a nod, I thought afterward, of mutual understanding—and I continued on to work.

I was surprised to learn that some women actually knew customers as more than a face behind the glass. There was a lawyer named Terry, for example, whom I had started to recognize from his regular visits, and who had started to recognize me. Charlotte, Maria, and I were onstage together on a weekday afternoon when the large corner window near the stage entrance began to open. Maria was closest, so she turned toward it, waiting to dance. But as soon as the screen revealed the customer, her underwater-slow movements came to an abrupt halt and she rushed offstage. I moved in to take her place.

From across the stage Charlotte saw that it was Terry. "He's going to tell you you're beautiful," she said, smiling at him, talking loudly enough for him to hear. She was right. Every regular was predictable in his own way. I danced a few feet away from him, waiting to see if he would stay. Sometimes they came to one window, scoped out who was onstage, then went to another, trying to get in front of a particular dancer. But Terry was lightly touching his groin now. He was going to stay.

Maria peered at me from offstage, and I nodded to signal that Terry was still there. She retreated back to the dressing room. The last time Terry had appeared during her shift she had done the same thing, and I had asked her what the deal was. I knew she wouldn't be back until he was gone. I moved in closer to the window, grabbed the plastic bar above it in my left hand, and crouched down so that I was at eye level with him, rippling my torso.

"You're beautiful," he mouthed. He undid his shorts.

Terry was pretty appealing as customers go. He was handsome and clean-cut, with full lips and short brown hair. He looked about thirty. He often came in wearing a suit, but today he had on a polo shirt and khaki shorts. I imagined he was on his way to go sailing, or to play a round of golf. Or maybe he just had a casual Friday.

Maria and Terry had met outside of work. They dated for a couple of months after meeting through a friend of Maria's who worked at Terry's law firm. She told him about her job at the Lusty, and he appeared unfazed. He had never been to a peep show, and he asked if he could come watch her. She said it would be fine if he wanted to come in once, just to see what she did.

They agreed on a time. He went and watched. Then, abruptly, he stopped calling her. She tried to reach him, but he wouldn't call back. She thought his behavior was bizarre, but she put it out of her head. She didn't expect to see him again. But several weeks later, a window went up at work to reveal Terry. She didn't know what to make of it. She was uncomfortable and refused to dance for him. He stayed, watching the other dancers.

She tried to call him to talk about it but she couldn't reach him. He appeared over and over during her shifts—so many times that she began to wonder if he was following her. How could he know her schedule? But he never called her at home, even though he had the number. Maria asked the show directors to refuse him admission, but they wouldn't, saying he hadn't really done anything wrong. As a compromise Catharine and Debra tolerated her leaving the stage whenever he appeared. He became enough of a regular that he had favorite dancers, including Charlotte and me.

Five minutes after Maria left the stage I was still dancing for Terry. I faced him on my knees, moving slowly. He had stopped mouthing endearments. His lips were parted, his eyes squinting, his hand moving quickly. He was almost done.

His window screen went down with a whir almost immediately after he came. He waved to me as it lowered. I watched his arm shrink to just his forearm, then just his hand, then his fingertips, then nothing but mirror. I was impressed with how well many of them were able to time it. They put in just enough money for exactly the duration they needed.

On my break I found Maria sitting on the dressing room counter scowling. Her arms were crossed, and she slumped against the mirror.

"He's gone," I said.

"I wish he would stop coming here," she grumbled. She hopped down and returned to work.

The stage was monotonous. Men with unusual fetishes, or incidents like Maria dodging Terry, were the sort of things that marked time. Sometimes the droning sameness had a soothing quality. There was nothing to be done about everyday worries onstage, so one might as well forget homework, children, or overdue bills for a few hours. The repetitive moves were meditative, like chanting a mantra. Up, down, turn, look, wink, ass, leg, shake, repeat as necessary until subject comes. . . . With mirrors on every surface—except the floor, we were spared that—I examined my own body as though it were something separate from myself, like a fine wooden boat or a thoroughbred horse. How did it look when I stood like this? Or like this? Could I move those two muscles independently of each other? Did the skirt flatter or detract? Should I have shaved there? This narcissistic concentration had the effect of clearing my mind, and I often emerged from daytime shifts with a buzz of invigoration.

Sometimes the monotony had a surreal effect. We weren't supposed to wear watches, so our only indication that a clock was ticking somewhere was the ten-minute span in which people came and went for breaks: April is on her break; April is back. Charlotte is on her break; Charlotte is back. That's twenty minutes I've been here. Maria is out; Maria is back. That's thirty minutes. Cassandra's shift is over. Blue is on break; Blue is back—forty minutes. Candy is on break. I'm next! But it was easy to lose track. It would have been rude to ask customers what time it was, but we often did ask them other things: Was it still raining? Was the sun out? The game over? The traffic okay? Girls in boxes couldn't be expected to know such things. Fantasies didn't have such mundane concerns; we didn't even have clothes. We were no more than a suggestion of humans; we were images hovering in a shiny red vacuum. Time, traffic, weather—these were beyond our world.

Chapter 7

For a while I had three jobs. I temped every morning, worked at the Global Affairs Council two afternoons a week, and fit the Lusty Lady in the rest of the time. I was busy but happy. I never had a whole day at one job stretching out ahead of me. No matter where I was, I knew I would leave soon. My private changeover moments, while I drove from one job to another, felt like suspended time. All my employers liked me, yet I didn't owe any of them more than half a workday. It gave me great satisfaction to be accepted in these unrelated little worlds, alone in my power to cross from one to another.

I started dressing more modestly outside of work, wearing overalls and loose sweaters. I got all the sexual affirmation I needed now in a few hours a day. I cared less than I had before whether men thought I was attractive or sexy. And I felt now as if I could control when I was looked at and when I wasn't, like turning a faucet on and off. I lapped it up at work, and the rest of the time I shut it down. I was the master of my own transformations.

I also became more comfortable blowing off men outside of work. If a man in a bar, for example, said something stupid or unpleasant, I no longer even pretended to be polite. If a man in a nightclub asked me to dance for a third time, I no longer felt I had to keep up a pretense that he was charming. I saw that for a long time I had lived as though there was a taboo against being confrontational or angry toward men, as though they had a right to patience and tolerance even when they didn't merit it. I had given too much benefit of the doubt before. I saw now that I could be *paid* to listen to insulting drivel. I could be paid to pretend that someone was the sexiest person I had ever met. In this way stripping gave me a gift. It helped me draw a line between what I would and wouldn't put up with in my outside life.

Secrecy was easy for me. Ever since I had told my first lie, almost accidentally, I had found silence comfortable. It happened when I was thirteen or so, and my mother had instructed me to ask another mother for a ride home from dance class. At the last minute I decided I didn't want to approach this woman. I felt as if I was imposing. I took the bus and let my mother believe I had taken the ride; this felt so natural a thing to do that I quickly forgot about it. A few days later my mother found out, and I was surprised and deeply aggrieved at her anger. It seemed unjust. I felt as if I had done what made everyone happy. I had gotten my quiet bus ride home without bothering anybody, and my mother, well—I didn't know why she wanted me to get a ride with this woman, but it seemed important to her, and I didn't mind letting her think I had.

But my mother's anger couldn't dissuade me from a tendency to let people believe what they wanted to. I thought it was a fine way to get along, and possibly the only way to buy a little unhampered time on my own. It wasn't just my parents I did this with. Reflecting people's wishes back at them made them like and admire me. I found that almost everyone wanted to identify with others, and that boys and men were looking for nothing so much as themselves. If I behaved like a mirror, they thought they were in love. What I didn't want, as a child or an adult, was to have to answer to any one person for everything I did. My parents were due a small piece of me; Erik was entitled to another, mostly distinct portion; and I guarded much of myself from anyone I thought would judge or make demands.

Being temperamentally suited to deceit meant it wasn't difficult for me to keep my dancing covert. My parents didn't know, and Vancouver was far enough away that it was easy to lie and say I was still temping. For years I had pretended to them that sex was not a dominating, gripping force in my life, and I had tried to conceal anything they would have thought was petty or manipulative. My impression was that they didn't wish to see flaw or frivolity in their children; I tried to show as little as possible. Not telling them about stripping hardly felt different from not telling them about everything else in the previous ten years. My brother, who had been at university in Seattle, left to teach English abroad shortly after I started at the Lusty, and I didn't tell him either.

I told a handful of friends, male and female. If anyone was taken aback, they didn't say so. The women peppered me with excited questions: What's it like? What do you do? What are the men like? I had a notion that certain friends thought it was cool; to know me said that they were open-minded and knew risqué people. One friend was so enthusiastic that, much to my dismay, she introduced me to her family as a stripper. She was bisexual, with many gay friends, and I knew she thought that it wasn't fair to out others. I wanted to explain to her that my position was similar in one respect: There was a stigma attached, and it should have been my choice whether or not to reveal my profession.

Despite my own concealments, I marveled at the trickery some dancers went through, actually living with families or boyfriends who didn't know what they did. A scrubbed and healthy looking blonde with the stage name Amelia started shortly after I did. Amelia and her boyfriend had just moved together from Minnesota to Seattle. When she told him she had auditioned, he cried, so she told him she wouldn't take the job. She did, though, telling her boyfriend that she temped during the day and, when she was scheduled for nights, that she packed goods for a mail-order company. She kept her wig, glittering jewelry, and dildos stuffed in her locker at work. What surprised me most about Amelia was her apparently wholehearted enthusiasm for the job. Right away, she took as many shifts as she could and started working in the private pleasures booth. She invested heavily in accessories and sparkling makeup. And though many dancers seemed to like aspects of their work, Amelia stood out in the way she talked about it with unqualified gusto. If this was so much a part of her, I wondered, how was she able to hide the entire thing? It was as though the secrecy of it, the danger that her boyfriend could find out any day, made her more excited to come to work than the rest of us. Still, I would have hated having to lie the way she did, in my own home, with the person closest to me. The effort not to get my story mixed up would have caused me too much stress. My deceptions were more like passive omissions; I left the facts vague so that people might think what they liked.

Maria had an even touchier situation. Though she still looked like a teenager herself, with freckled café-con-leche skin, she was actually twenty-eight and had two sons, ages twelve and fourteen. At home they were forbidden to enter her bedroom, where they might find hints of what she did. When she worked nights, she told them she was going out with a friend or working as a caterer. By day they thought she worked for a law firm, which she had done until she quit in 1996, planning to dance just for a little while before looking for another job. She had been the head of clerical services at the firm. She once told me, "If you're not a lawyer in a law firm, they treat you like shit."

But fissures appeared in her ruse from time to time. On the back of the schedules her name was marked with two asterisks. Dancers calling to trade shifts, though, sometimes made mistakes. Coworkers had called and asked enough times for "Emmy" that her sons were starting to wonder why. And once, she said, her older son had found one of her paycheck stubs. They didn't say "Lusty Lady" on them, but they did say "dance hours worked," next to "hours" and "total pay." She told him she had served drinks at a cocktail party as a favor to a friend. I asked her once what she would tell her boys when they got older, and she rolled her eyes and shook her head. "I don't intend to be doing this when they get older," she said.

Compared to Amelia, Maria, and others, I didn't have to lie much. But I was nowhere near as open as Zoe, a dancer with whom I became friends. She believed firmly in telling everyone. Her parents knew, as did her sister, boyfriend, and most anyone she met. I told her once that I didn't tell certain people because I didn't want to deal with their judgments and preconceptions. "That's why you have to tell them!" she said. "How are those stereotypes going to change if people like you and me don't talk about what we do?" She had an energy for changing minds that I lacked.

Occasionally, men I knew from my temp jobs came in to the Lusty Lady. I saw a project manager from the Bellevue construction company several times, but as far as I could tell he never recognized me. I didn't look dramatically different onstage from the way I had in the office, except for the obvious fact that I was naked. But being naked was a kind of disguise. After approaching him warily several times, and never catching a glint of recognition in his eyes, I assumed that even if I looked familiar the context must have been too different for him to place me.

And though the Global Affairs Council was only eight blocks away from the Lusty Lady, I never worried about seeing its employees turn up behind the glass. The few men who worked at the council were educated and politically liberal, which at the time I thought were dissuading factors. More important, aside from the director, they were young, which meant a variety of things: they had girlfriends and sex lives; they were less inclined to think that buying sexual services was normal; they had small disposable incomes; they hadn't had the time it takes to temper and burnish a true perversion. A slight majority of customers at the Lusty were middle-aged, and if you counted only the regulars, most of them were. The young ones were usually curiosity seekers, or drunk, or there on a dare.

The Global Affairs Council put on an annual reception at the Seattle Art Museum. It was held in a long, glass, street-level atrium across from the Lusty Lady, stretching from First up to Second. All the interns had been summoned to help out, and I found myself there in a business suit, adjusting national flags and taping signs onto poles. My boss, Simon, who was in his twenties, walked around sweating and fretting over last-minute details like getting the microphone to work. He gave me a small stack of Global Affairs Council business cards to hand out to anyone interesting or useful, which was, after all, the point of stuffing envelopes for free—to meet people who might help me get a job.

Waiting outside to greet guests I turned my back on the flashing marquee across the street. ("Have an Erotic Day!") I was talking to Simon when I realized that Zack, a talkative guy who worked at the front desk of the L, was walking up the sidewalk toward me. He was wearing his usual black jeans with a silver chain looping down from the pocket. Simon said something to me about the importance of networking just before I froze and stopped listening. Zack was getting closer. I stared at him and shook my head very slightly, willing him to disappear. I couldn't tell if he saw me, but suddenly he veered away, crossed the street, and walked into the Lusty. I hadn't taken a breath in several seconds. An unpleasant shiver shook my spine as my immediate surroundings came back at me in a rush of volume. Simon was talking about his microphone, and guests were arriving. We entered the brightly lit hall, which was now filled with a soft burble of clinking glasses, conversation, and violins.

I left the Global Affairs Council, crucial letter of recommendation in hand, and began another unpaid internship for a local magazine, where I fact-checked and was allowed to write short articles. Now making fifteen dollars an hour at the Lusty Lady, I made myself available for as many hours as the show directors would give me and turned down work from my temp agency. Stripping had become my sole source of income, I noticed with surprise. The fact that I had let that happen gave me a little thrill, as if I were walking close to a cliff edge. I couldn't call the job a sideline or an experiment anymore. It reminded me of a game I had played with myself as a child, on a beach my family went to every summer. I would swim out into the crashing surf and let a wave carry me in like a shell. Then I would take a deep breath, drop to the bottom, and let myself be dragged seaward in the violent suck of the undertow. When I started to run out of breath, I would kick the bottom and pop myself up like a cork, break the surface, and gulp air. I did it over and over until I was exhausted. Breathe, down, out, up, breathe, down, out . . . I swam in the surf every year until I was old enough to notice the water's paralyzing cold, and the current released me every time.

As I waded deeper into stripping, a blank spot grew in my recollections. I couldn't remember how I had lived before. I couldn't recall how I had organized my time or put up with the stultifying cycle of bus-office-bus-home. How did others do it? How did they make space for work they cared about, or that advanced their careers, when it didn't support them financially? How did they pay for school, or give themselves free time? Obviously they did; everyone managed, as I had before. But from inside my velvet- and mirror-lined job, I quickly forgot how it was done.

It had come so easily, this change from office girl to naked girl. I had expected more obstacles, if from nowhere else than within myself. There must be hurdles, I had presumed, or nobody would make such a fuss about the job. Because truly anyone who was female, breathing, and without major deformities could do this work. I had done no more than show up and sit through some interviews, and I was quickly learning from other dancers that the Lusty Lady was unique in requiring even that much screening. It was the willingness that made me different. Maybe I had once had some block within me of the kind that stops other women from becoming strippers, but if so it had disappeared years before. I felt like a misfit, as though I were missing some piece of DNA shared by the rest of society.

I arrived early one day for an opening shift, and a dancer named Tiffany came in a few minutes later. The dressing room was tidy and silent, freshly vacuumed and restocked by Jeff, whom I had passed on the way in. It felt peaceful. Tiffany looked bedraggled, with damp hair, wearing sweatpants and a too-large wool coat. She had given birth a month earlier, and I knew that her body was still showing strange stretch marks and sags, though on the whole it was snapping back reassuringly. She leaned her face close to the mirror and examined her cheek, where an immense, angry red pimple had erupted, and she said that on the bus she had felt as if everyone was staring at it.

"But you know, shit like this doesn't even bother me anymore," she went on. "Ninety-nine percent of people would think I'm a freak anyway if they knew what I did, so who cares if I look like one. I am a freak to them. We're all freaks."

I found that I knew exactly how she felt. I was a freak. Not properly socialized. But at least now I had company.

Chapter 8

I lived in two realities. In one I was the girlfriend of Erik, sharing a home and dutifully spending holidays with his family. But even while I helped his grandmother in the kitchen, or played with his niece and nephew, I felt like a fraud. I was indulging everyone, most of all myself, in a playacted life. In my other reality I had already projected myself into a future decoupled from Erik.

Erik, meanwhile, worked hard on the house, drafting friends now and then to help him. One of them, Lance, knew how to operate a backhoe, and they rented one and spent a week digging up the yard. They revved it up early every morning while I pulled a pillow over my head and tried to sleep off my late-night shifts. Our friend Matt came around to help Erik pour concrete, always a screaming and stressful operation. As I was leaving the house during their prep work, picking my way across what had once been lawn, Matt asked me where I was going, and I told him to my new job. He asked me what it was, and much later he would tell me that he had assumed I was joking.

Sometime in March I pedaled up the last steep block to my street with my thighs burning. I made it to the top and around the corner without dismounting, a first, and cheered quietly to myself while gulping air and coasting down to the house. Erik was working in the backyard, which now gaped like an open mine. Clutching the mail, I went inside and sat at my desk, which was wedged between a book-shelf and the hanging innards of the former kitchen wall.

I had been reaching for the mail with increasing anxiety over the previous weeks, looking for mail from what was, in the end, the only graduate school I had applied to. All my plans for departure now depended on getting into this one institution, and every day that went by without a letter was both good news and bad—good that I hadn't been rejected right away, bad that I still could be. This time there was a letter. I felt it, and it was fatter than one sheet, a good sign. I was afraid to see what was inside. I ripped it open quickly with shaking hands.

I was in. Not only that, they offered me a scholarship that amounted to almost half a year's tuition. I reread it five or six times to make sure I had it right. Something had paid off. No, everything had paid off. No more earthmovers, offices, rainy Seattle.

The screen door creaked and slammed, and Erik came in, trailing mud and small chunks of concrete. I calmly told him the news. He stopped still, and a tangle of expressions played across his face. Then he hugged me, enveloping me in sweat and dust, and whispered, "Congratulations." We held on for a long time. When he let go, he got a beer from the fridge and sat heavily on the sofa. His voice cracked when he asked me if I could defer my acceptance. "You could begin in January instead of September," he offered. I hadn't even thought of that. "I can't go in September," he said. "The house won't be done."

Inside I was ebullient, my blood racing. But I carefully separated my feelings from my expression and told him I would think about a deferment. His face screwed up into a wince, and he said, "Elisabeth, don't go."

If someone had asked me what Erik thought when I started stripping, I would have said that he didn't mind. But this would have been mostly a reflection of my opinion that he *shouldn't* have minded. It didn't occur to me that it was his right to hold an opinion on the subject. If he had chosen, say, to go back to school or change jobs, I would have supported his decision, and to the extent that I thought about it, I felt I was due the same consideration.

But I wasn't the only one who assumed Erik didn't mind. For a while he seemed to assume this as well. In the years that I had talked about stripping he had never said a word against it, and when I started he didn't voice any objection. He spoke fondly about a friend he once had who was a stripper, saying that she was "insane," a term he used to describe many of the people he admired most. I took this as encouragement.

Another close male friend of mine tried to discourage me from stripping at first, but he said finally that I should just do it and get it over with—he didn't want to know the details. Similarly, Erik seemed to make a good faith effort to tolerate my plan and even take pleasure in it. I was sexy enough and nonconformist enough, qualities that gave him a minor thrill. He wasn't happy about my stripping, but he couldn't object out loud without overturning his self-image, which was that of an open-minded and unjealous person. Jealousy had always been an unspoken demon between us, drawing strength from our refusal to acknowledge it. We had a longtime understanding that it was an emotion for other, weaker people.

I was slow to understand what many dancers have told me since: Lots of men like the idea, but few like the reality of a stripper girlfriend. Maybe I was stupid not to get this from the start, not to appreciate that what's desired at a safe distance isn't necessarily wanted in the home. But it suited me not to understand: I wanted the devotion of one man, and the admiration of many. At that time, if forced to choose, I would have taken the latter. Admiration from many meant no single one could make a claim on me.

So I was obtuse in my righteousness over stripping, but at heart it didn't matter to me what Erik thought. Had I wanted to keep the relationship alive, I might have asked, considered, and maybe altered my behavior. But I cared only to the extent that he occasionally made unpleasant comments. I wanted not so much understanding from him as quiet.

When in relationships, frequent sex had always been important to me. I enjoyed it physically but also needed it for more than pleasure. With sex, Erik and I expressed things that we didn't say to each other or even recognize. For example, I never told Erik that I always felt as if I was fighting to stay independent. But I had to know that he needed me more than I needed him. Continuing to have sex proved to me that he was still in my thrall. I didn't take anything—not his desire to live with me, marry me, or follow me, and not everyday kindnesses—as stronger evidence of his devotion than sex.

But while I semiconsciously wanted to prove that I was stronger than him, my need for sex weakened me. There had been a time early in our relationship when our sex life had fallen into a decline. For months, he fell asleep on the sofa in front of the television, and I would try to wake him and coax him to the bedroom; but he would open his eyes only long enough to growl at me, affronted. Tearful and self-pitying, I would take myself to bed, feeling that a great injustice was being done. I had the frustration of unfulfilled desire, and I also felt indignant and insulted. I was diminished because he didn't want me. The more he withheld sex, the more I needed him to desire me. Since I couldn't, by the implicit terms of our relationship, seek it elsewhere, I was left bereft. He had claimed and was now ignoring an essential part of me. As long as he didn't want me I was at his mercy.

Overall, working at the Lusty Lady didn't increase or decrease my physical desire for sex, but it did change my psychological compulsion. I stopped needing to turn on my boyfriend to feel whole. The customers showed me that I was desirable. At the same time, they helped me become a little more aloof from men's wants because I could see how capricious they were. Onstage I didn't care whether a man chose Cassandra or Maya or Leila. It seemed irrelevant to me, and dependent on the imagination of the viewer.

With the help of the Lusty Lady, I stopped needing Erik to desire me. This bolstered me for my getaway, giving me some of the strength I needed to walk away. I wondered what other women did when they wanted to leave a man. Maybe they never became as wrapped up in being sexy as I had. But what if they did? I knew women who were never without a boyfriend, who, in fact, overlapped boyfriends. Were they just lucky enough to fall in love again and again, or was something else at play? Maybe they feared falling apart if no one wanted them. How many women—or men for that matter—wanted to be wanted so much that it made them stay in relationships they would have otherwise left?

Since every love life was a secret, sex was difficult to know anything about. Books and magazines talked about it in terms of orgasms, because an orgasm, at least, was quantifiable. I tended to think this way, too—it was important to me to climax during sex. But by looking at my own relationships and at the customers, I was struck with how much of sex seemed to be more about being wanted than anything measurable. People were turned on by turning on. I had never faked an orgasm, but I understood the temptation. Every man I had slept with had been deeply concerned with giving pleasure, as though it went right to the core of who he was. At work my impression that men, like women, were aroused by causing arousal was confirmed. Our job wasn't just to be naked, it was to look and behave as though the customers really turned us on. For a convincing performance, men were willing to pay.

Chapter 9

Almost nobody looked forward to the Sunday morning staff meetings we were required to attend every couple of months. Management announced the meetings by taping signs to the dressing room mirrors, which the dancers read with weary resignation. At first I wondered how bad they could really be, but after going to a couple I understood. They were repetitive and always disintegrated into long-winded and inconclusive debates about workplace rules. Management paid us only six dollars an hour to attend. The meetings started at nine A.M. sharp and took up the whole morning, and the only acceptable excuses for absence were having worked the closing shift the night before, which ended at four A.M., or actually being scheduled to work during the meeting. After missing a meeting a dancer had to pick up a copy of the minutes, discuss its contents with three coworkers, get their signatures, and present the signed minutes to a show director.

Kim and Venus both held the title of performers' representative. In addition to dancing they were paid six dollars an hour for any time they put in to planning meetings, taking surveys, or acting as dancer-management go-betweens. An increasing number of dancers had been clamoring for changes to the scheduling rules and the tattoo and piercing policy. The performers were getting bolder, with good reason. Management was sensitive because of the unionization drive at the San Francisco Lusty Lady. Kim and Venus had been relaying demands to Catharine and Debra, who passed them up the chain of command to June.

Piercing policy was an issue dear to Kim's heart. Only three dancers were allowed to wear their body piercings onstage; the rest of us were forbidden. The three special cases had been around for so long that management had, as they put it, "grandmothered" them in when they banned bodywork. Lucia wore one nipple ring, Cinnamon had a pierced clit, and Belle wore metal in both nipples, her belly button, and clit.

Kim, whose stage name was Maya, wasn't so lucky. She had a small black female symbol tattooed on her hip and an allowable tongue piercing, but she had sacrificed a cherished nipple piercing because of her job. She had pierced it during her senior year of college when she felt she was getting ready to go out into the world. Before leaving her radical campus she wanted to reject what she saw as the status quo and mark herself as different. But when she got to the Lusty, she wasn't allowed to wear the nipple ring on stage. For a while she took it out for every shift, but after several months of removing and replacing, the hole became infected and it hurt too much, so with much regret she let it close over.

I had only four man-made holes in my own body, a very conventional two in each ear, the first pair of which I got on a long-awaited trip to a shopping mall when I was fourteen. I had the second pair of punctures made at nineteen. I had just returned to college after my very first solo trip abroad—a summer in Spain—and I wanted to exercise my newly felt freedom by branding myself. But I was unlikely to want any more, as my taste in adornment was conservative, and I had a deep fear of needles. I wasn't vexed by the Lusty's prohibitions.

It may have been just because I saw more of their bodies, but I had the impression that, as a group, strippers had more piercings than other people. Nose and belly-button piercings I empathized with. I thought they were sexy and was sometimes tempted to get one or the other myself. Nipple piercings I understood less, because I had sensitive nipples and was sure a piece of metal through one would put me in excruciating and lasting pain. The same went for clit and labia piercings. They suggested to me too much discomfort and pain on very tender flesh.

But I understood that everyone had her own taste and pain threshold. The only piercing that really confounded me was the third one Anastasia got in her tongue. She already had two bars through her tongue, side by side, with metal balls at either end that flashed and clicked against her teeth when she spoke. I was skeptical when she said she was going to get a third, all the more so when she explained that the tongue, unlike the earlobe or the flesh below the belly button, is a muscle. Rather than just shooting a piece of metal through the skin, the way most piercings are made, a hole in the tongue required that a chunk of the organ actually be removed.

Anastasia got her third tongue piercing and came to work later that day feeling ill. Over the course of her shift, despite painkillers, her jaw began to ache. Her alabaster skin went greenish and clammy. Her jaw swelled, her neck hurt, and she started slurring her words. Someone found her drooling morosely in the dressing room and urged her to call a manager and go home early, which she finally did without putting up much of a fight.

On a spring Sunday morning, I rode my bike downtown and locked it in front of the L. I removed the seat and walked two blocks north to the Pike Place Market, where management rented a room for our meetings. The market was sunny and peaceful, with vendors still setting up their wares. The throngs of tourists and Sunday shoppers had not yet arrived. I stopped at First and Pike to buy an iced latte and, on my way to our room, passed the fish counter piled high with ice and silver-wet salmon. One of the boys in his still-white apron called out to me, "Meeting today?"

Our upstairs room had a view of the bay. About fifty chairs formed a wide circle, beginning and ending at a table where Catharine, Debra, and June sat. A few dancers sat on the floor. It was refreshing to see everyone in real clothes. I had to stare at some of them for a few seconds until I connected the woman in front of me with the naked, doll-faced creature I knew from the stage. Hardly anyone wore makeup. The long hair that usually curled around shoulders and breasts had been scraped into ponytails. Absent wigs revealed fluorescent dye jobs, improbable spikes, and shaved heads. They wore jeans and overalls, thick-soled black shoes, homemade dresses and jewelry, army-surplus fatigues. Even though I saw them come and go from work, the effect of seeing everyone together was jarring. We looked normal.

Charlotte was an aspiring fashion designer and wore something of her own creation: striped thigh-high stockings and a ruffled, ass-skimming skirt made from shiny black PVC. She was standing in the middle of the circle looking for a place to sit when April yelled to her, "Hey, you dropped something!"

As she bent over to pick up an imaginary object, someone yelled from the other side, "No wait! You dropped something over there!"

She made an exaggerated bending-over motion, sticking out her ass and looking over her shoulder with fake wide-eyed innocence. More people yelled, "It's over there!," and she turned and bent over again. Everyone was laughing, including Charlotte. I was nearly doubled over. And when we realized we were all laughing, everyone laughed even harder. In subsequent years I would try to explain the hilarity of the moment and always fail. I think the butts of the joke were the men who looked at us. If anyone in the room had tried to explain it, she might have said, "They look at us, they whistle, they say things, and they don't realize how dumb they are." But it was no use, it was funny to us and no one else. That's what caused the second, louder round of laughter: The recognition of our freak status, the pleasure at having found an exclusive club of women who understood.

June didn't come to all of our meetings; her presence signaled weighty topics ahead. Debra handed out a numbered list of items to be discussed. "Trading and replacing shifts" was first, followed by "one-dollar raise" and "pay for prep time." "Tattoo and piercing policy" was fourth. Numbers two and three created a stir, and Debra had to ask us to quiet down.

Most meetings began with exhortations about stage behavior. We were told, usually, to focus on the customers, stop talking and singing onstage, wear more colors because men were scared by all black, and wear more garter belts because men liked frames. We were also told to put more sex into it—but not too much sex. No one wanted pussy juice all over the bars and mirrors, and showing too much onstage undercut the private pleasures booth.

But this time we skipped all that and went straight to the agenda. Item one, "trading and replacing shifts," was good news. Suddenly dancers would no longer be required to replace their shifts with a look-alike. A redhead didn't have to find a redhead and a busty didn't have to find a busty. It would now be easier for everyone to get rid of, trade, or pick up shifts.

Number two was as good as it sounded: one-dollar raises for all. The entire scale would be notched up. The new starting wage was eleven dollars an hour, and the new top wage twenty-five. And number three was more good news. Up until now there had been no recognition of the time we spent getting ready. Now we would be paid an extra quarter of our hourly wage for every shift, based on a presumed fifteen minutes of prep time. Most people took longer, but prep time pay was as much a symbolic coup as a financial one. Management was listening.

It wasn't hard to figure out that we were getting these unexpected bonuses to stave off any unionization attempts. The San Francisco dancers had fought, and we were reaping the rewards. We did have dancers in Seattle who wanted to unionize—Kim was one of them—but as many or more were opposed. My friend Zoe was against unionization. "Don't people get it?" she would ask. "It's a part-time job." She didn't think dancers should rely too heavily on the Lusty. Zoe had been dancing for about five years, much longer than Kim, who had worked for only about one. But the Lusty was Kim's only job, whereas for Zoe it was supplemental. She earned the majority of her income at bachelor parties.

After everyone had cheered the wage increases, we moved on to tattoos and piercings.

"This is a business," June began. "You think you work for me and for the show directors. But who are you really working for? The customer. Your customer is paying your salary." She spoke slowly so that every word could sink in. "So we have to cater to their tastes. We want women who look sexy and professional onstage."

Venus, a third-year law student, sat on the floor in a hooded black sweatshirt. Short red hair clung to her skull, and her cheeks had faint acne scars. "I have two points I would like to make," she announced. "First of all, what appeals to customers is entirely a subjective thing. Some customers like piercings. So we are catering to those customers by allowing piercings onstage. Second, it seems that there are a lot of ambiguities in the tattoo policy."

Other dancers murmured in assent.

Venus went on: "Are we allowed to have one if we cover it up? I know we're not supposed to get new tattoos while we work here, but some people do and then cover them with pancake makeup. I think part of the problem is, we don't really know what the rules are. And those of us with body work don't want to feel like we're discriminated against."

"Yeah, like are nose piercings allowed?" asked Nina, who wore one.

"We've said before that a very small stud in the nose is allowed," June said. Several people started talking at once. "Order, order," Debra called. April had her hand up. "April, go ahead."

"When I started, I got rid of my nose ring because the rules said I couldn't have one. Now my hole has grown over." Dancers mumbled and shook their heads in sympathy.

"I'm not concerned about nose rings," June said. "I am concerned about rings on the rest of the body. I have literally seen a man, an older gentleman, walk out in disgust at the sight of a nipple piercing. That's nothing against those of you who have them. It's a wonderful form of personal expression. But we are running a business here, and we have to think of the customer. It's just not a normal thing for many of them to see body piercings. They don't find it sexy."

The debate started to irk me. I sided with Zoe. I thought the L was as fair and well organized as any office I had ever worked in. It didn't bother me that there were dress codes; every job had dress codes. And I embodied one of the main obstacles to activism in the industry: I didn't plan to be here for long. To Kim, that was no excuse. "Someone says, 'Oh yeah, I'm just going to do it to pay off my bills,'" she told me once. "And six months later she's still doing it and hasn't dealt with the conditions."

In a fit of irritation I raised my hand.

"I think June has a point. We may think piercings are normal and acceptable, but if you look at the age range of most of our customers—"

Belle cut me off before I could finish. "Some of my best regulars are in their fifties or older, and they love my piercings. So don't use that argument." Despite her special grandmother status, Belle advocated more liberal piercing rules. That was the last time I spoke up in a meeting.

Ten people started talking at once.

"This is about changing standards of beauty!" said a new dancer named Frieda. She had a wavy black bob and caramel skin and had been around for less than a month. I had been onstage for her audition when she had worn a long, straight wig and a garter belt, which, I reflected, were unlikely to change anyone's standards. But I had to hand it to her, she didn't shave her armpits. That took some conviction. And her effusiveness made her good company in the dressing room. She was idealistic about stripping and was utterly sincere in her pronouncement about beauty standards. Her statement sparked a new round of debate, and I listened but kept silent. June reminded us that the Lusty went to great lengths to hire a diverse group of women. This was at odds with some of the Lusty's employment ads, which asked for "luscious blondes," but she maintained it was true.

The subject veered back to body art.

"This is about personal freedom," Belle said. "You trust us to make our own choices in costuming. We're adults, not children. You shouldn't assume that everything is going to suddenly look bad if you allow us to make our own decisions about how we decorate ourselves. We deserve that choice."

"Yeah," chorused a few people, but energy was fading.

The meeting went on until noon. It was decided that Venus and Kim, after consulting with performers, would create a body art policy proposal to present to June. June told us that wearing piercings or tattoos onstage before a decision was made "could affect scheduling and employment," ending things on a sour note.

In the way they dressed onstage, dancers at the Lusty showed a range of opinion on changing standards of beauty. At one end were dancers like Frieda, who flouted convention. They couldn't break the rules on hairstyles; if they had short hair, primary-color dye jobs, or dreadlocks, then they had to wear wigs. But some dancers had never touched a razor to their skin; a few went without makeup onstage; and while we weren't allowed to go barefoot, one danced in ballet slippers and a few others wore low- or flat-heeled shoes. Instead of wearing garter belts and stockings, some went completely bare or wore unusual belts and scarves.

Some dancers were more likely to notice what was "standard" than others. While I was at the Lusty there were never more than four black dancers employed at once, and roughly the same number of Asians, out of a total of around seventy women. Victoria, who was about five feet tall and black, had worried when she started that both her height and skin color would make the men more likely to reject her. That was one reason she had chosen to work at the Lusty rather than a club. Her height was less obvious, because she stood above the men, and being separated from them by glass meant she was less likely to hear what they said. She still couldn't help seeing their expressions, and sometimes when she approached a window a look of horror appeared on the man's face. If she was in the right mood, she made a joke out of it and said, "Wow, I sure gave you a shock." If she felt pained, she walked away.

But exoticism worked in her favor, too. In the private pleasures booth she started asking the customers if they had ever seen a black lady naked before, and they usually said, "No, you're my first." Entertainment and media didn't show black women much, she figured, and for a lot of men it seemed that what was new was erotic. In any case, being black brought her extra customers, and money, as well as driving a few away.

The Lusty also made her think that her body wasn't as strange as she had once thought. She had believed, for instance, that she had strangely shaped breasts, because they didn't hang in a perfect half circle like the ones she always saw in magazines. But surrounded by naked women, she noticed how varied their bodies were. It occurred to her that she wasn't unusual—it was just that only one body type was ordinarily put on public display.

In both looks and attitude, Betty was at the opposite end of the spectrum from Frieda and Victoria. If I had asked everyone I knew to describe a prototypical stripper and aggregated the results in a computer, it would have come up with Betty. Betty was the uber-stripper, the platonic ideal of stripper. She was the stripper one would arrive at based on market research. Not merely blond, she had long, platinum curls. Not merely busty, she had fake D cups. Her body was pink and creamy white and completely bald; her cunt looked like a baby's. A precisely lip-lined mouth and black-rimmed eyes enhanced the doll-like effect. She wore platform heels even when she wasn't working, and she tenderly called all the customers "sweetheart." She wore such an exaggerated stereotype of femininity that she reminded me of a drag queen.

In my appearance and outlook I was somewhere in the middle. By my mother's "accident of nature," I fit the convention of sexy that the Lusty Lady had determined sold best. I didn't go to cartoonish lengths to be blond and pneumatic, like Betty and a few others. But I didn't do anything unorthodox either—I wore makeup, shaved in the usual places, and bought different-colored thigh-high stockings and cheap platform heels. And while I admired Frieda's idealism, I didn't share it. Maybe she was right, and a few hirsute or pierced strippers could help change ideas of sex appeal. But I didn't think the Lusty Lady was about changing standards of beauty, as she had said. For the owners, the managers, and many of the dancers, it was mostly about money. I hadn't yet figured out what it was about for me. But I knew I wasn't out to evangelize on beauty to the customers. I was more interested in finding out if I could fill a role, written by someone else, called "stripper" or "sex symbol," than I was in reinterpreting it.

Chapter 10

Stripping put me in a new world with new conventions. Having ditched the moral framework of the outside world, I was now ethically adrift where nudity and sexuality were concerned. I actually felt as if I had divorced myself from the moral norm years previously, simply by growing up and becoming sexual. But when I entered pink-and-red stripperland, my departure became official. Having given up the old norms I needed new ones, and where none were provided, I had to make up my own.

I had to decide, now, whether or not to do the private pleasures booth. Onstage I was comfortable. I never had to talk directly with a man or hear him speak. If someone was rude, I could walk away. And we dancers felt bigger than the men in every way. We had all the mental fortitude that company provides, while they were partitioned into little boxes, each one alone in his black-walled universe. Plus the architecture of the stage was such that we literally looked down on them, and they looked up at us. We also held a sort of moral high ground, in the sense that we could explain our presence here, however disingenuously, in terms of earning a living. They, on the other hand, were ducking into cubicles where they paid money to watch girls fake arousal while they jerked off. What life existed behind each sequestered man I'll never know, but if we struggled with so-called normality, they must have done so even more. I suspected that, for the regulars in particular, something had gone wrong. Somewhere in the circle of sex, love, and society, something had broken down and tangled. But despite a sense of damage done, I was at ease with the stage patrons.

The private pleasures booth was a different matter. It was basically a miniature version of the stage that everyone called simply "the booth," or, occasionally, "the box" or "the cage." The dancer performed in a box lined with mirrors and red velvet, and the customer stood in a black-painted closet, separated from her by glass. Through a sound system, the customer and the dancer could carry on a real conversation, rather than the shouted or misheard kind that sometimes took place onstage. A second major difference was that the dancer was alone. She had no one to laugh with, and until she called the front desk for an escort at the end of her shift, she could not simply walk away.

And the men had needs. They had weird wants to be negotiated, mental trip wires that made them desire more than just visuals. They wanted to tell a girl what to do, or they wanted counseling, or they needed her to playact. Maybe they wanted to be looked at themselves. Whatever it was, they were guaranteed to draw on her mental energy in a way the men around the stage never would.

The booth was also more profitable than the stage, and less dependent on one's hourly wage. In the booth, the dancer made 50 percent of whatever the customer put in the bill slot, and above a certain amount she earned 60 percent. The resulting average among the dancers was between fifty and fifty-five dollars an hour, though certain women sometimes made as much as ninety. If a dancer drew few or no customers, she was at least guaranteed her hourly stage wage. The shifts were between one and two hours long. Some dancers, because they were low booth earners, could barely get themselves scheduled for one a week. And since it was draining work, even those who could get scheduled rarely did more than three a week.

I was intimidated by the booth, but mostly it was a mystery to me. No one knew for sure what anyone else did in there. Unlike the Champ Arcade and other peep shows, the Lusty didn't throw performers into private pleasures–style boxes right away. It was left up to each dancer to decide when she would start, and though they didn't have to do it, almost everyone did. While I waited, the mystery grew. In the dressing room I overheard women complain about, praise, and laugh at their booth customers. They compared the number of "shows" they did in each shift. They always seemed to head for the booth with grim determination, if not outright reluctance, and return exuding palpable relief. I often overheard one dancer or another on the dressing room phone, trying to give away her upcoming booth shift to someone who needed it more.

Considering the Lusty's overall slick micromanagement, the show directors were unusually silent regarding the booth. They ran through the mechanics of scheduling and earnings with new dancers but divulged little else. One dancer, Stephanie, told me that when she asked what the standard was for booth shows, they told her there wasn't one. They wouldn't even tell her what was legal. We had a vague notion that performing certain acts, like inserting things into one's vagina, under certain circumstances, like for a cop, could get you charged with violating obscenity laws. But we gleaned this only from dressing room word of mouth.

As well as the intimidation of the unknown, working the booth required learning a new set of procedures. Dancers had to fill out a form for each shift, keep an eye on the machine that tallied up shows, and negotiate with customers. Because of all this many dancers did a two-girl show their first time, known as a "double trouble." A new girl paired herself with someone more experienced who could show her the ropes. Double troubles were routine occurrences on the schedule. Girls sometimes did them for extra money, though they couldn't be guaranteed to make more than they would alone—they could charge more, and management let them take a higher cut, but they had to split the earnings. They also did them for company or out of boredom, or because they had a crush on another dancer and it was an excuse for physical contact. Triple troubles had been known to occur, and even the occasional quadruple trouble. We all lived in the shadow of rumored, legendary double troubles—multi-orgasmic shows in which the customer became no more than a pretext.

When I got into graduate school, I knew two things. One, I would be leaving Seattle, and therefore the Lusty, and therefore, most likely, stripping. Two, I could really use some cash. Not that any amount I could have earned at the Lusty would have been enough to cover tuition, but every little bit would help. I also had a growing sense of illegitimacy from just working the stage, as if I hadn't really pushed myself and as a result was missing out on something. And my boundaries had shifted since I started. As my work world became quotidian to me, the booth came to seem like the next logical step. Women I liked and admired did it, and so the idea moved from beyond consideration to actual possibility.

Enter Blue. She had an hourglass figure and long straight black hair with bangs cut evenly across her forehead. She looked like a nudie version of Veronica from the comic strip *Archie*. Blue owned a wide array of garter belts, among which my favorites were the lavender one and the see-through plastic one. After a shift she would face the dressing room mirror in a wide-legged stance, grab her hair by the bangs, and yank it off. Her perfect, elegant skull was shaved clean underneath. Blue had a tiny black triangle tattoo above one breast and a larger rainbow-colored triangle on one bicep. She carried around in her coat pocket a small vibrator, which she called the silver bullet. Outside of work she usually wore fatigues and black sweatshirts, though sometimes she turned up in a bright skirt and red lipstick.

"I know someone who likes you," Charlotte said to me in the dressing room, in the singsong voice of a six-year-old. It was Blue, of course. She had begun to flirt with me onstage. She would come up behind me and trace a hand along my side or my thigh. Sometimes she spanked me. Sometimes I reciprocated. It was mildly arousing, and wondering if she was going to approach me shortened the long hours. Lots of girls messed around with each other onstage, and sometimes it spilled out into the dressing room. I couldn't know for sure, but it appeared that much of the onstage flirtation was confined to work. Mine was. The stage was explicitly its own dimension, a sort of loophole in the rest of one's life. Onstage events subsisted on a peculiar oxygen not available anywhere else.

Getting dressed one day, Blue announced—loudly, as though to no one in particular, although she was standing very close to me—that she was getting bored and lonely in the booth and wanted some company. "I'll do it," I found myself saying. Opportunity had turned half-baked thought into reality. All we had to do was ask Debra to schedule it.

I got knots in my stomach in the week leading up to our slated day. Then Blue canceled two days before because she had an exam she had forgotten about. We put it off another week, giving me time to relax and then become worried all over again. Our shift finally came around on a sunny afternoon at one of those rare moments when light streamed in through the dressing room window. We got dressed in black lingerie. She put on her wig and asked for disposable latex gloves from one of the janitors.

"Oh no, I forgot to bring toys," she said.

Toys?

"Do we need them?"

"They're good to have because you can charge money for different stuff. I normally always use them."

Great, I thought. Not even out of the dressing room and already my first booth was going wrong. How could she screw up my first time? But there was nothing to do about it. One didn't lend or borrow toys. And I wouldn't have known what to do with them anyway, so maybe this was a good thing. Fortunately I didn't have much time to ponder anything else since Jeff came to the door with merciful speed. He escorted us down the hall and released us into the red velvet box where we would spend the next hour.

The booth had two windows: one that faced the customer cubicle, and one facing the hallway. Each could be blocked off from the inside with a heavy curtain. While waiting for customers we displayed ourselves to the hallway like cats in a pet store window, our best "pick me" expressions on our faces. We curtained off the hallway when a customer entered and turned 90 degrees to face the cubicle.

Once inside Blue calmly talked to me about what we should charge for specific acts. She asked me what I was comfortable with, and I didn't know how to answer. Finally I said that anything anal was definitely out of the question but that otherwise I was easy, though I didn't feel easy at all. I felt like I was about to submit to both a dental and a gynecological exam at the same time. Blue said there would be no actual oral sex since we had no dental dam but that we could simulate. Feeling dazed, I said, "Right, okay," as though she were stating the obvious. I didn't know how to simulate licking pussy. For that matter, I didn't know how to do it for real.

"You do the talking," I told her. I would follow her lead.

It was past midday, so the majority of the lunch-hour crowd had already gone back to their skyscrapers, but we had a few customers. I was mute while she confidently sweet-talked. "Would you like to see . . . ," "We'll need a tip for that . . . ," and, of course, "It's her first time. . . ." I did as she directed, which at one point involved her sliding a gloved finger inside of me. She explained technicalities related to light switches, timers, curtains, and counting cash, but not a word of it stayed in my head. I felt so unerotic that I couldn't even muster up a good impression of being turned on. The best I could do was to try not to look anxious.

My first and last double trouble was cold, sterile, and not remotely legendary. "Thanks," I said to Blue afterward. "It made me more comfortable to have someone in there my first time." I didn't want to appear ungrateful, but I also wanted to make it clear, through the tone of finality in my voice, that it would never happen again. This was presumptuous of me, since there was no indication that she had enjoyed it either, but I wanted to be sure.

We were back in the dressing room, getting dressed, the sun still shining in. Debra puttered in her overalls inside the open office door, and I went in and told her to sign me up for one booth a week. "Just one?" was all she asked, and I said, "Yeah, for now."

Blue and I never mentioned the double trouble, but we stayed friendly. I gave her rides home from work sometimes, to the house where she lived with a woman she called her wife, and later her ex-wife. Blue was studying graphic design, and I helped her get an internship with the art director at my magazine. Once she took me to a lesbian bar on Capitol Hill called the Wild Rose. We crowded into a table with a group of her friends, and she pointed things out to me like a proud native guide. You got a cross-section of society at the Rose, she said—from lawyers to blue-collar workers to college girls—

because it was the only good dyke bar in town. She complained about butch dykes who failed to treat the femmy ones in gentlemanly fashion, buying them drinks and pulling out chairs.

Over the next few months, Blue grew out her hair. She later started dating a man, left the Lusty Lady, and moved to San Francisco; we lost touch.

Late at night in early May, I walked offstage and punched out. Then I flipped my time card over and punched the other end to mark the start of my booth shift. I took off my shoes with relief and grabbed a yogurt from the refrigerator, laid a paper towel on the red easy chair, and sat down. I had fifteen minutes.

Simone entered the dressing room from the hallway, having just finished in the booth. She wore a see-through pink slip over a pale beige bra and panties. Her black female-symbol tattoo was visible through the slip. Straight blond hair fell below her shoulders, and bangs framed her delicate features. She was tall and skinny, graceful rather than gangly.

"How was the booth?" I asked.

"Good. Pretty busy."

It wasn't a very useful question to ask, I thought to myself, because Simone always did well in the booth. She had been doing it for three years and had a corps of well-paying regulars. One creative customer had given her a remote-control vibrator he had made himself. Simone brought the vibrator with her into the booth, and he brought the controls with him to the other side of the glass.

While Simone transformed herself to get in her pickup truck and drive home to her girlfriend—removing her wig to show closely cropped hair, pulling on jeans and a black sweater—I dressed for the booth. I put on a black satin push-up bra, out of which my breasts almost spilled; a black lace thong; knee-high black stockings; and my black fake-suede high heels. There were no costuming rules in the booth, so I could wear as much black as I liked. In fact, there were few rules of any kind once you were inside. I didn't buckle my shoes because I was going to remove them before I began. They were just to get me down the hallway.

I brushed my hair, powdered my face, and put on more lipstick, then clinically surveyed my image, which was framed in the mirror by taped notes:

"Sierra's Tuesday dance shift up for grabs. Call me!!"

"Mercy—Call Jesse at home"

"Anyone want to go hiking on Thursday? Call P.J."

And, from the show directors, a notice entitled "Sick Pay Questions."

I checked the items I would bring with me: a hairbrush, a plastic zippered pouch containing lipstick and powder, and a large piece of embroidered black cotton in which I wrapped the other items. I also brought a paper cup full of water from the cooler because I always got thirsty. I picked up the phone and called the front desk.

"Hi, this is Leila. I'm ready for the booth."

I stood for a few seconds by the dressing room door until I heard the metallic clink of keys outside in the hallway. The support staffers all wore voluminous key chains like armor.

"Whenever you're ready," said Chris, and I stepped from the warm bright light of the dressing room into the dark hallway. Chris stood back, allowing me to choose which way to walk. There were two routes from the dressing room to the booth, one usually busy with customers, the other one quiet. The busy route was the long corridor extending to the left of the dressing room door. On one side of it ten doors opened onto the stage-viewing cubicles; the other side was lined with private video stalls. The backs of legs were always visible below the cubicle doors, mostly with trousers rumpled around ankles. On each stage-viewing door was a sign with a cartoon drawing of two pouting, bare-assed women. Half of the door signs read "we can see you"; the other half "we can't see you." A few customers milled around in the hallway jingling change in their pockets, and beyond the long corridor was the entrance foyer; the front desk, where Chris, Jeff, and Zack exchanged large bills for small ones and made sure dancers arrived on time; the closed-circuit black-and-white monitors of other parts of the theater; a cash machine; a change machine where customers turned fives and tens into quarters; a magazine rack carrying *The Stranger* and *Exotica;* the wall of pornographic works that management called the Erotic Art Gallery; and the Polaroid display. The brightly lit glass display case showed every performer who worked in the booth in alphabetical order, from Apple Jack to Zenia. My photo had recently joined their ranks.

Later on I would usually choose the busy route past the foyer because it helped pick up business. I thought of it as running a gauntlet. The men in the hall stared and commented—"muy bonita!"—and without my protective glass wall I felt like bait thrown into the water. It was the same feeling I had walking parts of First or Second Avenue outside, feeling the predatory gaze and hearing the rough comments. And I walked the same way I did in the street—briskly, with eyes slightly down, determined not to notice.

But that night it hardly mattered which route I chose because there were so few customers loitering. I took the short, narrow hallway to my right, the one I thought of as the back road, and Chris followed. We then turned left, passed the customers' bathroom—a pool of bright white-tiled light behind swinging saloon doors—and walked down a hallway lined with video stalls. On the door to each, a pink sign read, "30 Channels XXX-Rated Videos." A light above each one indicated whether it was occupied or not. We passed all these doors and arrived at a glass window under a pink fluorescent sign that read, "Private Pleasures Booth." Next to the window a glass case showed my Polaroid, in which I stood smiling in front of a blue satin curtain, in lingerie identical to what I had on now. Under the Polaroid a laminated sign read "Leila" in large black letters. The support staff changed the signs and photos between girls.

Zinging a key out of his bundle, Chris unlocked a narrow wooden door, let me in, and then locked it behind me so that no one could open it from the outside. I was in the booth's anteroom now, a mini–dressing room of about five by two feet. I relaxed a little after the hall and kicked off my shoes. I had a final few minutes to savor before going on display.

The upper half of one wall was covered with a mirror. Below it, two shelves were stocked with supplies: baby wipes, rubbing alcohol, vaginal lubricant, window cleaner, paper towels, tissues, a pump bottle of an antibacterial liquid called Purex, and disposable paper sheets like the ones used in doctors' offices. The sheets were new: Ever since two dancers had contracted scabies, everyone had been encouraged to bring their own sheet, which was why I had the length of black cotton. If a dancer didn't bring her own, she could use one of the paper ones supplied. The week's schedule was posted on the wall, above an alphabetized file box that held all the Polaroids and laminated name tags.

I took one of the calculation sheets from a wooden box on the wall and started to fill it out:

Stage name: Leila
Date: 5/5/97
Time shift begins: 12:45 A.M.
Time shift ends: 2:30 A.M.

There were two meters on the wall, one that read "shows" above it and one that read "bills." Each one displayed a six-digit number that I recorded on my sheet. The "shows" reading counted the units of time each customer paid for and would help me determine how much I had made. The "bills" reading helped the managers count the cash.

Finally, I printed my real name and added my signature.

I ascended three narrow steps, entered the booth, and closed the door behind me. The entire back wall of the booth, including the inside of the door, was mirrored, and the other walls and the floor were carpeted in bright red velvet.

The window facing the hallway was draped off with a red-and-black rose-patterned curtain. The other window was larger, taller than me, and was hung with heavy red velvet. It faced the cubicle where the customer would stand wearing his headset. Clear plastic bars, strong enough to support my weight, flanked either side of the large window, and another ran across the top. A small shelf above the hallway window was used to hold more baby wipes, alcohol, and Purex. A telephone in one corner was set to automatically dial the front desk if I picked up the receiver. We were supposed to use it to call for an escort to the dressing room, a cleanup on the window, or the eviction of a problem customer.

I spread my black cloth on the floor and arranged the eight pillows the way I liked them: four small ones next to the hallway window, for leaning on while trying to attract customers; two large ones in the middle of the room, for leaning on while performing. I threw the remaining two into the anteroom. I opened the curtain onto the empty customer cubicle and carefully arranged the folds to hide the "PP Mistress 2000." The "Mistress" was a red metal box with two digital displays and three square red buttons. It recorded the amount of money the customer put into the bill acceptor and counted his remaining time. I had found that when the customers could see it, they became preoccupied with when their show was going to end.

Finally I opened the curtain onto the hallway, putting myself on display. A short Hispanic man stared at me intently for a few moments, then walked away. A young blond man in a windbreaker saw me from the other end of the hall and walked toward me. I lay down on my side, head propped up on my hand, my knee bent to make my hip curve. I inched closer to the window, where the light would catch me. I smiled at the customer walking toward me.

I was ready to begin.

The booth was not easy money. For every amiable, generous customer, there were a dozen who were rude, demanding, cheap, or some combination thereof. Even the most experienced performers got booth burnout at times and took themselves off the private pleasures roster for months.

Everyone—even the girls with followings of quirky regulars—saw countless customers with indistinguishable desires. These men wanted, simply, to see more. More body, more tongue, more tit, and especially more pussy, as deeply as they could behold. Sometimes I laughed out loud at this. I wasn't mocking them; it was just that I found it so absurd. More was never enough. You could have your labia nearly planted against the window and they still made "spread it" motions with their hands, bending and peering to get a better angle. There was one stage regular who always came equipped with a flashlight. What did he think he would find? The vagina was more or less a tunnel once you got past the opening. One dancer periodically intoned onstage, like a soothing subway announcer, "You have reached the cervix." Another dancer would lie back in front of a corner window, legs spread wide, and say cheerfully to some unblinking man, "Let me know when you find the pot of gold!" It felt as if they wanted to see our insides. One Seattle Web business, where several Lusty dancers had worked, was infamous for providing girls with a "dildo-cam"—a dildo with a camera on it, which enabled the remote viewer to see the pink wall of flesh inside.

The booth wasn't quite so extreme, but it was, among other things, a place to see more. The majority of dancers used toys—dildos and vibrators—and most developed a list of prices for specific acts of penetration. A sex toy was so de rigueur that management would reimburse new dancers who bought one for up to fifteen dollars. The women who used them lined up their bright-colored plastic playthings in the window to try to entice customers into a purchase. Performers also charged to use their fingers—so much for two inside, so much for three, and so on.

Some women were willing to talk about what they did in there. Anastasia didn't do any penetration at all, she said, even with her fingers, but she was still a midrange earner. She had dark flashing eyes and a taut body as well as a good deal of metal in her tongue, and once I saw her go to the booth wearing ripped denim shorts. She was sharp and thoughtful, and the customers paid because she was a good talker. Another woman told me she charged a forty-dollar tip for anal penetration, on top of the cost of the time it took, and she said it took her a long time. Belle, a top earner, had a speculum—the medical instrument used to widen the vagina—and charged thirty dollars to use it. This meant customers could actually view her cervix. Belle also had a set price to make herself have an orgasm, and she would really do it, not just fake it. Though I thought this was an audacious thing to charge money for, it didn't surprise me that there was a demand. They always wanted to see us wetter, to be convinced that we were really turned on.

Once again I was traveling without a map. There were no rules proscribing what to do in the booth, either from management, which stood to make more by being laissez-faire, or from social expectation, which said I shouldn't be there in the first place. I had to make it up as I went along.

The booth forced me to think about what I was doing in more direct financial terms than I had before. Though I appreciated my stage income, which was now in the high teens per hour, and lived on it, I had never thought of the stage exclusively in terms of money. It didn't just earn me more, for fewer hours, than other part-time jobs— I also found it more pleasant than temping, waiting tables, or working in a shop. I never went to work bracing myself, or thinking the cash was all that made it worthwhile.

I had to brace myself for my booth shifts, especially at first. With no one to tell me the rules, I could only go on a gut feeling of what felt right and wrong. But sometimes I had to bump up against the wrong to figure out what it was. In general, I didn't put my fingers inside myself, even when they asked me to. Once when a customer asked, I did and tried to charge him. But it felt like such a ludicrous topic for negotiation that I almost started laughing. He paid me, and I continued, and felt an immediate surge of anger toward him. Afterward I was left with the uneasy, unpleasant awareness that I had done something I didn't want to for money. The stage had never made me feel that way, and despite my jitters the booth usually didn't either. But I realized I had to approach the booth knowing my own boundaries. Otherwise I might be faced with a cash offer and a split-second decision, and make the wrong choice. A few decisions were easy. Toys, for me, were out of the question, because I found them alien and unerotic; I was almost a toy virgin. I had never used any unless you counted one of those electric drugstore vibrators that were marketed, either euphemistically or in willful ignorance, as massage tools. I knew that if I were to try anything so new to me, it would be in my personal life, with no money at stake. Double troubles, after Blue, were also out. Now that I was a booth worker, more customers would ask me to meet them outside, but that, too, would always be an easy no. The risk of meeting a stranger would have stopped me, but beyond that I was just never tempted. I never met a customer whom I wanted to know beyond the games we played in the box. I was, by the norms of my new world, quite conservative.

Still, whatever you decided your boundaries were, you couldn't be prepared for every request. Zoe had once been asked to pee. She said she could—there were small plastic garbage bags in the anteroom—but he balked at the forty dollars she demanded. A customer asked me to sell my panties to him, which I did for twenty dollars—they had cost me six—in an illegal move that required me to open the anteroom door and pass them out. As a stripper someone was always offering you more to do more. Because of this, my boundaries became more ironclad than ever. They had to be, or I would have been pushed until I had lost any sense of where the men stopped and I began. The customers would always test how far they could go because they, too, were off the map. I wasn't in the category "girlfriend" or "wife," characters they thought they knew. I was "stripper," a creature who did sexual things for money, and if I didn't tell them what the limits were, nobody would.

I made fifty or sixty dollars an hour in the booth, an average amount. At first I did just one a week and later two. Clumsily, by trial and error, I developed a modus operandi. I tried to encourage good tipping for a good show without charging act by act. I never penetrated myself. What I didn't mind, and sometimes even enjoyed, was talking and playacting. Sometimes customers complained that I had no toys, in which case I suggested they come back and see someone else.

I started to get my own regulars. They were on the whole more polite, interesting, and profitable than all the quickies who came and went. I started to remember their faces, their likes and dislikes, and even in some cases their names. The Lusty had a telephone hotline with a recording of the booth schedule. They would find out my hours and turn up, sometimes waiting in the hallway before my shift began.

There was one who, like the dancers, had a fantasy name for himself. He told me he was called Excalibur, which evoked a heroism that contrasted with his job as a baker. He wore glasses and had long hair, and he rambled philosophically but usually without making sense. He amused me but also had an insistent quality that I became annoyed with. He started leaving me gifts at the front desk, always strange collections of thrift store trinkets housed together in a little box or a paper bag. The items seemed disconnected—for example, a framed drawing, a ceramic statuette, and an embroidered pouch all came together one time. I wondered if they held some connection in his mind. Excalibur paid for lots of time—the booth cost a minimum of five dollars for two and a half minutes—but he didn't add much in the way of tips. I talked to him as though his every word fascinated me, and sometimes I took off my clothes. One time he came in acting dizzy and talking even more nonsense than usual, and said he was on acid. He gave me pages and pages of poetry, always painstakingly handwritten backward with the aid of a mirror. It would have taken me a long time to hold it all up to a mirror and read, and I never bothered. I shoved it in my locker with the rest of his junk and eventually threw it all out.

Another regular was a handsome, dark-haired guy named Phil, who always wore a red jacket suitable for climbing mountains. He said he was a computer programmer. He had a fiancée we sometimes talked about, a graduate student, who he said didn't know he came here. I got the sense that he enjoyed his little deception, so I goaded him on it. "What would she do if she found out?" I asked him, watching his dick get hard. He told me the reason he liked the Lusty Lady was because it was seedy.

So many of them just seemed to want to please. More precisely, they wanted to be sold the illusion that they were giving pleasure. They assured me over and over that if they could just magically pass through the glass they would make me feel unbelievably good, usually by way of their tongues, less often their cocks. For them I did virtually nothing but lie with my legs spread open while they bent their head to the glass and flicked their tongues back and forth. I said things like, "Mm, yes, I bet you're really good at that." Lying back on my pillows, I had lots of time to think. I thought about Simone and her remote-control vibrator, and Belle and her fee for making herself come. They wanted us to have orgasms. Was it because they wanted to please us? Or was it because an orgasm was a sort of surrender, and therefore causing one was a sort of conquest? From our side of the glass what they did looked a lot like worship.

One of my most reliable sources of income was a man who never told me his name, but whom I thought of as Navy Guy because he said he was a sailor. He looked about forty, had a neatly trimmed mustache, and usually wore a jean jacket. He would disappear for long stretches, then come in several times in a couple of weeks. I became a favorite of his because I played along with his exacting demands. He was precise about what he wanted and would happily spend a couple of hundred dollars if his fantasy was delivered just so. They always involved a similar plot line, usually pedophiliac.

He preferred me to wear clothes and only wanted me to remove them very slowly. He would ask me questions like how old was I, and where were we. The first few times, when I didn't know what he wanted to hear, a look of frustration would cross his face and he would bark at me. He didn't insult me, but he spoke brusquely. With a snort of impatience he would go over what he wanted as though explaining it to a child. After a while I learned what he liked, and he had to explain himself less often.

"How old are you?"

"Fourteen," I said. I knew he would rather have heard me say eleven.

"Who are you?"

His eyes were beady, and his hair was bristly. His face suggested a well-groomed rodent.

"I'm a schoolgirl. Your student," I said. "You're keeping me after school."

"Did you misbehave in class?"

I nodded. I was wearing a very short, black-and-white-checkered skirt, his favorite. On top I wore a black bra, not his ideal choice, a little too racy. We were going to have to imagine the shirt I wore.

I said I had arrived late for class.

"You're going to have to be punished. You're going to have to stay after school."

"Do I have to?" I asked. "I don't think I should." He liked resistance.

He put a hand on the bulge in his still-zipped jeans. He liked to wait. He started stroking himself.

"You have to stay. You're going to have to do what I tell you to," he said.

"Are you going to tell anyone?"

"Not if you do what I say." He undid his pants and reached inside. "Come over here and sit on my lap."

I moved and kneeled by the window. Absentmindedly, out of habit, I started to remove my bra. He shook his head in frustration, let go of his penis, and quietly commanded, "No, leave it on." I had broken character.

I enjoyed the schoolgirl fantasy more than I expected to, I think because of the coercive quality, which had never existed in my own sex life. Coercion was taboo and therefore exciting. Sometimes he wanted me to play somebody's little sister. Not his own, I insisted. A friend's, perhaps, or the next-door neighbor's. Then we would pretend to be in the bedroom of a family house, where I would be innocently shocked by his nakedness and by my own desires. I would undress very slowly, I would masturbate, I would put my face to the glass and pretend to suck on him. Whatever the scenario it always contained secrecy, punishment, his dominance and my submission, and my initial reluctance followed by enthusiastic lust. I never had to ask for tips; the bills came in unsolicited. If things were going especially well and he wanted to make sure they stayed that way, he would pause to slip in a couple more twenties or a fifty. My job was just to play a role, which suited me. I still didn't like the hustle of asking for money.

I wondered if my little restrictions on his fantasy mattered at all. What difference did it make if I was eleven or fourteen? It was all imaginary. Sometimes I thought we did a service to society in there, keeping potentially dangerous appetites locked up in a safe environment. But then maybe we just encouraged them. Or as Kim, an expert booth performer, had once told me, "I am hopeful that it's a safe redirecting. I am not 100 percent confident."

Navy Guy turned up one day and put in an initial bill to start the show. I pressed the button that turned on the light and sound, and I smiled and asked how he was doing. He fumbled with the headset for a moment, and when he got it on, he hesitated.

"Do you think I'm perverted?" he asked. I looked quickly to his face and saw that this wasn't part of the game. His guard was down and his expression vulnerable.

"Do you think I'm sick?" he asked.

I spoke carefully.

"If you did in reality the things you pretend to do in here, I might think you were sick," I said. He nodded. It seemed to be enough of an answer for him, because then we began the fantasy.

A few days later I was in the dressing room when Gypsy came in after her booth shift. She had years on me in age and experience, and I regarded her as a real pro.

"You wouldn't believe the obnoxious customer I just had," she said. "He wanted me to pretend to be some sort of schoolgirl. He was ordering me around, trying to tell me what to do." She took off her wig and brushed it furiously.

"Was he kind of shortish with a mustache?" I asked. He was. "Did he have on a jean jacket?" He did. "I know that guy," I said. "He always wants you to be his little sister or something."

"Yeah, that's him. He told me what to do so many times I finally just told him that I was running the show. He had the nerve to tell me I wasn't doing a very good job. *I* wasn't doing a very good job," she repeated. "Then he sort of shook his head as though he were disgusted, and walked out before his time was up."

Indignantly, she threw her shoes into her locker and began to change clothes. I didn't say anything because I didn't want to admit that I didn't mind this guy too much. I felt something I couldn't quite put my finger on. It was partly surprise, because I had considered her an unflappable old hand. Then I realized what the rest of it was. Pride. I had handled that guy. I had given him what he wanted and earned his money. I looked down at the floor and smiled. For whatever it was worth, I was good.

I always felt a vague anxiety before my booth shifts. I couldn't say exactly what I feared, just that a man would say or do something terribly disturbing, and I would be stuck facing him, alone. And the booth *was* more difficult than the stage, because I had to focus on my façade the whole time I was there, whereas onstage I could tune out. But my trepidation invariably outweighed any problems. The booth always held some possibility of being interesting, and the hours there usually passed more quickly than they did onstage. As time went on I became more comfortable saying no. My worst episode ended quickly. The customer ordered me around, coarsely and with little cash incentive. I balked. He said, "You're rude"; I said, "No, you're rude," and shut the curtain on him, then called the front desk to make sure that he left.

Much later, years after the last time I had seen him, I learned something about Navy Guy from Anastasia. She had asked him outright why he always acted out the same fantasy. He told her that his sisters and mother had raped him. When I heard this, I felt sharply sad. I pictured him saying it in the same way he had asked me if I thought he was perverted, blankly and without defenses. Of course, I had no way of knowing if it was true.

Chapter 11

When I told Erik I had started doing the booth, he told me he thought it was wrong. "You shouldn't do it," he said glumly, sitting on the desk chair next to the hanging wires and insulation. "You said you wouldn't." I couldn't remember if I had promised that or not.

At first, I was incredulous. He was proudly unbound by laws, morals, or rules of any sort, but suddenly they suited him. Unequivocal words like "it's wrong" never came out of his mouth, which was why it took me some time to be convinced that his sadness and anger were real. When I realized that they were, I stopped telling him anything more than necessary about work. Before I had told him anecdotes I had thought were amusing but insignificant; now I held back. Whereas at first he had sometimes picked me up and dropped me off at work, he started to refuse. As the Lusty Lady became more and more mundane to me, its every detail took on twisted significance for him. There was a bitter edge to his voice when we talked about it even cursorily. I rarely told him when I worked a booth shift, letting him think they were few and far between.

There were many things wrong with us. I had one foot out the door on my way to leaving for good. We squabbled and tried to manipulate each other; we lived amid encroaching mess; we had leftover jealousies about the people we had dated when we were apart. Above all, we had no will to change or compromise; any reciprocal desire to please had collapsed into "you go first." Some people, I have heard, have angry sex, checked-out sex, or just-putting-up-with-it sex; I had never been that way. All this emotional caving-in numbed my desire to sleep with Erik, so it became an occasional event. When we did have sex, he complained that I wanted it from behind too often, suspicious that I must be fantasizing more when I faced away.

Erik started to blame stripping for everything that was wrong. It was true that I didn't need him to want me as I once had, and that that was related to dancing. But the job had only helped a breakup that would have happened anyway. He was blind to attribute the tensions of four years to my relatively recent pursuit. It was as though by focusing on stripping he could block out everything else.

Sometimes he tried to seduce me, and when that failed he begged. In the mornings when I was barely awake he pulled me to him and asked me to touch him. When I said no, he masturbated anyway, under the covers beside me. I ignored him and pretended to sleep, or I asked him in exasperation to stop; but he wouldn't, and I would become angry at being made to participate without participating. I felt helpless. I questioned whether I had a right to be angry at him and tried to convince myself not to care.

I sometimes became aroused during booth shifts, but only fleetingly, and by the time I got home the hunger had usually passed. After one shift, though, I took the feeling home with me and found him on the sofa half asleep. I wondered if he would rebuff me. I removed my outer layers of clothing and mounted him, and after a few moments of surprise he reciprocated with enthusiasm. It was a relief for both of us to want the same thing at the same time. I told him afterward that I had come from the booth, as though to say, See? They're not so bad. But I had made a mistake, because I didn't want to have sex after work again, and in the following months he asked me repeatedly, "Why then?" and "Why not again?" He briefly and optimistically reconsidered his opinion of the booth, but when I lapsed back into reticence, he hated the idea once more.

If my sex life was misfiring badly, at least my sense of entrapment was falling away. As spring turned into summer I plotted my departure, which I had started to think of as an escape requiring no less strategy, precision, and tenacity than a military maneuver. A new, single life beckoned, and I nearly salivated thinking about it.

We started splitting up our things. When I looked around our house, I realized there was very little that I wanted. He could keep the furniture we had bought. He could have the glasses and dishes we had received for Christmas and our hand-me-down beige pullout sofa. I would have no use for any of it in my student apartment. The only thing I coveted was a smooth departure.

One life of mine was coming to a close. But I still felt at risk, as though it could mire me down if I made a wrong move. As I looked around the house I thought of all the things Erik had taught me. With him I had learned to sail, drive a stick shift, cook perfect rice. A man was a whole world, I thought. I could attach myself to him and have his life—his family, his pastimes, his obsessions. For a short time I could make myself the woman of that man—letting him wash over me, soaking him up. And still he would only ever know a fraction of me. Men—people—never seemed to see what they didn't want to see. With Erik I had talked about my simmering, defensive urge for escape hundreds of times. But he still seemed almost surprised when I left.

Without the weight of the future, our relationship was lighter, and much of the time we got along. Whereas in the past we had argued—about money, about housekeeping, about smoking—nothing was worth a fight anymore. When I realized that I was going to be able to leave in peace, every box I packed made me feel giddy. In August my parents went abroad, and I went to stay in their house. I drove up to Vancouver with my car packed so full that I could barely see out the rear-view mirror. One of the best things about having a home, I had thought, was that it was a place to put things permanently. But now that I was back to shifting boxes and suitcases around, I found that I didn't mind.

Erik, in the end, released me. He agreed to pay the mortgage for the next three years and then buy me out of the house. We put it in writing and signed. I felt the rush of freedom again, mixed with deep gratitude to him for letting me go.

Aidan was an old friend of Erik's. I had met him briefly when I was a college sophomore, but it wasn't until several years later, after I started dating Erik, that we hung out. Erik, Aidan, and I started scuba diving together. Once Aidan came to the San Juan Islands with us on a long weekend, and we went out diving during the day, then skinny-dipped in the steaming hot tub at night to melt the cold out of our bones.

After university Aidan had moved to Vancouver to live with his girlfriend, an artist named Karen, and together they launched an art-supply website. I called Aidan when I was back in Vancouver, and a few days later he greeted me at his door with a warm, tight hug. He was a hugger. He hugged all his friends, male and female, so I didn't attach much meaning to this physical contact. Karen was out of town, but Aidan spoke excitedly about a new exhibit of her work that he wanted to show me. We drove to a downtown gallery. It was closed, but he had the key. Half of the showroom was devoted to Karen's latest project—wall-sized paintings of people's mouths in garish rainbow shades. I found myself staring at a grainy display of bright blue teeth. Near it an engorged red tongue, taller than either of us, glistened with saliva. Obscene mouth parts greeted me all around the room. Aidan sat down on the cushioned bench in the middle of the gallery, and I made a conscious decision to keep my distance. I observed him from across the room while we chatted. He was tall and broad-shouldered, like Erik, with dark curly hair cropped close to his scalp. He had the kind of features that when picked apart didn't add up to handsome but that together were appealing. I was pretty sure my attraction to him was one-way, and in any case I had no intention of acting on it; he had a serious girlfriend, and he was close to my barely ex-boyfriend. I just let my appreciation idle. I noticed the tattoo of a moon on his forearm. He said it matched one that Karen had in the same place, marking their status as soul mates.

We went to a Japanese restaurant and ordered noodles and sake. He asked me what stripping was like, and I talked at length. I still found it so interesting that I could talk endlessly about it—about the customers, the managers, the hours, the money, and, most of all, the women. I took pleasure in every little myth I could counter with my observations. And on some dim level I was aware that I was talking about sex with a man I was attracted to, and it was perfectly innocent because I was answering straightforward questions about my job. No bounds of propriety were breached.

But I started to feel self-conscious. Almost always, I much preferred to ask questions than to talk about myself, and few people were able to turn the tables on me. I liked to let personal information fall drop by drop over time rather than to release it all in one great avalanche of confession. I felt vulnerable talking to Aidan, as if I was exposing too much. In my head, stripping ricocheted back and forth dizzyingly between normalcy—the way it had come to be for me— and freakishness—the way the rest of the world perceived it. I tried to remember that he was the rest of the world.

I attempted to steer the conversation in another direction, and it turned to Erik and Karen. I told Aidan that Erik and I were more or less over, which was more or less true. Aidan told me that he and Karen had an open relationship, and he began describing to me in detail the rules by which they played. They had what he called the 50K radius rule, which stated that neither of them could sleep with another person if they were within fifty kilometers of each other. They also had a don't-ask, don't-tell policy. And they were going house hunting the following week. They were moving in together. I wondered if Karen thought their arrangement was as perfect as Aidan seemed to believe.

He drove me back to his place, where I had left my car. He seemed unsure of whether he wanted me to come in or not. Earlier he had mentioned that he had some photos he wanted to show me of a road trip he had taken with Karen. But when we got to my car, he didn't say anything further, and I was surprised and disappointed. I realized I had wanted to go in, then chastised myself for being so silly. Of course he wasn't going to invite me in. We were just friends. There was nothing going on.

"What about the pictures?" I asked, and within moments we were inside his house. He showed the photos to me, and as I went to leave, he hugged me close and this time kissed me on the cheek. He would have kissed my lips if I had offered them. I was reluctant to pull away, but I had to; to stand there any longer would have been to admit more than platonic intentions.

I went down to Seattle for the weekend, where I worked a few shifts at the Lusty and packed some more belongings into the car. Erik had landed a full-time job as a boat builder, and he loved it. It made me happy to see him with a steady paycheck and a job he enjoyed, as if I was leaving him less bereft. It meant, though, that he had stopped work on the house, and all the digging and demolishing was now in a state of suspended animation. We had sex in our bed. I asked him to fuck me from behind and imagined it was Aidan.

When I got back to Vancouver on Tuesday, I had a message from Aidan, and I went over. The weather was warm, and I wore a T-shirt, overalls, and bare feet. I showed him photos I had taken, some of them inside the Lusty Lady, in some of which I was half naked. I was ostensibly showing them to him because of his anthropological interest in peep shows, but I enjoyed the way he looked at the photos of me in my girl-in-the-box attire. He showed me his backyard vegetable garden, and then we went out to eat.

He asked me more questions about work over dinner, and again I felt slightly put upon. It felt one-dimensional to be talking constantly about sex and the L. I drew the conversation to a halt and started asking Aidan about his business. They had recently won a new contract, and I congratulated him. I sipped my water, he sipped his beer, and we fell into a silence.

"So I guess you see a lot of different masturbation styles at work," he said. His non sequitur made me feel suddenly exasperated. I didn't want to talk about it anymore. I now saw the fascination I had enjoyed as annoying prurience. "Yeah," I said, and excused myself to go to the bathroom.

We went to a movie after dinner. When I dropped him off afterward, I expected him to go inside because he had been saying all evening that he had work to finish that night. We stood by my car and hugged, then our lips met for a fraction of a second too long.

"You better get to work," I said.

"Or," he murmured, "we could play."

I decided to play.

He poured large glasses of tequila and orange juice, and we went outside where he laid out a blanket next to his vegetable patch. We stretched out and looked at the stars. We talked about the trees and the weather and other inane things for a while, and he began to touch me. He ran a couple of fingers over my hand, my arm, and then my side, in the gap between my top and my overalls. At first I was nonplussed and a little surprised. I asked him something about Karen—what was she doing in New York?—and he drew his hand away.

It was soon back. Stalling the hand's advance, I asked him to give me a back rub. We listened to his loud neighbors, who were drinking on their back porch. When they left, it was quiet. I sat up after my massage, now over the initial shock of what I was about to do. It had been a long time since I had been with anyone other than Erik—a year and a half, since the end of our six-month separation. When Aidan touched my shoulder, I turned my head so that his fingers entered my mouth.

We kissed for a long time, and I savored his new feel and smell. Then I stopped him.

"Don't you feel awkward about this?" I asked, looking him in the eye. I had a fear of Erik's sadness, and, also, I wanted to emphasize our misbehavior because it gave me a thrill. This was new for me—before the Lusty Lady, I had never given much thought to the arousing potential of illicit sex. Now I was intrigued. We assured each other that no one would tell anyone anything, and we resumed our touching. Between kisses I told him I had been thinking about him while I was having sex the previous day. He said he had thought about me while masturbating that afternoon, on the sofa in his living room, after we had spoken on the phone.

Aidan pulled off my overalls. I wore a thong underneath. I lay on my stomach, pulled him around behind me and told him to kiss my neck. I thought to myself that the nice thing about a new, unserious, and short-lived affair was that I could tell my partner what to do without fear of judgment or hurt feelings. We were explicitly not going to spend all the time in the world to get to know each other's bodies. He was rubbing himself against me. "Do you want me inside of you?" he asked. "Not yet," I said. I urged him to continue, and he came on my back.

Afterward I asked him: "Is a kiss on the neck sex? Is sucking on your fingers sex? Is a back rub sex? How about looking into someone's eyes?" In the drowsy, thoughtful mood I was in, I believed they all were—or at least that they could be. He agreed with me, which probably had less to do with what I had said than with an amiable post-ejaculatory haze. "People think what they can't see is sexy," I said. In some places, I told him, men are turned on by the sight of a woman's ankle, because it's rare to catch a glimpse of even that much.

We went inside, and he became hard again. In the bedroom there were sex stains on the red flannel sheets, and I made him leave the light on. He fingered me. I pushed him gently down on his back and asked him to show me how he touched himself, and he did. He looked like a marionette, I thought, with his jerking limbs and crooked elbows and knees. Watching him, I started to touch myself— I wanted to look at him from a distance. But he sat up and did it for me again. When I became loud, he told me his walls were thin, but I made no effort to be quiet.

"Penetration?" he asked nicely. I pulled away and collected myself. I was tempted but decided not to cross the line. Instead I made him come in my mouth. We lay there for a few minutes. He was tired; I got dressed to go. He walked me to the front door, and we kissed on the porch. I drove away still vaguely aroused. No two people have the same idea of sex, I thought. The foot fetishists, the submissives, Navy Guy, Aidan, me—we would each explain it in a different way. I hadn't fucked Aidan in the allegedly normal way. I wondered what difference my line made, whether it was arbitrary, and whether it mattered at all. Maybe it didn't matter what the boundaries were—I just needed to be certain that I had them.

Aidan and Karen moved into a house together, and they rented a studio where they ran their business, which became a success. They got married. I saw Aidan a few times during visits to Vancouver in the following years. Once he invited me to pick him up at their house.

Karen, I thought, knew only that I was a friend of his from college. She was there when I arrived, said she had an appointment, and had Aidan drop her off at a bus stop as we drove to lunch. Another time I called Aidan at their studio. He said Karen was with him and invited me to come have lunch with both of them. Good, I thought, I'll finally get a chance to talk to her. My sexual spark for Aidan had disappeared, and I was curious to know Karen—the artist, the "soul mate" with the moon tattoo. When I arrived, though, Karen had already left. Aidan and I went out alone.

Over lunch I asked him how married life was. I was half joking and half curious to know if he took it seriously in the traditional monogamous sense. He told me that they had continued with their 50K rule. He said that knowing they had an open relationship had enabled him to be more faithful to her than he had been previously with anyone in his life. He hadn't had sex with anyone else in over a year, since before their wedding.

Karen had though. She had met someone when she was in another city for an art show, and then met up with him again, always outside of Vancouver. She had developed an intense relationship with him by phone and e-mail. Aidan told me he didn't mind. Once, though, when she had been having a long phone conversation with her lover in the bed she shared with Aidan, he had asked her to stop—it was too much.

I saw what I was. With her tacit agreement, possibly out of guilt, I was to be his extramarital affair. That was why she kept disappearing when I came to see him. In their eyes, it was his turn, and he told me as much. He said that he wouldn't have an affair with anyone among their group of friends—a group I had foolishly thought that I might join. Just as I was for the customers at the Lusty Lady, I was in a special category for Aidan—not "wife," not "girlfriend," and not, it turned out, "friend." Because I was a stripper, I had cast myself as someone who was sexually open-minded—someone of whom he could request the unusual. He was asking me to have a sexual affair with him but to otherwise keep my distance. I had to admire his honesty, but now I felt completely cold toward him.

When I left that day, I remembered something he had told me early on, when he first invited me into his house while Karen was away. He said that he had thought about me sexually ever since he saw me in the hot tub after one of our dives. And because I liked to tell myself that my naked body didn't inherently, necessarily, always stand for sex, I was surprised.

Maya

I love working in the peep show because I've never worked with so many women with college degrees, mostly in women's studies and philosophy. It's like they figured out what to do about patriarchy: Take their money.

—Julia Query, *Live Nude Girls Unite!*

Chapter 12

Erik's friend Lance was a real estate agent turned construction worker who had a knack for procuring all sorts of things. As well as backhoes, these included building materials, concert tickets, and drugs. Lance once joked about getting business cards made for himself that said, simply, THINGS ARRANGED, which would have been entirely appropriate. He had a collection of fine wines and a night blue Volkswagen bus decorated with handmade curtains. He was slim and handsome, with brown eyes and long wavy hair. He always seemed to have ample time and cash on his hands, which he said was because he could work few hours at a high rate of pay.

On an early fall night in a Wallingford wine bar, Lance told me at length about a woman named Kim he had dated over the summer. They had taken a blissful road trip in his van. When he talked about her, he rolled his eyes and shook his head as though besotted. She was "supersmart," he said, and was planning to go to medical school. She owned her own house, a small place in the Central District. Lance said they were intense together. He described everything about her as intense, but especially her eyes. Her tongue piercing offered certain sexual possibilities that, he said, were definitely intense.

The next time I saw him he had just gotten his own tongue pierced. He was lisping and could only swallow liquids and ice cream, which he used to down his painkillers. He had to turn his tongue stud several times a day and swish a cleaning solution around in his mouth. He hadn't seen much of Kim recently, but he still talked about her. He said she was tanned and had long brown hair and beautiful eyes. He tried to describe her breasts. "Like this, like this," he said, making points with his hands, and concluding, "big areolas." There was another unusual thing about Kim: She worked as a stripper, at the Lusty Lady. "She didn't have a mother to teach her right from wrong," he explained.

The next time I saw him he referred to her as "that bitch." It was over between them, and it seemed she had taken up with someone else. He said he had no regrets about his now-healed tongue piercing, adding that it would bring untold pleasure to women. A few months later he cut his hair short, which changed his appearance so dramatically that I almost didn't recognize him. He stopped wearing tie-dyed T-shirts, replaced his night blue van with a sport utility vehicle, and started talking about going back to real estate. It was as though his breakup with Kim had closed a chapter on a whole identity.

When I started at the Lusty, I tried to figure out which one was Kim. I didn't yet have connections to any dancers outside of work, and I was curious to see who this woman was who was tangentially linked to my own life. At least five dancers had tongue piercings but one in particular caught my eye. Her stage name was Maya, and when I saw her eyes, I understood why Lance kept using the word "intense." They hovered somewhere between robin's egg blue and mint green, and they appeared to radiate light. They looked as though if you were caught in their beam, you'd be sucked into an alien spaceship. These mesmerizing eyes were set in a chiseled, tanned face, framed by shiny chestnut hair flecked with gold around the temples. Her street clothes consisted almost entirely of coarse wool sweaters, hiking boots, and well-worn jeans, with long underwear peeking out through the ripped knees if it was cold. She had big areolas.

I surreptitiously checked the time cards, standing at the punch clock much longer than necessary and feeling like a spy. There were around eighty cards, organized alphabetically by last name, and I didn't know hers. I scanned until I spotted "Maya." When I saw "Kimberly" handwritten next to it, I knew she was the one. I felt sheepish for having ferreted out her name.

A few days later we were standing side by side facing the makeup mirror. "Are you the one who was dating Lance?" I asked. She froze for a moment, fixating on me with her rays. She looked wary, and I

thought maybe this had been a bad idea, but then she spoke. "Yeah.
How do you know him?"

I babbled in relief. "Well, I was just wondering because I know him
through my boyfriend, Erik, and he said you worked here, and I saw
that your name was Kim. . . ." I trailed off.

After I had broken the ice we talked whenever we saw each other
in the dressing room, though for a long time she regarded me suspiciously. I tried to impress on her that I was really more of an acquaintance than a friend of Lance's and didn't side with him on any
breakup-related issues.

Kim recalled our meeting differently than I did. Years later she was
convinced that I had come up to her and said, "So you're the bitch
who broke Lance's heart." The fact that she remembered it this way
told little, I thought, about the way we met and much about Kim's
worldview. She had an air of being braced for disappointment. When
bad things happened to her—a theft, say, or an injury—she spoke
about them with a calm and control that I found intimidating.

Kim grew up in Stamford, Connecticut, and her parents split up
when she was a child. Her mother continued to raise her until
December 1984, when she was shot in a parking lot by two young
men. She died the next day, on Kim's thirteenth birthday. Kim's father
didn't step in to rear her, but his devoutly Catholic mother did, and
with great vigor. Kim went to live at her grandparents' house, where
rosewood rosary beads decorated the entryway, Jesus stared down
from every wall, and an unforgettable portrait of a shimmering St.
Lucy hung in the upstairs hall. It was a hologram showing the
Christian martyr with her eyeballs held out to the viewer on a golden
platter; they appeared to follow Kim as she walked by.

Far from never having been taught any conventional version of
right and wrong, Kim had attended catechism every week for some
ten years of her childhood, and her grandmother founded and induct-
ed Kim into the Stamford chapter of Junior Catholic Daughters of
America. Going to church as a teenager was like a bout of cognitive

dissonance. People gossiped meanly about one another while leaving mass. Boys and girls kissed in the bushes after youth group. Kim had sex with her boyfriend, felt guilty, had sex with her boyfriend, felt guilty, sex, guilt, sex, guilt, sex . . . she also imagined, sometimes, that her mother was watching.

She was accepted at Wesleyan University in Middletown, Connecticut, which though nearby was culturally a world away, and left home. She stopped practicing religion and started studying it as her major.

She spent the summer between her junior and senior year in Seattle, and then visited again on her way home from a semester in Thailand. She fell in love with the city in the way many people from the crowded, conservative Northeast did. It left an overall impression of greenery and friendliness on her, and with no understanding of the dismal, sunless fallwinterspring of Puget Sound, she packed her belongings into her car. On the day she graduated, she drove west.

Wesleyan, a hothouse of activism, had left Kim with the feeling that she should do something useful in the world, and so on her arrival in Seattle she got a job in an abortion clinic. She saw it as a peerless cause, despite having once been required to attend a convention in Ohio where they handed out cards with little plastic fetus feet pinned to them. Kim was, in part, inspired by a story told to her by her grandma Janie—her mother's mother, the less Catholic one. Grandma Janie had told Kim about the time she had to make a three-hour drive to an illegal abortionist, fearing the whole time that if something went wrong, her body would be unceremoniously dumped.

Working at the clinic also fit in with Kim's plans for a medical career. Seattle, fortunately, was just the sort of place to have a prominent school of naturopathy. But while Bastyre University rejected the limits of Western healing, it didn't let applicants off the hook in terms of scientific preparation. She had had little as a religion major, so she signed up for college courses in statistics, genetics, and biology.

Upon reaching adulthood, Kim had come into a small inheritance from her mother. She used part of it to pay for college, and much of the remainder to buy a house when she got to Seattle. She paid

$95,000 for a place in the Central District, a dilapidated neighborhood that some reckoned would be the next big real estate thing. During her first two weeks in her new home, her car was broken into twice. Then a rock was thrown through her window, hard enough to dent the opposite wall, and a short while later thieves stole her stereo and jewelry that had belonged to her mother.

Kim was introduced to the Lusty Lady during a once-a-year event called Playday, which served as a combined staff party, open house, and, with the income it generated, year-end bonus for the dancers. It was organized not by the management but by the performers themselves, and for twenty-four hours turned all of the Lusty Lady's carefully wrought rules upside down. I had first heard about Playday when I was hired. I had just filled out my employment forms, and Catharine told me that it was coming up and asked if I wanted to participate. She said that the dancers got very excited about it, and that some customers saved up for months in advance. But as I asked questions, she became reticent, offering to give me the phone number of one of the dancers doing the organizing. "Basically all these rules I just went over with you go out the window," she had said. I told her that I would pass.

A woman with whom Kim had gone to college had also moved out to Seattle. Susan, an aspiring midwife, worked at the Lusty Lady under the stage name Gloria, and she brought Kim as a guest on Playday, which was the only day of the year when dancers could bring outsiders backstage. Kim sat for hours in the privileged inner sanctum of the dressing room, her chin on hands, absorbing the atmosphere and musing on how fascinating and gorgeous Susan's coworkers were. She tried to figure out what it was that drew her to them. They were beyond confident. They were brazen. It was not at all what she had expected from a peep show.

Kim returned on a calmer day, slipped into a booth, and deposited a fistful of quarters. *Cling-cling. Whirrr.* A brunette with ringlets and rosebud lips—Clara Bo—materialized in front of her window and said, "Sweetheart, what are you doing here?" A crush briefly ballooned in Kim. When Clara Bo left, Kim's eyes wandered the stage and came to rest on a long, taut body. As her eyes traveled upward, she was astonished to recognize the attached face. Marybeth, also of Wesleyan. Kim had seen her on campus dozens of times. If Kim came to work, too, they could practically form an alumni club.

Between getting straight As in her science courses and working at the clinic, the winter started to wear on Kim. She split up with her boyfriend, Allan, and started spending all of her free time in the gym as she tried to mend her heart. She noticed, after a while, that she was in great shape, which gave her a new surge of confidence about her body. She had been terribly shy about it as a child. She thought about Susan and Marybeth, about how they made more money in fewer hours than any entry-level job would pay. She thought about how much naturopathic school was going to cost, and about how good it would feel to ease up her schedule. Her first Playday visit had been in December 1995. The following May she bought a pair of platform shoes and danced around her house naked. She watched herself in the mirror to see what looked good, and when she felt ready she went down and auditioned.

When she tried out, she was acutely aware of the hot zone around her body but not of much else. She did some of the things she had practiced at home and tried to copy the others. Excited and nervous, her temperature rose, and her face flushed red. When she came off-stage, a girl who introduced herself as Venus asked Kim if she had danced before. Kim said no.

"Well, you look like you have," Venus said.

Kim felt good. And sexy. Some of that fuck-you confidence she had witnessed on Playday welled up inside of her.

The show directors assigned her a locker right next to the door to the hallway, which she quickly dubbed the suicide locker. If she was standing in front of it and someone opened the door too fast, she got squashed. On the plus side, she didn't have to share it.

Kim felt that she didn't want a typical girl's name, the kind that made up about 70 percent of the dancer list. She seriously considered the nature-invoking and non-gender-specific name Cypress. But she settled in the end for Maya. She had studied Mayan civilization in college and wanted to pay homage to its advanced ancient culture. Customers didn't get it, of course, but no matter. She felt that words held some power. Occasionally the men did ask what her name was all about, and sometimes that led to intellectual dialogue, which, as far as Kim/Maya was concerned, was never a waste.

Her nervous excitement about performing continued through her first weeks. Every time she went onstage a thrilled, transgressive voice in her head whispered, Oh, my God, I'm naked. It was months before this thought disappeared entirely, to be replaced by the more hum-drum, I'm going to work.

What didn't disappear was the sense of power of which she became conscious. It was a simple construct: I control it + you want it = I'm in charge. Controlling it wasn't the same as just having it. She had always had it—though usually well hidden under scratchy sweaters and denim, it was always there. But being desirable had always seemed double edged to her. You could never be sure if morality, cus-tom, law, or force would do its job and physically protect you. At the Lusty Lady, those who looked as if they *might* cause harm could not. Kim couldn't help but be struck by her own position of control.

Chapter 13

By her late twenties Kim was an experienced landowner. First there was her starter home, the house in the Central District. It had been small enough, and the Central District seedy enough, that she had been able to buy it outright, with no mortgage. After she started dancing she worked through the summer and fall, put money in the bank, and put off applying to naturopathy school. In January she took a leave of absence from the Lusty and went traveling in Central America, where she soon found her way to the Honduran island of Utila, in the Caribbean. Utila had sandy beaches, jungle, clear blue water, and not much else. She snapped up two and a half acres for $55,000. To finance her little piece of utopia, with its 287 feet of south-facing waterfront, she took out a $30,000 loan against her house. Much of the rest she borrowed, at extortionist rates, from another American with property on the island. She returned to Seattle and to work.

Kim had never really intended to do the booth. She had been in it only once, to do a double trouble on Playday—her first Playday as an employee—right before she took her leave. The booth, she thought, seemed precariously revealing. You had to give brain stuff in the booth, rather than just offer up something to look at. On her return from Utila, though, she took a cold look at her finances and noted that for the first time in her life she had debt. She decided to start doing the booth.

Despite her reservations, Kim turned out to be a booth success. She didn't have that pneumatic Barbie doll allure that worked so well for some performers—she was muscular, brunette, small-breasted. She had strong and solid thighs, though, which certain customers considered her best feature, and she had those eyes. More important, she was an expert fantasy spinner. It was simply a matter, she worked out, of being smart enough to figure out what someone's gig was and then playing it. Sometimes a guy's gig was right out front: "Look at me, I'm wearing ladies' underwear," or "Pretend to suck my cock." But some of them were as shy as turtles and needed to be drawn out. Kim proved excellent at fetish discernment and on-demand acting.

She became one of the booth's top earners, often taking home eighty or ninety dollars an hour when the average was in the low fifties. And she had what may have been the highest level of booth tolerance ever, because at times she would take not only her three scheduled shifts in a week, but also try to pick up one or two more from dancers giving them away. This was known as maxing out. No one knew how she did it and stayed sane, but if anything her sane qualities—frugality, industriousness, single-minded devotion to purpose—intensified over time.

Kim attracted the talkers, the guys who would slip in twenty after twenty just to talk philosophy with a half-naked woman. She built up the usual cadre of regulars with unexceptional tastes. But her favorite customers, though few and far between, were the ones who came to be dominated. She knew that in her life as Kim she had a tendency to be bossy, but she tried to keep a lid on it. In real life she tried not to be cruel or tell people what to do. She espoused kindness as a value; she really did. But she was aware that there was a part of her that was not kind. She was a little ashamed to admit it, but she truly loved to humiliate people. She found it deeply satisfying. And at work, on some very lucky days, she was able to let herself go.

In the booth, obviously, physical abuse was not possible—which was why her coworker Stephanie referred to domination at the Lusty as "McDom's," or "Dom-lite"—but Kim became very good at verbal debasement. She was out and out astonished at the things some of the customers enjoyed. She would tell them, for example: "I'm going to strap on this dildo and fuck you with it, and then you're going to suck on it! I'm going to ram it down your throat!" Or: "How dare you look me in the eyes!," while staring into the man's eyes. Or: "I'm going to christen you with my scat so that everyone knows that you're mine!" She was creative. And all the while they panted, salivated, begged for more.

But most customers weren't that much fun. Kim had had her share of boring booths and depressing ones. She had never felt that someone else was making her do something, but she had watched herself give up her own boundaries for money. When she had done something she didn't really want to do, she confessed it to others as soon as she got back to the dressing room. Someone was always there to commiserate and laugh with her.

In truth the booth often made her feel vulnerable. Even though she distinguished her persona, Maya, from Kim—Maya said all sorts of things in the booth that Kim thought were stupid or vulgar—she felt exposed. Sometimes certain customers tempted her to prove something—she wanted to show that she was more than a sexy girl in a box, and so she would start talking about her degree in religion or the property she owned, baring more of herself than she had planned to. And then, even when everything she said in there was a lie, there was a reason she gave those particular lies and not others. If someone looked hard enough, she feared, he might see through her façade and pick up something about who she really was.

I never felt Kim's urge to show a man that I was more than a sex object. In fact, I was determined to show them nothing but—it was part of the boundary setting I went through when I started the booth. I never told the truth about my personal life; usually I wouldn't even lie, I just didn't answer. I wanted to protect myself behind an image. A selfish undercurrent ran through this decision. The customers didn't have a *right* to know me. I looked down on them for wanting the trite stereotype that I could so easily put on. They made me feel superior, but I also felt bleak over their simplemindedness. It was similar to the first stirrings of power mixed with contempt that I had felt toward boys as a teenager. Those feelings had been dormant, and never elicited by Alex or Erik, both of whom I had seen as complex. The booth reawakened a forgotten hostility.

Out of this malice I resolved unconsciously not to give customers anything more than the fantasy they came in for. If *that* was what they wanted, that was all they would get. A customer once said to me, while zipping up his pants, "I bet you're a psychology student or something like that." "Something like that," I replied, and shut the curtain. It was the most I ever told.

Kim said she often felt like a healer. One man told her that his wife wouldn't do anything that required her to look at his penis. Kim felt sorry for him. Maybe coming to the Lusty enabled him to stay in a relationship he would have otherwise left. Maybe she was saving his marriage. The booth also gave her much cause to consider the question of nature versus nurture. It couldn't be natural to refuse to look at your husband's penis. Could it? The customers told so many similar stories: We never have sex. She won't touch me. She would never do that. (Had he asked her?) Where did the women get these ideas?

But if she wondered about the women in the background, the ideas of the men in the foreground boggled her even more. Why, for instance, were they so obsessed with their own come? Kim worried sometimes that she perpetuated a certain stereotype: namely, that women liked it when men came on their faces. She was sure that there were women in the world who did like it, but she herself happened to think it was gross. Was she encouraging it? Was she part of the problem? Why did so many customers get off on that image? Was it just because porn movies endlessly reiterated it? She started to think that biology—nature—played a much larger role in sexuality than she would have ever allowed when she was a radical. She didn't give up on culture and education—nurture—entirely. But there was a big gap, she concluded, in the nurturing men and women received regarding sex. It was as though women learned about sex from an unfortunate combination of religion and romance novels, and men learned about it from porn flicks. Men came to the Lusty, with their woeful tales of dispassionate wives, because they were living the romance novel in their relationships.

Kim raised the question of whether, by what we did, we caused harm. As individuals we all reaped something, whether money, or a lifestyle, or some murky psychological reward. Like most people, we did our jobs for selfish rather than altruistic reasons. And I may have been more selfish than others—I was never spurred by wanting to change standards of beauty; I never, like Zoe, told people that I was a dancer to try to change their idea of one. But did we somehow make life harder for other women?

I wasn't sure. It was true that we fulfilled a clichéd idea of femininity, whether in our young, taut looks or our buyability. On the other hand, as many strippers were quick to point out, so did a variety of feminine jobs. Most models and quite a few actresses presented a sexuality determined by market forces. They, like us, delivered paid, passive fantasy rather than the truth. A lot of strippers felt as if they could hardly be blamed for stereotypes of women when faced with the billboards and magazine covers they saw every day.

And I was tempted to see sex work as more of a symptom of social illness than a cause. The sex biz was nothing more than a sophisticated arbitrage operation, dealing in morals rather than financial instruments. The greater the difference between the sort of sex people wanted and the sort that was socially sanctioned, the more business thrived. It exploited the spread between lust and deeply ingrained social expectation. At some point women had become artificially divided into two types—the good and child-bearing ones, carefully trained to disdain sex so that they wouldn't stray, and a separate, pro-sex class. The second group were despised and disparaged so that the good women wouldn't want to join them. One group of women ended up with respect but no freedom, and the other with freedom but no respect. But economics abhors a vacuum, and the whore class—which over time grew to include strippers, peep-show girls, telephone talkers, rub-and-tuggers, porn stars, streetwalkers, call girls, escorts, models, showgirls, pro-doms, pro-subs, and many, many more—rushed in to fill the chasm between men's actual desires and the social structure that they, with women, had built. I didn't think the divide between the two types of women would go away until all girls were raised to be free, responsible, and unashamed of sex. And until society had bridged the sex-ed gap—porn for boys and religion and romance for girls—there would always be Lusty Ladies.

After paying off the most usurious portion of her Honduran debt, Kim decided it was time to rethink her Seattle home. She dreamed of building herself a castle. She thought about adding a second story but instead opted for new premises. At twenty-six Kim moved out of her starter home and into her project, her baby, a spacious and run-down two-story dwelling that was probably a farmhouse before Seattle encroached on it. It was in a neighborhood which, though farther from downtown, was looking like a more promising real estate bet than the Central District. She was right. After Kim bought the house, the area acquired an ale house that served pricey salads, a lesbian-owned Sicilian bistro, an art gallery, and that crowning symbol of economic arrival, a chain coffee shop.

Kim bought her second home with the capital from selling the first one, plus a mortgage. Then she borrowed an additional $175,000 and embarked on a remodel. It was no ordinary fix-up. After overhauling the siding she painted the exterior in teal green and turquoise. She stripped, stained, and polished the wooden floors to a texture as smooth as silk, and the one in the kitchen she tinted purple. She covered the countertops with glazed green tile and had the veneer on the cabinets made from the finest bird's-eye maple. She made at least one artisan whose efforts didn't meet her standards rip up his handiwork and start again. She installed a bathroom on the main floor, and upstairs she built a floor of heated tile to go under her enormous claw-foot tub. She replaced windows and doors and endowed the house with such elegant details as crystal doorknobs. Some walls she painted pristine white and others she washed in pastels. She had a deck built—a second one; there was already a cozy sleeping porch upstairs—and ordered custom-made French doors. She started whipping the brush on her property into tidy shape, planting, mowing, and building a brick path with a trellis arching over it. She went into more debt than ever before, but Fortress Kim was becoming exquisite.

Chapter 14

For Stephanie there had first been curiosity, then inspiration, then need. She had dated women who stripped. One ex-girlfriend of hers had worked at the Lusty Lady fifteen years previously, back when it was called the Entertainment Center. Another worked at the topless club Razzmatazz before it turned into a Déjà Vu. They, and their stripper friends, piqued her interest because they weren't what she expected. They seemed confident and well balanced.

When Stephanie was twenty-eight, a girlfriend took her to the Fallen Women Follies, an annual burlesque-style revue of skits, dance routines, and trapeze work, and there Stephanie first laid eyes on Lara. Lara, sinuous and pale with inky black hair, did a pole performance that had the audience enthralled. She became an acrobat suspended in the air, climbing the pole to the ceiling, hanging right side up and then upside down; legs together, wrapped around the pole, or in the splits; arms supporting her effortlessly or splayed out in a cross; finally alighting back on earth as though in a casual nod to gravity. If that was stripping, Stephanie thought, it was the most beautiful thing she had ever seen.

She knew herself to be something of a show-off, exhibitionist, and performer. She had done various kinds of dance for years, salsa being a favorite, and was serious about martial arts as well. Plus the whole idea of exploring a female sexual arena—not necessarily in a lecherous way, not to get dates, but just to see what women did in that environment—appealed to her. And she liked the fact that it was an underbelly-of-society sort of job. Didn't everyone want to be a little bit of a bad girl? She certainly did.

Five months after Lara's performance Stephanie found herself without a job for long enough that she needed to make some money. That turned out to be the kick in the pants she needed finally to give stripping a try. She called the Lusty Lady and was hired. She cut a dramatic figure onstage, long and lean, with streaks of red and gold in her dark hair. She first named herself Paige, in honor of Betty Page, the 1950s pinup girl. Shortly after starting at the Lusty she landed a thirty-hour-a week job working for a nonprofit organization that distributed money to other nonprofits. It was satisfying work, rifling through grant proposals for good causes every day. Financially speaking, she could have quit the Lusty, but she chose not to. When she made a conscious decision to remain a sex worker, she changed her stage name. She wanted something that reflected her onstage persona, and the thought that always ran through her head at work was, You are here paying to see my pussy, so you better be nice to me, you better say please, because I'm in charge, and I'm going to walk away with your money at the end of the night. She chose the name "Mercy." As in "you are here at my mercy." As in "beg for it."

For Playday 2000, Kim and Stephanie ran a dungeon. They complemented each other perfectly. Stephanie loved to flog. Kim liked to do more of the ordering around and verbal humiliation, handling the insults and the instructions to crawl, bark, and lick boots. It was Kim's fourth or fifth Playday—she had lost track. It was Stephanie's second, as well as her second dungeon; she had done one the year before with Abby, who had stopped doing domination since it had become an exclusivity zone reserved for her boyfriend. Savvier this time around, Stephanie had been diligently advertising her Playday schedule to her booth regulars for months. Kim had been doing the same thing, and they were guaranteed a busy, profitable, and hopefully entertaining couple of hours.

Stephanie wouldn't do a dungeon with just anybody. Girls who didn't play on the outside—use dominance and submission in their real sex lives—would be harder to work with, she thought. She would just end up looking after the girl *and* the customer, when they both should have been focusing on the customer. Since Stephanie wasn't a pro dominatrix herself—she was just somebody who liked to play—she wanted to work with someone as capable as she was or more so. Kim, though she didn't play on the outside, seemed to have a preternatural gift for domination. At any rate, she was a pleasure to work with. She was supremely businesslike, very good at pretend games, and took the work seriously. Not that Stephanie could say she knew Kim that well. They talked onstage and occasionally on the phone. Stephanie had asked her point-blank once if the real Kim was anything like her stage character Maya. "No, I'm pretty much a prude," Kim had said. Stephanie was impressed with the way she was able to max out week after week. She didn't think she could have done it herself.

When Stephanie started doing the booth, she had let the managers advertise her as someone who would do a dom show, but she didn't anymore. She found that the customers seldom knew exactly what they wanted, and it was hard to negotiate in the short amount of time what they were willing to pay for. Plus the no-touch factor left only verbal abuse as an option, which was not her forte. Stephanie felt uncomfortable insulting them without taking the time to find out what their limits were. What if she had a psychiatric case on her hands? What if she pressed the one button that did serious damage? She didn't want to risk it.

Playday was different. It was still Dom-lite as far as Stephanie was concerned, since the guys paid for only twenty minutes or so—it was twenty bucks for five minutes—but at least she could get into the physical side of things. Stephanie worried far less about bruising flesh than she did about setting off mental tripwires. And twenty minutes gave them enough time to go over a few ground rules. Had the customer ever done this before? What were his limits? Was he into pain or humiliation? Would anyone ask questions about marks on his skin? Did he know to say red for stop, green for go? What would be their safe word, their accepted mode of crying uncle?

The Playday decorating committee had converted the windowless smoking room into a torture chamber. They had draped the walls with heavy black plastic and covered the fluorescent light with pink cellophane so that it emitted a sickly glow. Manacles hung from the wall, and a low black table resembling a menacing dentist's tray displayed an array of devices. As well as handcuffs, a cane, a cat-o'-nine-tails, and several other whips, they included "zippers," which were long strings of clothespins that could be fastened to the skin in a row and then pulled off all at once—snap-snap-snap-snap-snap!—and Kim's very own clover clamps, which consisted of two metal vises attached with a chain. The vises were for attaching to nipples, and when Kim pulled on the chain they tightened.

Kim wore shiny black vinyl pants, which looked to have been vacuum-sealed on, and matching boots with painfully tight triangular toes. Framing but not covering her breasts, she wore black leather straps dotted with silver studs, and each nipple was marked with a black X of electrical tape. Her eyes were on high alert, looking as though they should make light-saber noises when she changed the direction of her gaze. Stephanie also wore things that were shiny, tight and black, only her outfit included a bustier and a leather cap. She cradled a riding crop in her arms.

They were, as expected, busy. Jules marketed them out in the hallway, solicited a trickle of daring first-timers who lined up side by side with the regulars, clutching their dollars. The regulars were oh-so-polite. These men had waited patiently, the hour marked on their various Day Planners, kitchen calendars, and Palm Pilots, for the pleasure of being obedient to Mistresses Mercy and Maya. They looked forward to the delight of submission, of being overwhelmed, of abdicating, of shrinking one's world to "yes mistress" and "no mistress," eyes downcast, if only for a little while.

Kim and Stephanie had fun that afternoon. Only one customer was difficult. As near as they could discern, he wanted Stephanie to knock him out in a fistfight. They threw him out in frustration. A guy called Reggie also worried Kim a little. He was a regular visitor to her booths, where he put in lots of money and talked. He also went to Betty's booths, where he usually explained to Betty, the uber-stripper, how much he loved Kim. He often told Kim that Betty knew all his secrets, so Kim finally asked her what the deal was.

"Oh my God, he's so in love with you," Betty said. "All he does in my booth is tell me how wonderful you are."

Kim suspected that perhaps Reggie had trouble with the fantasy-reality divide. Her suspicions were reinforced when he appeared at ten in the morning on Playday, the moment the windows went up on the main stage.

"Are you going to be in my dungeon?" Kim asked him.

"Yes."

"When is it?"

"Four o'clock."

"Good boy," she said. Then it occurred to her to invite him onto the stage. On Playday customers could pay twenty-five dollars to sit for two songs on the blue velvet stool known as the hot seat.

"Are you going to buy a hot seat?"

"Nah."

"Sissy."

He left, and she thought she wouldn't see him until four. But fifteen minutes later he was on the stage, and Kim thought to herself, Fuck. She realized she didn't really want him up there sharing her air space, two feet away, when she was naked and whipless. She didn't like it one little bit. "Fyre, help," she pleaded. And Fyre—skilled party girl and Web mistress—took over and did her bachelor-party lap-dance routine on Reggie. Kim kept her distance. "I just love those thighs," Reggie groaned in Kim's direction while Fyre worked him over, but generally he behaved himself, and Fyre escorted him offstage after his two songs.

Though mildly concerned that Reggie showed signs of incipient obsession, Kim felt differently in the dungeon than she had onstage. In the dungeon she and Stephanie wore clothing, carried weapons, and occupied a well-girded frame of mind. He bought twenty minutes, dropped to his knees upon entering, submitted to the collar, and remained silent until addressed. He turned out to be a model sub, taking hard-core pain and using his safe words when needed. "He's fun," Stephanie said afterward. "I would play with him in real life."

With a half hour remaining of their shift, Kim and Stephanie took a breather and awaited the arrival of Francis. They got cold while they waited—the dungeon was air-conditioned, perfect for working but too chilly when they stopped. Kim ran to the dressing room to get a space heater and a snack. When she got back, Francis had arrived.

He was a corpulent older gentleman rumored to work at Boeing. He had occasionally visited Kim in the booth, often in drag. For Playday, Francis had been ordered to visit Kim and Stephanie by their coworker Vivian, who was his full-time mistress. Francis was a slave, a status that lay somewhere between hobby and lifestyle. He had previously belonged to Mistress Tawny, who had quit the Lusty Lady and moved far away from Seattle with her husband and children. When she left, she willed him to Vivian.

Mistress Vivian made him do things, like deliver food, stick address labels on letters, and wash her car, the last while wearing a bikini. For Christmas one year she had taken him to get his cock pierced, and now he wore a dog tag through it that said "Property of Mistress Vivian." She made him shave his body, paint his nails, sometimes dress as a woman, and keep a twenty-eight-day cycle during which he wore pads at the appropriate times. He was on various heart medications, and Vivian had ordered him to walk every day and stop eating meat. She made him do things in his own best interest, noted Kim, herself a vegetarian. It struck her as a positive relationship, as slave-mistress ties went.

Vivian had given Francis specific instructions for Playday. He was to make himself a bridle, and before her own arrival at seven P.M., he was to visit Mistresses Mercy and Maya in their dungeon. He was to take instruction on how to respond to riding commands, and he was to receive three visible marks across his back.

On his arrival, Kim examined the bridle and found it impressive. It was a piece of black leather with reins attached that fit over his head and neck and fastened with three buckles. A metal bit fit in his mouth. Kim had him put it on, and they ordered him to his hands and knees. Stephanie, who had had some experience with horses as a child, mounted him and rode him around the room, instructing him on physical cues for right, left, faster, slower, stop. She used her riding crop to drive home the most important points.

"Now you'll remember this for your mistress, won't you?"

They worked on Francis past the scheduled end of their dungeon shift. Soon it was a quarter to seven, and Stephanie left. Kim could have legitimately gone, too, but Vivian had not yet arrived to take over. Kim had scheduled herself for the daytime to avoid the ramped-up chaos of the night. Her feet were killing her, and she longed to go, but she felt that she couldn't leave Francis. He took this stuff seriously and just might feel abandoned if left on his own. As Kim saw it, she had an implicit contract with him. She was in a position of responsibility, the way a parent would be with a child, and she decided it would be uncool to break her word. She would hand Mistress Vivian her property in person.

When it was almost seven, Mistress Maya took the reins and had Francis walk through the back hall, which was packed with customers waiting for lap dances and triple troubles. In the dressing room she made him strip back down to his black underpants and the leather corset that he wore, his white flesh pouring out all around. She had him drop to his hands and knees, mounted him, and rode out to the middle of the red velvet stage floor, where she handed the reins to Vivian.

Everyone, on- and offstage, was electrified. The windows barely shut for the next forty minutes while Francis circled the stage like a circus freak. Girls clamored to ride the pony and did so in turns, moving him along with big giddy-up spanks. Dancers who had been in the dressing room or hallway flooded the stage, cheering, clapping, and taking pictures.

Her mission accomplished, Kim prepared to go home. She peeled off the vinyl pants, removed the torturous boots with a sigh of relief, and winced briefly as she ripped the electrical tape off her nipples. She reassembled herself in her painting overalls and an oversize wool coat, clipping her hair into a knot behind her head. Playday was over. She slammed her locker, clicked the combination lock into place, and gave it a tug to be sure, then stepped out into the hallway. A man who had come to the dungeon as a novice was lying in wait. He stared, wide-eyed, as she emerged, and then silently handed her fifteen dollars.

Kim sighed. "That's not how Playday works, sweetheart. Watch this."

She carried the fifteen dollars up to the front and tucked it into the communal cash box. "See?" She stepped out into the December chill and drove home, where she phoned a friend, took a bath, and went to bed. A few weeks later she taped a snapshot up among the photos and magnets that decorated her well-organized refrigerator. It looked at first glance like a reddish blur, but on closer inspection it showed a woman in black vinyl astride a pale, fleshy man on his hands and knees, holding his bridle as though he were a bucking horse.

Chapter 15

Kim had a history of relationships with slackers. It began with Allan, her first boyfriend in Seattle. She was fresh out of college, and he had just finished high school. She got him straight from Mom and Dad; he had never bought toilet paper or paid rent in his life. Then there had been Evan, but Kim started at the Lusty Lady two months after they began dating. He objected, she wouldn't quit, and they split up. Lance the procurer came next, also somewhat anti-Lusty, followed by a laggard named Wayne, who Kim eventually had to kick out of her house, after which she took a long relationship hiatus, punctuated by trips to Honduras and brief foreign affairs.

She met Shawn online, and they had a series of instant-message conversations. As they progressed to telephone, then face-to-face, he courted her patiently and persistently, though she insisted at first that she didn't want a boyfriend. He turned out to be tall and blond with heavy eyelids, and a soft, lopsided mouth. He wrote her poetry that she thought was surprisingly good, and his passion for her was convincing. She succumbed.

He was in the military, stationed at a base near Seattle. Iron discipline seemed to govern his life, which was run on a tidy blueprint and was refreshingly industrious. When he visited her on his days off, he went on eight-mile runs. He didn't smoke pot. Not that Kim objected to pot per se, but she took exception to the stoner lifestyle. He did smoke the odd cigarette when they met, but Kim told him she didn't date smokers, so he instantly quit. He said he wanted to be a firefighter when he became a civilian.

In his unit, only married soldiers could live off base, so they married, and he moved in with her. At the time it seemed to Kim like a lighthearted decision to make—reversible, even, in the peculiar love logic that makes anything appear possible. She put him on the title to the house and what was hers became theirs. Kim realized she was happy. She had found a partner for her palace. A vision of the future started to take shape in which Shawn featured prominently. It occurred to her, for the first time in her life, that she might like to have children. His children. Shawn the poetry-writing, firefighting dad.

Then two things happened.

First, Shawn left the military. Fourteen months after they married he was discharged. In the absence of Uncle Sam's supremacy, Shawn was a different man. Much to her dismay, he turned out to be the sort who played video games, bounced checks, and slugged around the house when he should have been job hunting. It irritated her that he sometimes stayed up until two or three in the morning playing video games, then slept in when he was scheduled to work the next day. He had one of the many work ethics in the world that would never match Kim's. He told her she was obsessed with money. It wasn't about money, she said. If he had a million dollars and sat around the house all day producing nothing, learning nothing, helping nothing, she doubted she would have been pleased.

Perhaps Shawn's greatest sin was that he failed to embrace the house project with appropriate enthusiasm. He would only clean, paint, or fix under duress. His style of garden work was to rake for ten minutes and break for fifteen. One might think, with Kim's authoritarian streak, that a man fresh out of the army would have suited her perfectly. But what she found was that while she certainly did boss him around, she hated doing it. She wanted an ally and accomplice; instead she got a recruit who budged only in response to threats.

Shawn worked part-time in a restaurant and started training to take the fire department's physical test. He produced a share of the vast mortgage every month, but even so they were financially strapped. In addition to maxing out at the Lusty, Kim took contract work for the Department of Labor, collecting census data, correcting maps, and taking surveys. She could do it on her own schedule and it brought in a little extra cash—her best-paying contract with the department paid more than seventeen dollars an hour. It was tedious, but at least she could get the work. They knew she was reliable.

In the back of her mind Kim was always trying to think of ways to make money and of careers to segue into, which weren't necessarily the same thing. She didn't want to work in a traditional strip club because she didn't want to deal with customer contact or what appeared to be vicious, backbiting competition. Plus Shawn disliked the idea, and she didn't want to make him uncomfortable. She thought about working at ExoticTan, an establishment where several dancers from the Lusty Lady were also employed. It was the type of business that advertised "lingerie modeling" services and was sometimes called a whack shack. At ExoticTan a performer and a customer entered a private room, where she kept her underwear on and he masturbated. Hidden cameras enforced no-touching rules. It was the sort of place that drew on the kind of fantasy-talk skills at which Kim was good. And she understood that at ExoticTan they actually gave interested performers training in domination.

As for careers, Kim was still drawn to medicine, if not medical school exactly. She bought a prep book for the Graduate Record Exam but it sat mostly idle in her bedroom's bay window. Every time she thought of more schooling, she thought of more debt. She knew she could get government-backed student loans, but they threatened to swamp her just-barely-afloat financial ship.

The more Shawn pursued firefighting, the more it appealed to Kim as well. The earning was good, and firefighters worked only eight days a month. Plus, with firefighting experience she could move into being a paramedic, which she thought she would enjoy. She had occasionally faced emergency situations at the abortion clinic and knew that she thrived on them. Passing the physical test would be a killer— you had to be able to drag a charged hose a hundred feet—but Kim started training for it. She figured that even if she failed the first time around, the exam would allow her to gauge herself and prepare for the next time. In need of a workout partner, Kim convinced Zoe to try out as well. Zoe had half an eye on future job options, too, but what persuaded her to do it wasn't so much becoming a firefighter as the prospect of a physical challenge. Zoe often set herself physical goals, usually long-distance bicycle rides.

Kim trained and Shawn trained, but it didn't bring them back together. She worked on the house. He started smoking again and spent hours cruising the Web and playing video games. A power struggle emerged between them that was particularly prone to showing up in bed. Before Shawn, Kim realized, she had never had a boyfriend as determined as she was to be the powerful one. She suspected he did it because he felt emasculated in other areas. It was Kim's house. Technically, the house belonged to both of them, but it felt like hers. She made more money than he did. She worried that he worried that she was smarter than he was. Perhaps he was trying to level the playing field, but whatever it was, something drove him to try to dominate her in bed, and not in a game-playing way. Games would have been all right. Kim would love to have played in her personal sex life, to have brought a little bit of the dungeon home. It wasn't even that she wanted to be in charge; she found something exciting about being a bottom, too. When she was fifteen she had asked her boyfriend to tie her up, and he had positively freaked. Kim was pretty sure she was a switch, someone who could be either dominant or submissive. But there was no game playing in her sex life with Shawn because the struggle for control was too real.

The nature of her work started to become a problem for Shawn. In particular, he blamed it when their sex life went awry. Kim believed his reasoning was flawed. She had, after all, been working at the L when they met, dated, and got married, and everything had been fine. It wasn't as though her work was new to either of them. It had been there in good times, and now it was there in bad ones, too. It was just an easy thing for Shawn to blame, she felt, a convenient focus for much larger pains.

Which all came back to coming on her face.

Oh god, she thought, you're just like those jerks. You want the same fucking thing. It was messy, yes, it got in the eyes and hair, but, more important, she didn't think it was sexy. She thought it was degrading.

It was true that hundreds, perhaps thousands, of Lusty Lady customers enjoyed getting off while imagining coming on someone's face. It was also true that Kim saw these customers regularly, and it was true that she objected to Shawn coming on her face. So Shawn concluded that Kim disliked getting come on her face because of her work. The Lusty Lady was ruining Shawn's opportunity to enjoy this pleasure with his wife. It was hurting his sex life. Kim, on the other hand, insisted that she had already disliked getting come on her face before she started working at the L, that she had found it distasteful long before stripping and long before Shawn. It wasn't as though her capacity to love it had been trampled by a sordid occupation; it had never been there in the first place. Kim would go so far as to suggest that the breakdown in their sex life had been caused by failures in their emotional life as a whole.

Result: impasse.

Over time, Kim's threats grew to include divorce. They filed the necessary legal documents, but never followed through. She did, however, ask Shawn to move out while she got her head together and he got his act together; in June he left for his home state of Colorado.

That was around the time that Kim discovered the Landmark Forum, which was the catalyst for the second big change in their marriage. The Landmark Forum was a revised version of est, a self-help movement founded in the 1970s that had been criticized for being cultish. After withering media reports, it shut down in 1985, then reappeared as Landmark, which went on to thrive. Tens of thousands of people took Landmark seminars every year, shelling out hundreds of dollars for each beginning, intermediate, and advanced course. Landmark Forum literature peddled it as "not a lecture on motivational techniques or therapy, but a powerful, accelerated learning experience," and claimed that "more than seven out of ten participants found the Landmark Forums to be one of their life's most rewarding experiences." There was another element to Landmark: it brought together groups of more than a hundred people in its courses. These people spent fourteen-hour days together. Apart from the content of the seminars, the sessions generated intensity from their sheer length.

As well as examining their own lives and contacting estranged loved ones, participants were strongly encouraged to share their experiences with everyone else. Microphones were provided at the front of the assembly rooms so that people could do just that. In short, though a secular commercial enterprise, a Landmark Forum class bore a striking resemblance to a religious gathering.

A friend introduced Kim to Landmark. Thinking it might help their marriage, she convinced Shawn, who was living in Colorado, to enroll in a $325, three-and-a-half-day course with her. They flew to Los Angeles to take it together. She found that it changed her outlook on things. A more Catholic Kim emerged. She began to take her marriage vows very seriously. She acquired a new solemnity about her word, which she had, after all, given to Shawn. All of it—the marriage, the promises, the once-shared dream—suddenly became terribly fraught with meaning. They became heavy. She even considered calling her father, whom she hadn't spoken to in ten years.

Shawn returned to Colorado after the course while Kim returned to Seattle. She began the summer a little worse off than she had been financially. She maxed out furiously and worked her Department of Labor jobs. Her Landmark course included once-a-week follow-up sessions, to which she applied herself with diligence, doing all the take-home assignments. She took out a twelve-thousand-dollar loan in August and devoted the little free time she had to working on the house.

Kim found a contractor in a surprising place—the Lusty Lady. He was one of an exclusive group of customers famous or infamous enough to warrant a nickname. As well as the Barbie Doll Man, there was the Candy Cane Man, the Fucky Fucky Man, and Stan Stan the Buttman. Kim met him the way everyone did: Gloria—Susan from Wesleyan—called her over to a window where a slim, moon-faced man smiled wildly. His eyes were scrunched up, and he appeared to wobble, bouncing around his narrow booth as though only the walls were holding him up. "Stan, have you seen Maya's butt before?" Susan asked him. Kim bent over, shook her ass, and Stan grinned some more.

Stan the Buttman was a late-nighter who always came in drunk, high, or both. He struck Kim as a fool. He was always flailing and overenthusiastic about whatever you said to him or showed him. His heyday at the Lusty was waning by the time Kim started, but he was notorious, both for his ass fetish and obvious abuse of booze. He was friends with Randy, a support staffer with a zillion tattoos and one gold tooth who, according to dressing room reputation, was a great lay. Through Randy, Stan came to meet a number of Lusty Ladies outside of work and even became friends with a few of them.

Kim had a contractor problem. Nearly everyone she hired overcharged and did shoddy work. She lamented this fact to Randy one day on her way into work, and he told her that Stan the Buttman was an exceptional carpenter.

"He's a good guy. Ask Ellis," Randy said. Ellis toiled somewhere in the Lusty's corporate hierarchy and had hired Stan in the past. He told Kim that the Buttman was slow and kept screwy hours, but that he was highly skilled and honest to a fault.

All that proved to be true. The first time Kim asked him for a bid, on her molding, it took him two months to get it to her, by which time she had already had it done. But then she had him bid on her closets—some custom shelving she had had designed—as a test run before larger projects. He bid low and turned out beautiful work.

Stan, it turned out, was a dream contractor. True, he sometimes showed up at five in the afternoon, worked for three hours, then disappeared for two days. And a significant chunk of his income went to alcohol and harder drugs. But Kim concluded that not only was he a highly skilled craftsman, he had more integrity than just about anyone she knew. He cleaned up at the end of the day, which many contractors didn't. In possession of her credit card to buy materials, he filed receipts by date and kept detailed work journals. At the end of every job he presented it all to her, and it always lined up perfectly with her credit card statements.

He was scrupulous. Kim asked him how much it would cost to have him do a particular extra task. He said it would take him about an hour, and his hourly rate was thirty-five dollars. She gave him forty and left. When she got his statement weeks later, she saw that he had carried the extra five dollars and credited it to her. Another time, he ran out of caulk one night and asked if she had any. She brought him five tubes that she had in the house. On his next statement he had credited her the value of the caulk, at a total of ten dollars and some cents. Somewhere in his Montana-born past, Stan had trained as an accountant, and it showed. He was kind, too. On the days when he rented a lawn mower to mow his own lawn, across town to the north, he loaded it in his truck, along with his dog, and drove down to mow Kim's lawn as well. Nowhere in his contract did it say he should mow her lawn. "Well, I rented it," he reasoned. "I might as well get my money's worth."

Stan, who had been falling off in Lusty Lady attendance, stopped going altogether. He said he didn't want to jeopardize his professional relationship with Kim. After her initial meeting with Stan-as-contractor, when she reflected that it was a little weird that he had seen her butt, it never crossed her mind again. She was thrilled that he never botched a job, and that, if he made a mistake, he fixed it at his own expense, not hers. His carpentry, though slow, was perfect. In short, Stan did a good job not because anyone told him to, but because he took pride in his work. Kim, a grudging dispenser of respect, bestowed it wholeheartedly on him.

Brian: a twenty-nine-year-old, divorced air force alumnus with some university education. Tall and white, clean-cut, moderate good looks. A native of Kansas and a Seattle resident of three years; an accountant for a coffee shop chain. Pastimes: going to bars with friends, watching public television, writing poetry. Foreign language: French, self-taught. Proud of his refined tastes, Brian could tell you the difference between a gladiola and a stargazer lily, or a Burgundy and a Beaujolais. Average number of visits per week to the Lusty Lady: two, though considerably more when flush.

Brian was not your usual customer. The most obvious difference between him and his peers was that he kept his hands either planted in his pockets or visible on the windowsill while watching the show. He was an admirer, and that was all he was. He preferred to think of his visits in sensual rather than sexual terms. He wanted to stare at women, but he saw himself as a nice guy, which meant he couldn't just ogle strangers on the street. So he went where he could gaze guilt-free. At the Lusty he could stare without invading personal space or causing offense—quite the reverse, they would be offended if you didn't look at them! He smiled and stared, stared and smiled, hands often on the edge of the window to display his innocence. They got paid, and he was sure that at least some of them, some of the time, had fun, too. It was a win-win situation. His strange behavior stood out, and the women started calling him "Nice Guy Bri." It came to the point where several of them even spoke to him, offering little bits of small talk and flirtation through the glass on a regular basis.

Brian had a deep aversion to being seen as a typical guy. It had been dramatically reinforced the time he had gone to see the movie *Thelma and Louise,* and as the only guy in the audience he found himself pelted with a cup of soda as the closing credits rolled. Him! Nice Guy Bri! He felt as if he was offering a positive example of manhood to the dancers, and this pleased him. He knew that the vast majority of customers had no qualms about exposing themselves and believed that many of them were rude and domineering to boot. He suspected they were very self-centered about it all, considerate only of their own needs. He felt as though he offered a polite and appreciative alternative.

It wasn't that Brian had trouble acquiring girlfriends. Aside from his ex-wife, there had been at least six who were semiserious. He dated women who approached him first, never the other way around. He was terrible at introducing himself and fearful of making passes at strangers. But once the ice was broken, he lured them with his nice qualities. He had something of a bad rep among his buddies for having tempted not one but two girlfriends of friends into ditching their partners and going out with him instead. The women he dated tended to be smart and on the mousy side. They had what he thought of as a simpler sort of beauty.

But to stare unabashedly at women whose beauty was not of the simpler sort, he went to the Lusty. It was his personal solution to the state of flux men and women found themselves in. Change was afoot. Brian had been convinced of women's power from an early age. His mother—grindingly poor, not an altogether good person—had never had a qualm about getting what she wanted by whatever means. She had been exceedingly open about sex. He respected those qualities. The first time he visited the Lusty Lady and saw the gorgeous naked girls, he had a moment of honest-to-God jealousy. He wanted, for a moment, to be them, to be able to do what they did. He wanted that power.

Now, he had noticed, women were starting to work it out. They were cottoning on to their own possibilities. The majority were still in ignorance, true, but it was only a matter of time. Women were wising up, figuring out that they ran the one show men absolutely had to see. They were realizing that entire civilizations had been predicated on putting pussy at men's disposal. Brian thought it had been a brilliant scam, really, while it lasted. But that era had ended. The means of enforcement that had made the whole machine function were slipping out of men's hands. Their monopolies on money and authority had dwindled, and now the psychological tactics—all the shaming, all the dividing and conquering—were starting to fail, too. Male power was heaving its last gasps like a tubercular prehistoric beast.

Brian decided that the only thing that would get one laid was being nice. He was at an advantage, being, as he saw it, one of very few truly good guys, an articulate, warmhearted charmer in a sea of schmucks. He put himself forward to women as an exception. And while he was getting all the action, he would save men from themselves. Nice guys like him would prevent the pendulum from swinging too far the other way. Being amiable, reliable, good in bed—these were the only things that would prevent women, once they worked it all out, from establishing a feminine republic of fear.

Kim started to recognize Brian from his regular visits. She noticed his hands on the window and his constant smile. What really got her attention, though, was that he had a tongue piercing and often wore a suit. One or the other sartorial choice on its own wouldn't have meant much, but the combination was out-and-out sexy. It said, I'm responsible and my life is together, yet I'm a wild man. It said, I'll bring home the bacon *and* lick your pussy. Kim told him as much while she shimmered in front of his window. "A tongue piercing and a suit, damn that's hot, I don't see that combination very often." He blushed and smiled some more. She flirted with him with complete sincerity.

For a long time after she first noticed him—five months perhaps—she didn't know his name. She would say to the others, "Oh look, the nice man is here. Hello, nice man." And she would come to his window and talk.

There was a night in August when meteor showers were going to arc across the sky. Kim, who was working until three in the morning, entertained herself by telling everyone, "Meteor showers tonight, best time to watch after two A.M." Brian came in early during her four-hour shift. Fyre, who knew of Kim's fixation on his tongue piercing/suit combo, saw him and said, "I bet you anything he's got tattoos, too." When Brian nodded, Kim said, "Let's see." He loosened his shirt and showed her a hieroglyph-style eye, and another marking that she didn't recognize but that someone else onstage said was a tarot card character. Brian nodded again. "It's the Magician," he said through the window. Kim loved symbols and the meanings of things; she was even more intrigued now. She wanted to know what his tattoos meant to him, but, separated by the glass, it was easier just to ask where he was from. The answer—Kansas—surprised her; for some reason she had had him pegged as an East Coaster. Maybe it was the suits. Maybe she had begun to identify with him, and so had given him an East Coast background like her own.

"Meteor showers tonight," she told him when he left. "Be sure to watch."

Brian came back twice that night, much to Kim's delight. His last visit was at ten minutes before closing. "He's here because he wants to see me after work," Kim said to Fyre. She said to Brian that it would be nice to watch the meteor showers, would it not? She put it in such a way that it could have been taken as an invitation, if he were listening for one.

The live show ended at three that night. The last window closed, the girls turned off the stage lights, and Jeff shut down the music. Only video booths would be available until the next morning. "I think he's going to wait to see me," Kim said to Hannah while they got dressed. The last four women walked out en masse and escorted one another to their cars. Kim was parked on University, next to *Hammering Man*. She looked around before she got in, but there was no sign of Brian.

"It's good that he's not here," Hannah told her. "Don't you think that's good?"

"Yeah, I guess."

Kim drove away slowly, and instead of turning south on Second, her normal route home, she drove up to Third, went north a block, and looped back down to First, which would take her past the Lusty Lady. And there he was, right in front. She slowed and rolled down the window.

"Hey, Nice Guy Bri," she called. She was excited and scared, but for some reason what she was doing felt right.

"Do you want to go watch meteor showers?" he asked. She said sure, and he climbed in. A friend of his who lived nearby had offered Brian the use of his roof deck and telescope, and Brian suggested they go there. Kim said no, she would rather go somewhere where she felt safe and comfortable. On reflection she decided she felt safest at her house.

She was open with Brian: She didn't know what her agenda was, she hadn't decided whether to divorce Shawn, but she was drawn to Brian. They spent several hours at her turquoise chateau talking and watching the sky, during which time he turned her on with his big vocabulary. She drove him home at sunrise, her faith in humanity ever so slightly restored.

Brian's girlfriend, who knew he went to the Lusty Lady, was disturbed when he told her he had actually met a dancer in person, that Maya had walked offstage and had become trusting, unhappily married, home-owning, star-gazing, flesh-and-blood Kim. Brian and his girlfriend soon split up.

Kim and Brian became friends. He agreed not to watch her at work anymore, and he tried to avoid going during her shifts. He developed new favorites. He liked women who were unafraid to make eye contact. He watched with his hands in his pockets or on the window ledge, smiling; because he seemed so nice, and because Kim said good things about him, other dancers started to talk to him, too. He thought they were some of the sweetest, warmest people he had ever met.

Not long after the meteor showers, Kim called Shawn in Colorado and told him she was thinking about dating someone else. Shawn came right back and said he was ready to make their marriage work. He was sorted out. They talked it through, and Kim welcomed him back with half-open arms. He was not to smoke, was that clear?

Kim sublimated the attraction she felt for Brian into friendship and made a good-faith effort to fix her marriage. She had dinner with Brian every so often, a fact that made Shawn unhappy. In Kim's view Shawn was paranoid, though the way she raved about Brian's intelligence didn't help.

She finally reached her father. After ten years of trying to get his approval and ten of acting as though she didn't give a damn, they had a conversation. She didn't tell him about the dancing. The only family member who knew about stripping was her grandma Janie, the one who had been to the illegal abortionist, who came to visit once a year. One year Janie had even come with Kim to the Lusty Lady and watched the show. But Kim wasn't ready to tell her dad. She and he talked about marriage, the first such conversation they had had as adults. She told him about her beautiful house. They talked about furniture Kim now owned—an armoire, a brass bed—that had once belonged to him and her mother.

In September Kim enrolled in the advanced Landmark Forum course, in Seattle, though Shawn wouldn't take it with her. On the final evening they were required to invite friends, and Kim, along with bringing Shawn, invited Zoe. The idea was for participants to share the transformative experience they had just had, as well as to sell more courses. Kim's irises spun like little pinwheels that night, but so did those of all the Landmark graduates who were milling around, excited by their recent discoveries. Zoe sat down for the first lecture beside Kim and a slack-jawed Shawn. Participants in the advanced course lined up at the microphones and made emotional revelations. At the end of it, the veterans were required to turn to their friends-recruits and offer an example of how Landmark had changed their lives. Then the recruits were supposed to identify a part of their life they wanted to change.

"We're due to finalize our divorce on Monday," Kim told Zoe as Shawn gazed into the middle distance. "But I'm not going to do it." Zoe, who had not been even remotely sold by the preceding lecture, but who figured she might as well participate, responded that she wanted to resolve lingering conflicts with her own live-in boyfriend, which was true. Both Kim and Zoe were ready to work on their relationships. They wanted to make things right.

Cassandra

Once I decided most of what my culture had told me about sex was wrong, I set out on a prolonged walk on the wild side, and by now I've walked into more secret places than I ever knew existed.

—Carol Queen, *Real Live Nude Girl*

Chapter 16

Claudia, Judith, Cassandra, Zoe: These were the names I would know her by, though I would think of her mainly as Zoe. Her penchant for name changing had started young. When she was fourteen and visiting an aunt and uncle in Israel, she told boys she met on the beach that she was called Paulina, the name of a supermodel whom she adulated at the time. Zoe gave the boys her phone number, which prompted much fury from her relatives when they called the house asking for Paulina.

She was named Judith at birth but started divesting herself of the label in her early twenties. She had originally used Zoe as a stage name, but on a trip to Hawaii she started introducing herself as Zoe outside of work. Later on an extended trip to Europe, she told everyone her name was Zoe, and the identity was born in earnest. Her parents were unimpressed when letters addressed to Zoe started arriving at their house, and they continued to call her Judith, despite her requests that they stop. She had chucked any notion of what they might have considered an appropriate lifestyle, and now she was discarding the name they had given her as well. By the time I met her, she was fairly well established as Zoe, though old acquaintances sometimes slipped up. I was in a Fremont café with her one day when she ran into someone from high school who called her Judith. "Oh no, I got rid of her," Zoe replied airily. "It's Zoe now."

I first knew her as Claudia, her stage name when I started work. She was a tall, lean dancer with plump breasts and one of the fittest bodies I had ever seen, all sleekly curved muscles. Straight, glossy dark hair fell past her shoulders and bangs fringed her forehead. She had dark brown eyes, an impish face, and liked to shave her pubic hair into odd shapes. I was onstage with her and three others when she announced that it was her twenty-sixth birthday. Twenty-six and still a stripper, I thought to myself with condescension as I stared blankly in the mirror. Then I checked myself—I was twenty-five.

After her shift she sat on the dressing room floor packing up. She took a rice and tofu dish out of the refrigerator and sniffed to see if it was still edible. Her backpack, cycling helmet, and bicycle seat lay around her.

I was getting used to dancers' transformations between stage and street, but hers was especially dramatic. The straight, well-disciplined hair I had first seen her in wasn't hers at all. The only similarity it bore to her own was that it was black. Her natural hair was a shock of thick, tight curls. She didn't often wear it down, and now she had tied it into a ponytail so that it sprouted from the top of her head, making her look vaguely punk rock, except that she also wore a thick pair of glasses. Whereas many people I knew pretended they didn't care how they looked, Zoe appeared truly not to give a damn. Even as I arranged and rearranged her hairstyle in my head, trying to settle her into a prettier, more conventional appearance, I was impressed. I admired that sort of freedom. Contradicting her hair, she had a high, breathy, and surprisingly girlish voice.

Zoe started working in a peep show when she was a freshman in college. She went to Evergreen in Olympia, the wet, green state capital an hour and a half south of Seattle. Her parents, who lived near Portland, Oregon, gave her four hundred dollars a month for rent. She worked in the school cafeteria but was not quite able to make enough to cover tuition, and she had just taken out a five-hundred-dollar emergency loan that had to be paid back over three months. During her winter break in 1990, she went to the Lusty Lady to ask about work and found it very businesslike. The Lusty's interview and audition process sounded lengthy. She could not afford to wait, so she thanked them for the information and walked three blocks up First Avenue to the Champ Arcade. She had passed the busy downtown corner hundreds of times and seen its "Live Girls" sign. This time she walked in to find a brightly lit room lined with racks of magazines and videos. She wondered where they kept the live girls and what the girls actually did. A short woman with wire-rimmed glasses asked Zoe if she needed help, and she stuttered in response. The woman asked her if she wanted a job and she nodded yes. Zoe was told that she could start the next day; all she had to do was arrive at five with her driver's license, a sheet, a combination lock, and some lingerie. Zoe walked back outside with no idea of what her new job would entail.

The dressing room at the Champ was littered with day-old greasy hamburger wrappers and take-out containers. Ashtrays overflowed with lipstick-stained cigarette butts, and dark stains dotted the red shag carpet. The bathroom faucet dripped, the cracked toilet seat felt oily, and there was no soap in the shower. When her shift began, she chose one of five performer booths. With no ventilation it reeked of stale smoke and cheap perfume. She saw fingerprints on the glass. Wearing a black lace teddy and a wig, she threw down her clean pink sheet and climbed in.

She made $178 that night, in cash, for seven hours of work. One hundred and seventy-eight dollars for acting coy, for being naked and touching herself. For pretending. To make that much at the college cafeteria would have required working over thirty-seven hours. After she was done, since it was too late to drive home, she slept at the youth hostel near the Pike Place Market. In her rented bed she folded her money by denomination and put it in a velvet pouch, which she tucked under her pillow.

As well as five private boxes, the Champ had a larger stage where two girls danced for ten windows. But performers spent most of their time compressed into the one-window booths, working for tips. The shifts were long and the boxes were dirty and so cramped Zoe couldn't even straighten out her legs or stand up. The men came on the window, one after another, adding to the soupy puddle of semen that dripped onto the floor. She wrote in her notebook between customers, logging each ejaculation in brief detail.

For a long time she viewed the whole experience as a wonderful sociology experiment.

Zoe worked at the Champ the following summer, during which she saved four thousand dollars. She worked at the Champ again over the next winter break, and throughout the two summers after that. Thanks to her notebooks she knew that by the time she was nineteen she had watched 1,392 men unzip their pants and masturbate. She stopped keeping count.

In college she saw herself as different from the career peep-show girls who worked alongside her. She was paying for an education. But when she graduated, with a degree in Spanish, she immediately started working more. She worked four nights a week, Thursdays through Sundays from six until one. A month after graduation, feeling burnt out, she quit the Champ Arcade.

The Lusty Lady down the road had iconic status in the peep-show world, largely thanks to its reputation for being run by women. This time when Zoe walked in, she filled out the five-page application form, answering questions such as "How do you feel about men?" and "Are you comfortable with your sexuality? Explain." After two interviews and her onstage audition, she was hired. The dressing room looked immaculate to her after the Champ. She was dazzled by the couches, microwave, refrigerator, coffeemaker, huge mirrors, and two telephones. It even had a window that looked—across an alleyway, over buildings, and through a double-decker freeway—out over Puget Sound.

Years later she wrote in an essay:

Frequently I found other jobs. I cleaned hotel suites, typed official documents, tutored Spanish students. The hours were longer than I was used to, the wages lower. Twice a month I deposited a check into my bank account and, like millions of people, extracted cash from a machine for a two-dollar fee. I used credit cards and wrote checks. My financial transactions were traceable. I missed always having cash lying around, bills to iron and fold and paper-clip together in bundles of fifty.

Mostly I missed being the center of attention. It doesn't matter that my parents and friends celebrated whenever I reentered the normal workforce, because those brief periods left me cheerless. Since that first night, when I made $178 and the men lined up and waited, not for Velvet or Fyre or Cinnamon but for me, I was hooked. Irrevocably I thrived on the attention, it energized me. Even when I berated myself for not using my degree—for not following through on the job interviews, the career opportunities—I was thrilled with the deviant status, the double life, stripping gave me. And so, inevitably, after a month or two or three of timecards and social security deductions, I would return to the booth.

After five years in the business Zoe was being chased in her sleep by larger-than-life throbbing penises. She cursed men and their anatomy and never wanted to have sex. Her family and boyfriend, Cameron, thought she needed a lifestyle change.

She paid off her credit cards, sold her car and mobile phone, and bought eight thousand dollars in traveler's checks, nearly draining her bank account. She didn't fill out a leave-of-absence form at the Lusty Lady because she didn't plan to be back. Instead she quit, abandoning shaved legs, wigs, and fake fingernails—for good, she thought—and left. She packed her bicycle, which she had christened Natasha, and flew one-way to Barcelona. "What I craved was an epiphany, a clearer sense of myself, in which my body as a commodity had no relevance," she wrote. "This wasn't a crisis of self-identity, not exactly, but more a conflict between me, societal expectations, and future security."

It was pouring in Spain. She pedaled south along the coast for four wet days, then paused in an Alicante campground to wait out the weather. She walked the streets of the beachside city, visited its hilltop fortress, and one day, out of curiosity, drifted into a place called the Costa Show. Less than a week after leaving Seattle she found herself working in a Spanish peep show. "I postponed the disengagement process in favor of a fast buck," she wrote. She spent her earnings on prawns, expensive red wine, and chocolates, and she began to wonder if she was cut out to be a budget bicycle tourist. "Maybe this trip was a farce," she wrote. "Or maybe, after three weeks of rain and masturbating Spaniards I needed to bite the bullet and make a move."

She did, heading south, then north. She would ride for six hours a day, set up camp, eat, write, and drink beer. She found it monotonous and alienating, but at the same time she was pleased to be free of train schedules and queues and loved the thrill of mountain descents. At least once an old man dropped his pants as she rolled by. Occasionally she met other solo cyclists, always men. She made her way north into France, then on to Belgium and the Netherlands.

Amsterdam held mythic status among sex workers as a progressive, sexually liberated nirvana, mainly because it allowed prostitution. Zoe had high expectations of the city and wasn't disappointed. She was delighted with the heady combination of permissiveness and bicycle-friendly roads. "There were bike racks in front of every shop, bicycles locked to trees, lampposts, canal railings, chain-link fences," she wrote. "Everywhere I looked there were women on bikes. Sexy women on bikes." She couldn't wait to see the red-light district.

The narrow streets of Amsterdam's sex quarter were crisscrossed with canals and lined with glowing red-glass boxes where hookers waited for business. The thronged streets suggested they didn't wait for long. Mostly male tourists swarmed the alleys and footpaths, ready to spend. In and among the prostitutes' windows were live-sex theaters, cinemas, toy stores, video stores, and businesses catering in one way or another to every permutation of every fetish imaginable. To Zoe, being a stripper suddenly seemed very tame. "After all, my clients only watched, only imagined. In five years of working in the sex industry I had never sold my body for sex, and yet I spent altogether too much time worrying about being a sex object."

She couldn't resist becoming a part of the surreal landscape. She wanted to say she had worked there. For the first time since Alicante she put on high heels and what she called her "submissive little girl voice." Zoe's voice was breathy to begin with, the little girl version even more so.

"My experience in Amsterdam was spiritually rewarding though financially disappointing," she wrote. She made the equivalent of five hundred dollars in four five-hour shifts, an amount she considered abysmal. American dancers often said that there was no money in Europe. Zoe used the earnings to buy waterproof panniers and a clipless pedal system for her bike. Six months after leaving home, she pedaled out of Amsterdam, continuing on to Finland, Sweden, Denmark, and England.

In Lahti, Finland, she stayed with a former exchange student to her family's home. A local newspaper ran a story about her trip and a photo of her with her bike, Natasha. In the black-and-white picture she looked healthy and plump faced, with sun-bleached streaks in her dark mop of hair. The reporter asked her about the potential dangers of riding alone. "I haven't been riding at nighttime and I haven't been sleeping just anywhere, so I haven't been in dangerous situations," Zoe was quoted as saying. The reporter wrote: "In her journey she hoped to meet some other woman traveling by bicycle, but she did not see even one."

By the end of her trip her odometer registered 6,483 miles. Zoe wrote, "This was proof of something, wasn't it?" When she returned home in August, she was happy to discover that the Lusty Lady would rehire her. I met her there three months after her return.

Zoe, who wanted to be a writer, had published a story about her bicycle trip in a small travel magazine. One day when I came into work I found a copy of it taped to my locker. I was impressed and a little jealous.

I was obsessed with the idea of travel—not so much to see specific places, but rather because I took pleasure in upheaval. I thought constant deracination was the only way to know who I was, as though by moving around I could distinguish myself from the web of people and routines that quickly enmeshed anything still. I wanted no precious objects, no ingrained habits, and no responsibilities to others. Just the thought of leaving—leaving Erik, but other leavings as well—intoxicated me more than a first kiss.

But these were ideals. In reality I needed people; I let myself be tied down. Zoe, I thought, lived closer to perfection than I did. All friendships begin with seeing some of oneself in another, and I thought I saw some of myself in her. She was wandering, adventurous, and self-contained. She had achieved the kind of independence that I aspired to—exactly as I would have described the perfect lifestyle when I was around twenty-three. Most years she worked for four or five months and spent the rest of the time traveling. She always went alone. I was dazzled by her self-reliance, which was both psychological—solitude could be difficult—and physical. Her sheer strength and fitness, her ability to ride 6,483 miles, fix her own bicycle, and set up a tent and cookstove, made a deep impression on me.

In her spare time when she was home from traveling she took classes, read books, and tried different jobs she thought might lead to a future career, though with little urgency. She moved frequently even when she lived around Seattle, and she often ended up in situations where she paid no rent. When I met her she lived with her boyfriend, Cameron, in a house he had inherited from a grandparent, but a few months later she broke up with him. After nine years together—they had met in high school—she moved out while he was away and left him no way to get in touch with her. While Cameron was still gone she took a road trip in his car and, while passing through the farming town of Ellensburg, met Marshall, the owner and chef of a local restaurant. She bounced around Seattle in the spring, and then returned to Ellensburg and moved in with Marshall for most of the summer. She slept on his sofa, ate in his restaurant, and enrolled in a writing class at the local campus. At the end of the summer she moved back to Seattle, despite Marshall's attempts to persuade her otherwise.

Zoe was frugal. By the end of her twenties she had amassed a savings account of about fifty thousand dollars. Moreover, she had no stuff. This I admired greatly. I once picked her up from an empty West Seattle house that a landlord friend of hers had said she could crash in. The two-story home held not a trace of furniture except, in one bedroom, an alarm clock, a small stack of books, her sleeping bag, and her bicycle. Her leopard-print bachelor-party dress hung neatly in the closet.

The bulk of Zoe's income came from bachelor parties, which made her unusual. Except for her and her friend Abby, almost no Lusty Lady dancers regularly worked parties. Zoe had started when she was still in university. The Champ Arcade was an hour and a half away in Seattle, and she could work there only during holidays and some weekends. So she called a party agency she found in the Yellow Pages and asked if they needed any dancers around Olympia, and they signed her up. Bachelor parties varied a lot in income but were much more lucrative than peep shows. The majority took place in the summer, which was how Zoe's schedule evolved into working summers and taking winters off.

Most dancers, myself included, based their decision not to do parties on some simple facts: parties required performing in strangers' homes, often in the company of many drunk men. Most club and peep-show strippers saw these as risks that were not worth the reward. But Zoe often told Lusty coworkers that they should reconsider their aversion. When they said they didn't like the idea of the men, the houses, and the booze, her answer was, "You can't live in fear."

You can't live in fear.

She said these words to me in the dressing room, stopping short anything I might have said against bachelor parties. The idea of not living in fear struck a deep chord in me. I had long resented the implication that I should live my life as though I were in danger. I became infuriated with anyone who told me I would be safer in male company, even if it was true, and had adamantly refused to let friends walk me to my car at night. I once became explosively angry with a boyfriend because he had used the word "vulnerable," quite kindly, to describe me. I stalked out of the restaurant where we were eating and back to our hostel, through desolate night streets, in part to prove my point but also out of sheer fury. I thought I would rather not live than live in fear.

I felt Zoe's words so deeply that I stared at her when she said them, speechless. My admiration for her had just expanded like an inhaling lung. Yet she was using my words—that's how I thought of them, as my words—in support of something I wouldn't do myself. I had to wonder if it was fear that prevented me from living Zoe's life or something else.

If I romanticized Zoe's lifestyle, she sometimes seemed to do the same. She often said that stripping was ideal. Having the ability to travel, all the free time, and an income of nothing but cash was perfection to her. She was happy to have found areas of the industry where she felt in control. Her party agencies took a fee for each booking, their compensation for advertising and fielding calls, but no one told her how to run her show. The amount she could make at a party was unlimited, and she felt no one profited unfairly off of her. The Champ Arcade and the Lusty felt fair to her as well, like well-functioning free markets. A guy walked down the hall, looked at the goods, and made a choice. No one told her what to do or what to charge; it was all between her and the customer. She had tried working in lap-dancing clubs—once she and Abby had gone to Montana for a week—but found them brutally difficult. The long shifts, tiring stage dances, and constant competition wore her out. At bachelor parties, on the other hand, there were only one or two women to tip, so all the money flowed their way.

Zoe and I started hanging out together over the spring and summer. Occasionally she slept on my living room couch if she was stuck in Seattle without a bed. In physical activities she was always stronger and faster than me, but she was benevolent about it. On a hike up Mount Si, we were three-quarters of the way to the top when I wanted to turn back because of blisters on my heels. She obliged with a shrug. "I don't have a completion complex," she said.

At some point every stripper has to ask herself the question, How much longer? I started to look at other dancers and wonder what their plans were. To what end were they working? Aside from any psychological toll the job might take was the glaring physical fact of age. Very occasionally a stripper pushed on into her forties, like Debra's sister Candy, if they had exceptional wit or skill. But relatively few even worked into their thirties. It was a young woman's field, no question, and it would always have a voracious appetite for younger, smoother, firmer flesh.

Zoe and I talked for hours about what she planned to do next. She faced a problem common to the long-term stripper, namely, a growing résumé gap. She knew it was going to be awkward when she had to explain to a prospective employer what she had been doing for the last seven years. While we were riding up and down the steep hills on the west side of Vashon Island—she slowing to my pace—she told me about a fantasy she had. At the age of thirty or thirty-one she would throw herself on some potential employer's mercy, explain her circumstances, and say she wanted to make a clean break. The idea that some male employer might see himself as rescuing her made her laugh. I wanted to laugh with her, but I didn't think the scenario was as funny or as likely as she did.

But she did have options. She had skills. She had traveled widely, spoke Spanish, and could write. She also had ideas about leading cycling tours. I urged her to take her clips and try to get my magazine internship when I left. Seattle, like much of the country at that time, was in an economic boom. Companies were proliferating in every suburban basement and downtown loft, handing out jobs like candy. Zoe was optimistic and unhurried.

The summer before I left for graduate school she had come to visit me in Vancouver, pulling into the driveway one afternoon with her bicycle in the back of her car. She wanted to go bike riding and sightseeing, specifically to a place she had heard of called the Cannabis Café, which sold pot paraphernalia and hemp clothing, her new favorite fashion, and to Vancouver's one nudist beach. She also planned to visit a guy she had met in Europe.

That night my friend Kristin came over with her boyfriend, and the four of us stayed up late, sipping wine and talking in the living room. After I said good night to my friends at the front door, I got the sense that Zoe would have stayed up later, chatting more, and felt strangely defensive against this possibility. I hastily said good night and went downstairs to bed.

The next day we rode out to White Pine Lake, about an hour from my house. By the time we had skirted the end of Burrard Inlet and were riding up through the woods, I was at pains to keep up with her. She had been training all summer for a grueling one-day ride around Mount Rainier, and her body showed it. We turned off the main road and rode through more pine forest down to a sandy, uncrowded beach, where we dismounted, took off our shoes and T-shirts, and stretched out on the sand. I guzzled from my water bottle and lay back, enjoying the sun. I rolled over and rested my face on my arms, burrowed my toes in the sand, and was just starting to doze when Zoe's voice floated over to me, sweet and syrupy.

"You know," she began, then paused for a long time. She always spoke slowly, with long pauses. "Last night I sat at the top of the stairs for a long, long time, after you went to bed."

My body prickled with cold. I considered pretending I had not heard. "Why is that?" I asked, resigned.

There was another long pause. "I really wanted to come downstairs and kiss you good night," she said, then let it hang in the air.

After a while, looking down at my forearms and the sand, I said, "Well, I certainly would have been surprised." I remembered my strange flash of anxiety at bedtime the night before. I had ignored it because I couldn't identify it, because it had been so out of context. I thought I could usually tell when men were sexually interested in me. I could smell it. But my radar wasn't tuned for women.

We got back on our bikes and rode home. By the end of the ride she had pulled far ahead of me, and I arrived at the house a full twenty minutes after she did. Zoe wanted to go out dancing that night, but I said I didn't, so she put on a new minidress, with fake fur trim around the neck and wrists, and went to meet her European friend.

The next day we went out to Wreck Beach. She was a vegetarian, so I found a meat-free restaurant where we picked up lunch. I didn't know exactly where the beach was, just that it was below a wooded bluff near the University of British Columbia campus. We both brought our cars because she was going to leave straight from the beach to make an evening shift in Seattle. We parked in a campus lot, and after trying several paths that led to nowhere, we found ourselves on the steep wooden staircase that led down to the beach. Signs on the landings warned that anyone likely to find nudity offensive should turn back.

On the beach we spread out towels and ate our curry and rice. It was a hot August day, and we were surrounded by naked people, mostly men and couples. I remembered hearing that the beach was heavily frequented by gay men. After eating I was about to take off my dress and stretch out in the sun, but I was briefly hit with a pang of modesty, not because of the other people but because of Zoe. Because she had expressed a sexual interest, I wanted to hide myself from her. To my mind, she had become predatory. But my pang was plainly ridiculous; we had seen each other naked dozens of times at work and certainly would again. I took off my dress and lay down. No one paid us any attention. It was great to be naked in the sun and ignored.

Later, we climbed back up to our cars in silence. I felt as if I had to say something but couldn't figure out what it was going to be. At the last possible moment, just before she got in her car, I confronted her. I seldom had the courage to do this when men made unwanted advances, but they were usually expendable as far as friendship was concerned.

"It's hard to find new friends," I said. "I don't want to risk a friendship for some sexual adventure."

She said airily that she had just thought it would be fun to fool around. I was surprised. I had been worrying about it for twenty-four hours and to her it was apparently nothing. I was relieved but also confused. I gave her a hug, and she got in her car and drove away.

While I was driving home from Wreck Beach I remembered something she had said around the time she was abruptly pulling up stakes from Cameron's place. He had inherited a jumble of furniture and artwork along with his house, and among these was an extensive collection of Hummels, a type of widely collected ceramic figurine. Zoe, who thought they were ugly but knew them to be valuable, told me she intended to keep some and sell them, for a total of perhaps a couple of thousand dollars.

We had spent a lot of time in the dressing room empathizing over boyfriends and commiserating about breaking up. I had sympathized with her over many small trials involving Cameron. When she said she was going to take the figurines, I thought I must have missed something. Maybe he owed her money, or had committed some outrageous injustice. But I asked her, and she could say only that she and Cameron had been together for a long time. There was nothing else. She just felt they were owed to her.

I made an effort, after Zoe's pass at me, to feel tolerant about it. But the more I thought about it, the angrier I became. When I stopped trying to be open-minded, I was left with gut-level revulsion. I was appalled by what she had just done, and the ease with which she had blown it off. I tried to understand why her pass, in particular, upset me so much. Other women had done it, and I had been flattered or amused. Blue's attention was sweet, even though I couldn't return it. But with Zoe I was consternated. It was partly, I thought, because I didn't take her seriously as a lesbian. She had fooled around with women, I knew that, but mainly in the booth. She had never had anything like a relationship with one. And she had given no hint of sexual interest in me until this weekend. I felt like an afterthought.

Moreover, Zoe knew that I wasn't a lesbian. I felt violated by a stealth maneuver. Under pretense of friendship she had made an under-the-radar assault on my sexual boundaries. One of the best things about platonic friendship, in my view, was that it was free of sexual tension. Zoe, I thought, didn't get this. She seemed willing to risk our friendship for the sake of some trivial exploit. Either I didn't matter to her as a friend, or she was being reckless. She had treated me the way she would treat a man. And her casual dismissal of the whole thing was even more disturbing—it was as though she didn't care whether she had sex with me or not. In which case, how could it have been worth the risk? I had no sense that I had been the object of real desire. I just felt expendable.

For a while these were the thoughts that erupted in me whenever I thought of her. But maybe, I started to think, we just had different points of view. I didn't think of being straight as something I wanted to push and prod around. I had assumed, blithely, that this was obvious, and that I wouldn't have to explain or defend it. Whereas to Zoe, perhaps, sexual limits were fluid, and sexuality all for experiment and play. I still admired her for an independence of thought and action that I saw in very few others. I still wanted to listen to her and follow her adventures. Gradually I started to trust her again. But I knew that I understood her less than I had thought.

Chapter 17

If Zoe hadn't encouraged me I might not have gone to Playday. I had moved away from Seattle three months previously and enrolled in school in New York, where I had submerged myself in studying. I didn't know if I would ever return to the Lusty Lady. But Zoe, who was diligent about keeping in touch, sent me an e-mail saying that Playday was coming up. She wanted to know if I would be there.

I calculated the dates. If I left right after my last exam for the semester I could be there just in time and spend my winter break working. I called the Lusty and reached Debra, who said she would put me on the schedule for December and January. Then she gave me the phone number for Belle, one of the dancers organizing Playday. Belle told me the theme this year was Space Odyssey, costumes optional, and ran through a roster of cash-making events: door elves, triple troubles, dressing room tours, the hot seat, panty sales, home movies, table dancing, slave training. Every dancer had to put in six hours to qualify for her Payday cut, and I signed up for two stage shifts of two hours each and one shift guarding the dungeon. All proceeds would be pooled and distributed equally among the dancers, after a small portion of the total had been donated to charity. The previous year the dancers had given five hundred dollars to a battered women's shelter.

The Seattle sky was gray and threatening when I arrived on the Friday before Christmas. Both sides of the Lusty marquee announced "Playday!" in large black letters. I had arranged to meet Zoe in the dressing room at the end of her morning shift, and at noon the entrance already frothed with dancers and customers. Jeff was behind the desk, and I wondered if he, or anyone, would remember me. With the exception of a handful of dancers, turnover was high, and I thought I might have been forgotten among all the appearing and disappearing faces. But as I walked in, Jeff said, "Hi, Leila" right away, matter-of-factly, as though I had been in the day before. Then Gloria, who was just inside the door, burst out, "Leila!," and kissed me. "How was New York?" she asked. She was doing a shift as a door elf. They operated in teams of two throughout the day, greeting customers and asking for tips to fill a Christmas-decorated coffee can. "All the money goes to the performers," they said sweetly to everyone who came in. Gloria wore sparkling silver makeup in keeping with the space-odyssey theme and had her hair pulled into a ponytail on top of her head. She had marked each of her nipples with a black X of electrical tape and wore a see-through plastic vest and a zip-front shiny black miniskirt. She introduced me to the other elf, a new dancer named Neco, who wore a Santa Claus hat and a red velvet bikini with jingling bells. Blow-up dolls dressed as angels hung from the ceiling.

I walked down the hallway, which was littered with glittering metallic confetti, and Jeff buzzed me into the dressing room. A parody of "Walking in a Winter Wonderland," called "Walking 'Round in Women's Underwear," played from the stage. The dressing room was packed with dancers, their guests, and customers who had paid for dressing room tours and hot seat excursions. It was the only day of the year nonemployees were allowed backstage. One of the sofas in the back had been replaced with a table that was covered with homemade food and two-liter bottles of soda.

"Leila! You're back! How's New York?"

It was Maria, and she was beaming. I wasn't more than a foot in the door. We hugged, and from the other side I heard Marilyn: "Leila, you're back!" I would hear that all day. Some dancers would ask me how the clubs were in New York, assuming I had gone for work. But I had no idea. I spent my time almost exclusively within the square mile around my university, and I had not set foot in a strip club. Everyone seemed to have a piece of news. One dancer was moving to New York, another to Los Angeles. Maria was having a baby, and Kim was recovering from knee surgery. A dancer who had gone to my new school as an undergraduate asked me how I liked it.

People had taken the space theme to heart. Marilyn wore a fuzzy, light blue, A-line minidress with a *Star Trek* emblem over her left breast. Gypsy looked as if she had stepped out of a *Jetsons* cartoon, with a disklike collar and a shimmering blue-and-green cape. Anastasia had devised a dress out of copper wire. It was shaped like an old-fashioned hoop-skirted ball gown, but with no fabric covering the swinging metal frame. Under it she wore a G-string, fishnet stockings, and Band-Aids over her nipples. She had painted purple teardrops below her eyes. She may or may not have outdone herself: for the previous Playday, I was told, she had made a smock out of pieces of Barbie dolls.

I kicked off my shoes but left on my black overcoat, then climbed the three steps to the stage, which contained Gypsy, Clara Bo, Satin, and at the far end, Zoe, finishing her shift. Balloons and streamers filled the top of the room, metallic confetti was strewn across the red floor, and shiny drugstore "Merry Christmas" signs were taped to the mirror. Clara Bo and Satin demanded that I sit on the hot seat, the blue velvet stool in the middle of the stage, which, on Playday, customers could pay to sit on and, if they were lucky, get a lap dance or two. I sat down, drab and coated amid the flashy naked girls, and Clara Bo and Satin showered me with kisses. Clara Bo grabbed Zoe's camera and took a picture.

There were new faces, some with unlikely names—Slip, Fantasia, and Devonshire. Old dancers had changed their names. Zoe had changed her stage name from Claudia to Cassandra, to prevent Cameron from finding out when she worked. Nina had changed her name to Nyx, "after the Greek incarnation of darkness and chaos," she told me, adding that the show directors didn't need to know that. She had tacked a sign near the telephone picturing a heavily fanged mouth in place of a vagina between two spread thighs. "Unwanted shifts?" it read. "Nyx will snap them up." A dancer who formerly went by Chelsea had changed her name to Agent 99, but everyone called her 99 for short. It made me imagine for a moment what it would be like if we all had numbers. I wondered if it would make a difference to the customers.

When she was finished onstage, Zoe and I went to one of several new restaurants on Western Avenue. To get there we walked down fresh concrete terraces past burbling fountains, all part of the Harbor Steps, the complex that now bordered the Lusty. Over lunch I told her about New York: I was studying, making new friends, and still contentedly single. Zoe told me about the trip she was planning to Venezuela, her new nipple piercing, and her new boyfriend. She had been placing personal ads, and one had resulted in Hans, an Austrian engineer.

Zoe spoke of personal-ad dating as though it were a form of entertainment, like reading the reviews, checking the schedule, and then going to a movie. She talked about the amusing restaurants and bars that various dates had taken her to. I didn't understand the appeal. A column inch of newsprint struck me as a sterile way to find someone compatible, whether for life or just an affair. I didn't think of myself as romantic, but when it came to meeting men, I was attached to ideas of chemistry and coincidence. I was convinced that sex and love would follow naturally from other things I did—work, hobbies, or friends. By definition they would be unplanned and messy, but all the more exciting for it. I couldn't understand why I would want to engineer an affair as though I were buying or selling a used bed.

But Zoe argued that when we carefully planned so many of the important things in life, like money, education, and work, it was only natural to try to plan romance. When I visited her later, at Hans's place, I saw that he had taped an enlarged copy of her ad to the wall. It began, "Naughty twenty-something, with hard body, literature degree, unmanageable curls, two bikes, three tents. Incurable wanderer . . ." It was a brilliant, seductive piece of self-promotion, but nevertheless it took me a few seconds to connect it to Zoe. The ad was accurate, which I thought must have surprised and delighted some of her dates. But it was also a fiction, in the sense that a few carefully chosen facts can't convey a true picture. It was no more real than Cassandra was—or than Leila was—when she lay behind the glass, spread her legs, and flattered a customer in a singsong voice.

After lunch Zoe left to meet Hans. I returned to the Lusty in the early evening for my scheduled shift. I didn't have any space gear but I wore a bright, obviously fake platinum wig, and when I got onstage and broke into a light sweat, the pink-and-silver glitter that was on the floor and in the air started sticking to my body. By the end of the evening I was covered, and those glimmering specks would prove to be tenacious. My body twinkled when I went to sleep that night. Pieces clung to the covers, and for the next week, even after showers and changes of clothing, I would find glitter on my skin and hair. It would make its way into my things so that for months afterward random sparkles would turn up in pockets and between the pages of books.

The stage was crowded, and I couldn't tell who was scheduled to work and who was just there for fun. Every window was open; it seemed as if none closed for more than a few seconds during the entire night. Several dancers wore angel wings on their backs. Cory, who was Asian, busty, and very short, arrived in the middle of my shift. She had painted her entire body, scalp to toe, in silver. I couldn't see an inch of flesh, and when I asked her just how much of her was silver, she bent over to show me that her outer and even, it appeared, inner labia were painted. She gained considerable height from both her blue platform boots and a bright blue twelve-inch-diameter afro wig, and she wore antennae with silver stars on the ends, blue-and-silver mirrored sunglasses propped on top of the afro, a silver garter belt, and long tinsel eyelashes. "I am the mistress of galaxy four-twenty!" she hollered at customers.

Former dancers often showed up on Playday. Benny had left to work in Internet porn before my time, but her reputation for outrageousness still lingered in the dressing room. She suddenly assaulted the stage in a black gown, thick glasses, and leather jacket. She screamed, "I want to eat some alien pussy!," whipped off her jacket, and dove between Cory's legs, resurfaced with silver paint all over her face, danced around, lifted her gown, screamed at customers, and attacked Cory again. They fell to the floor and rolled around, with

Cory panting and squealing and Benny yelling obscenities. Someone told me they were old friends.

Gloria led a man to the hot seat and sat him down, which meant that for the first time I was naked and at close quarters with a customer, with no glass between us. He was about two feet away, here in our little red room, like a Trojan horse seated midstage. I blushed from head to toe and felt hot, as though even without looking at him I could feel his presence. But he was fat and docile and wore the beaming expression of a kid in an amusement park. Betty gave him a lap dance. She and others lavished him with physical attention, straddling his lap and touching his shoulders and thighs, which surprised me.

Betty ushered in her skinny, pockmarked boyfriend to take a turn in the hot seat. In the general bedlam—ten people onstage, Cory and Benny screaming—a surge of exuberance made me feel as if I could do anything. I approached him warily and minced around in his personal space without really committing to a lap dance. But when he reached out and touched my thigh, I recoiled and disappeared between the streamers, glitter, and bodies. Outside of my comfort zone, where I was physically separated from the men, I felt disoriented and unsure of how to behave.

During my break from the stage, Cory and I walked up the alley to the Alibi Room, under the Pike Place Market, for a drink. She put a nylon track suit on over her silver body, but otherwise left her costume intact, so passersby stopped to stare. The Alibi Room was crowded, but she asked two men if we could share their table, and they shifted their chairs to let us sit down. While we drank they snuck sidelong glances at her, which she ignored. "This is it. This is the day," she told me in a low, conspiratorial voice. "You want to have sex onstage, you want to do anything you want with a customer, today is the day to do it." She had been working for several years versus my one. When we returned, I went back out onstage, both more guarded because of what she had said and more excited by the sense of possibility.

After my shift onstage and before I took over sentry duty outside the dungeon, I spent some time wandering the halls. I wore a black bra and heels, pink-sequined hot pants, and my helmetlike platinum wig. Surrounded by fully dressed men and half-clothed women, I felt as if I was walking through an exotic bazaar. A well-behaved line of customers waited outside the lap-dancing room, a converted storage closet, where Betty now performed. Another performer stood outside collecting twenty-five dollars from each man.

In the private pleasures booth the hallway curtain had been thrust open; inside, three women were piled on top of one another like tiger cubs. One of them, Serena, called over the intercom to a three-hundred-pound man who stood staring: "Kevin . . . oh Kevin . . . have you ever had three women at once, Kevin?"

I was on a high. My sense of self had expanded to fill the space around me. "How are you guys tonight?" I asked two bewildered-looking men in their twenties. They were surprised that I had approached them. "Is this your first time here?" I asked with a smile. Being polite was a sort of armor—they were confused about how to behave, and so would be courteous in return. I sauntered on, smiling. I moved swiftly, choosing my targets to talk to, knowing that if I paused for too long one would choose me first. I felt utterly confident, as though released from vulnerability. Here I was in control, relieved of the notion that my very nature put me in danger. I was free from all the terrible whispered things men would allegedly do to me, free from the message that I should travel in male company, free from the leaflets on my new campus that read, simply, "Men Rape." I had stared down the worst men had to offer, and it wasn't threatening at all. I was in charge here, and it was *because* of, not despite of, my sexuality.

When I returned to the dressing room, I collapsed into a chair by the buffet table and curled up. Chips and paper cups littered the floor. The surge of adrenaline had abandoned me, and now I was exhausted. Conversations floated above me, one of them about outrageous Benny, who, it seemed, had ripped a girl's dress and made her cry. I sat and rested, getting ready to go out again.

I waited to use the dressing room telephone, which was busy tonight, and then called my friend Matt. He was someone whom Erik and I had met together several years earlier, and he had been a friend to both of us, helping Erik work on the house and inviting us to his parties. Sometimes during my last year in Seattle, when Erik was out of town or had gone to bed early, Matt and I had gone out alone. He had a broad face and long flaxen hair. I found him attractive.

He was a commercial fisherman in his thirties. He had worked in Alaska through some of its most lucrative seasons and had plowed his earnings into buying an old house with an expansive view of the city and mountains. Like Zoe, he had an unorthodox work life, making all his money during an intense summer period and then traveling or simply resting through the winter. He was social and outgoing in large groups, never hesitated to introduce himself, and always carried cards with his name and address printed on them. Every time he left his house, it seemed, he ran into someone he knew. But he was close to very few people and spent much of his time alone. I had told him once that I worked as a stripper, but he had assumed I was joking, and neither of us mentioned it again. Somewhat whimsically, with an idle curiosity as to what might result, I invited him to Playday.

I met him at the front desk, where he put on the required name tag that identified him as "Leila's guest," and escorted him back to the dressing room. It was crowded with naked and costumed women talking loudly. He remained reserved at first, with his hands thrust into the pockets of his canvas workman's jacket. When he was invited to go onstage, he declined. But when I left him for a few minutes and returned, he had rallied and was talking to two dancers, one of whom, it turned out, knew someone he knew. Before we left the dressing room he handed her one of his cards.

It was my turn to guard the dungeon. The two leather-clad mistresses entered the black-walled room, and the security guard from the shift before me handed over the wooden lock box that contained the money. Matt walked around the halls and then came to stand with me, and we chatted when I wasn't taking money from customers. Then Zoe arrived with Hans, whom she wanted to show around her workplace. With the three of them hanging around and other dancers coming and going, my shift passed quickly, feeling more like a party than work.

Matt, who had two spare rooms, invited me to stay with him, and I spent most of the rest of my winter break in his home. It was a dark, roomy, creaking house, filled with carvings and carpets from around the world. I worked four or five days a week, a pace that over the long term might have been too much, but I felt I could throw myself into it since my time was short. Some of my regulars from before—Excalibur and Navy Guy among them—rediscovered me and started coming to my booths, asking where I had been. Their tastes and needs hadn't changed, nor had the parade of stage customers. There were new faces, but they might as well have been masks over the same old eyes, which still pleaded and winced, and new clothes on the same old pumping, bucking bodies.

I started to experiment with my booth customers, who no longer made me as anxious as they had before. I wasn't as worried about doing my job right, or as eager to please, or as afraid to confront the men. Instead I tried to have fun and do more of what I wanted. To the extent that I could get away with it, without being too obvious, I moved and spoke according to fantasies scripted in my head. I steered the customers into ideas that turned me on. If they bored or annoyed me, I closed the curtain or ratcheted up my fees until they went away. If they clicked with my vision, I tried to keep them for as long as possible.

For the first time I was working at the Lusty Lady without any boyfriend, even an estranged one, to go home to. I had gone for months without sex, and though this fact hadn't struck me before, it did as soon as I started work. I was in an environment thick with eroticism, surrounded by parodied and playacted sex. I turned people on for hours on end, and yet I had no real sexual connection to anyone.

So it was almost inevitable that I would sleep with Matt. I had been staying at his house for about a week when I finally came to his bed on some pretext, and we proceeded to indulge in a small, cozy affair until I left.

But it was Zoe who ended up with him. I went back to New York, and in the late spring Matt called and told me he had been seeing a lot of her. Remembering Zoe from Playday, he had called her months later to ask if she would work at a bachelor party he was organizing for a friend. They talked and agreed to get together, and they met one after-noon outside the Lusty. They walked up First to the market, bought fresh food, and had a picnic overlooking the ships in the sound.

"It's good," he told me. They were expressive words for him. Zoe confirmed the same. I felt pleased, like a matchmaker. I was relieved that Matt was falling for someone, because it removed a lingering, sheepish fear that he might have remained interested in me. And Zoe said she was having a wonderful time. Their lifestyles seemed to mesh, and they talked about traveling together. She loved his playfulness, and their sexual chemistry was better than she had ever felt before.

By the time the bachelor party rolled around they were an item, and so instead of Zoe doing the entertainment they hired her friend Abby. Soon afterward Zoe, who had bounced from house to house after splitting up with Cameron, moved in with Matt. They desig-nated one of the upstairs rooms as her study, painted it yellow, and decorated it with Turkish carpets and carved masks. Together they built her a desk out of an old door and shellacked an enormous map of the world onto it. They moved a futon into the room and bought a bookcase, which she filled with her ever-growing library, and the room became her haven for reading and writing. The house became the most permanent home she had had in years.

Chapter 18

Getting a job as a party girl was easy, but learning to run a show confidently and profitably took time. Zoe developed a repertoire of tricks and games to keep the crowds entertained and the money flowing. She often took satisfaction in her party work, in the way she was able to take a bunch of guys who were interacting with one another in their usual way and turn the evening into a memorable event. She enjoyed looking around at the guests having fun and knowing that she had helped make it happen. And she wanted to make sure that when the grooms were sifting through all their memories, they could think about their bachelor party and smile, preferably without embarrassment. Parties did sometimes become unpleasant or out of control, in which case she left in a hurry. There were some crowds so odiously rude that her task felt more like baby-sitting. But she estimated that she pulled off good parties at least 80 percent of the time. There were always enough good parties to make the taste of the bad ones go away.

She was pleased to be able to present her job in a professional way. She knew the men didn't really see her as a complete human being, but even if all they saw when they looked at her was a sex object, at least they saw a sex object who was well organized and in control. She wanted to leave an impression of strippers as sharp and competent.

Agencies like LiveWires, Vixens, and Affluent Affair charged the customer an initial fee and kept 50 percent. Not all the calls they took were for bachelor parties. People hired strippers for birthdays and anniversaries, and the agencies also booked girls for private shows, performing for just one customer in his home or hotel. The up-front fee depended on the length of time and number of dancers, ranging from $80 for a fifteen-minute strip to lingerie—popular at co-ed events—to $140 for a full-hour, two-girl show. But dancers made the vast majority of their money in tips. Guests couldn't expect much of their strippers if they didn't pay well beyond the initial fee.

Zoe did a lot of parties with her friend Abby, whom she had first met when an agent booked them to do a show together. The deal was that Zoe was supposed to arrive first and start her routine. A half hour later Abby was supposed to come in posing as a police officer and arrest her for indecent exposure. Never having seen her before, and without planning to, as soon as Abby walked in and saw Zoe, she gave her a big hug, and Zoe returned it as if they were close friends. It was as though somehow they had instantly felt a bond with each other. Their first instinct had been right, and they quickly became close.

Zoe turned out to be the first stripper Abby met whom she didn't think was either insecure or just a plain bitch. She was also the first outdoorsy, athletic stripper Abby was to meet, which clinched the friendship. They complemented each other perfectly. They had similar styles of dancing, which Abby thought of as not too naughty and not too nice. They taught each other different party games. Abby was loud and boisterous, Zoe calm and collected. Abby was an up-front negotiator, while Zoe was subtle and acquiescent. Abby barely stopped to inhale when she talked, whereas Zoe spoke in slow motion. When they worked together, if a party fell to pieces, they knew they had each other. If they were apart and one of them fled a party in disgust, she knew she could call the other to vent at any time of the night.

They met just as demand for two-girl shows was growing. Booking girls to do dyke shows and toy shows was relatively new in Seattle, taking off only in 1998 and 1999. There was a lot of money sloshing around the city, and, it seemed, there were growing numbers of women out there competing to do more for more. Zoe and Abby had an advantage: Their agent could tell customers they were that rarity, "Two girls who actually like each other."

At Zoe's encouragement Abby started working at the Lusty Lady. Abby also worked across the border in Vancouver clubs in the winter, and she was trying to get an Internet porn venture off the ground. But though it earned her the least, the Lusty became her favorite workplace.

It was safe, reliable, and, most of all, she loved the women. She found adapting to the peep-show format easy. The masturbating men gave her a sort of goal.

Zoe was likewise invigorated when she met Abby. She had done plenty of double shows and had never connected with any of the women. Quite the reverse, she usually came away thinking, Who are these people? Abby was thoughtful, organized, and ambitious, and she said her goal was no less than to revolutionize pornography. They could talk about the minutiae of stripping together for hours. And even though they had, in Zoe's estimate, one misunderstanding a week, they became the best of friends.

Unfortunately for Zoe, Matt took an instant dislike to Abby. When she did the bachelor party he had organized for his friend, Abby put on one of her regular shows, in which she worked the room for tips. Zoe hadn't warned him that this was the way it worked, and Matt was embarrassed to see her hit up all his friends. In retrospect, Zoe realized, they should have arranged to pay Abby a healthy up-front sum and had her do her show without asking for extra payment. Subsequent occasions when Matt met Abby didn't erase his first impression, which was that she was money-grubbing. So from very early in her relationship with Matt, Zoe tried to keep her best friend and her boyfriend apart.

Zoe had a party scheduled with Abby for eight o'clock on a Friday night, but it was already eight when Abby, who lived an hour and a half north of the city, arrived at Zoe's place. Abby rushed into the living room while talking on her cell phone to her mom and dropped a large black duffel bag and a plastic garbage sack on the floor.

"There's my girl," said Zoe, who was already dressed and made up. She reclined on the couch in a long black tube skirt and a leopard-print blouse.

Still talking to her mother, Abby flipped through the pages of a binder until she found a handwritten note with a phone number on it and handed it to Zoe. "Call and ask for directions," she whispered loudly, covering her mouthpiece with her hand. Zoe called the house where they were scheduled to appear. She got directions from a man named Darren and reminded him to have salt, tequila, and whipped cream on hand.

Abby clamped her cell phone between her cheek and her shoulder, dropped her overalls to the floor, kicked off her panties and began to rummage around in the garbage bag. "Fuck," she said to herself, then pulled on a pair of shorts and ran back outside to her car to retrieve a missing garment. When she returned, she whipped off the shorts and continued undressing, still talking on the phone.

"No, it'll be totally safe, Mom. It's fine . . . we can kick their ass," she said. She put on a black bra and hooked a garter belt around her waist. "I love you, Mom. 'Bye," she said, and ended the call. Abby often talked in a long monologue, in contrast to Zoe, and while continuing to dress she told Zoe about her mom, her drive down, and their schedule for the night. She put on a thong, a minidress, stockings, and a leather coat, all black. She undid her thick, sandy hair, which fell to the middle of her back, and brushed it with vigorous strokes for a minute before tying it back up in a ponytail, where it had been in the first place. Her belongings from the two bags had spread out across the living room floor. Now Abby compressed them all back into the sacks and was ready to go. Just as she was about to walk out the door she noticed a run in one stocking. "Fuck," she said, and sat down on the floor to fish a new one out of one of the bags. She changed it and they left.

The party was in a two-story wooden house with a west-facing view. It was on a hillside where the streets dipped and curved and dead-ended, so it was tricky to find, and Zoe and Abby drove up and down, trailing each other in their two cars until finally they found the address. They pulled up in front of a house with warm, yellow-glowing windows, with no visible sign of activity inside.

"Maybe if they partied a little harder," Abby said as they walked up the steps and knocked on the front door. A man opened it, and they stepped into a living room softly lit with different-colored lamps. Paintings of primitive shapes in primary colors dominated one wall, and the others were lined with books and compact disks. The windows looked out over a sea of suburban lights. It was a small party, only seven guys, and they were scattered around the living room drinking beer. Some of them waved as the girls introduced themselves. Zoe said she was Claudia, and Abby—who went by Delilah at the Lusty Lady only because they insisted she use a stage name—said she was Abby.

The house belonged to Darren, who was in his forties, and he shared it with two younger roommates. One of them showed the girls downstairs to Darren's bedroom, which would be their changing room. Low light came from behind a divider made of hand-painted silk, and the scent of sandalwood incense permeated the room, which had its own terrace and the same sloping-away view as the living room above. A screen saver moved sleepily across a computer screen, which sat on a small desk stacked with papers. A theater brochure topped the stack. In the room and in the hall just outside it were floor-to-ceiling bookshelves. One bookcase was packed with books about plays and actors. They learned later that one of the younger housemates was an actor and that Darren ran a recording studio.

Abby and Zoe opened their duffel bags on the bed. They touched up their makeup and talked about what they would do upstairs and what they would charge for. They were each other's favorites to do parties with, and they had a well-honed routine together. Darren brought down an envelope with the "pickup" in it—$450 in cash. It was the initial fee for one hour, which was to include a lesbian show. Abby, Zoe, and their agent, Shannon, got $150 each.

"All set? Let's go."

Abby headed for the stairs, but Zoe wandered down the hallway and peered into another bedroom, then a bathroom. "C'mon," Abby said.

At the top of the stairs Zoe scanned Darren's extensive music collection and found a favorite compact disc that she also owned, called "Asian Travels." Darren put it on, complimenting her on her choice. The men sat around the living room on chairs and a sofa. Abby and

Zoe seated the groom, Brent, on a chair in the middle of the room. He had a sweet face, an ash blond buzz cut, and was due to marry in a week. The two women started their routine to a trancelike wailing with a synthesized beat.

Abby and Zoe didn't do much actual dancing, but their performances were big on acrobatics, audience involvement, and physical contact. Zoe stood behind Brent and ran her hands over his chest, neck, and scalp while Abby wiggled in front of him. She slithered between his legs, bumped and ground on his lap, straddled him, and got on her knees between his legs and put her head inside his sweater. He wore brown overalls underneath. Then the women switched places, and Abby massaged while Zoe writhed.

All of the guys watched the show attentively except for one, who chattered for most of the party, bugging whoever was nearest to him. He was a paralegal about to take the bar exam, he told the girls, and he kept telling them he could help if they ever needed legal advice. Later he handed them each bushy green heads of fragrant cannabis, which he said he grew himself because he had an eye condition. He was the only guest wearing a wedding ring.

The striptease began when Abby reached behind her head and with an elaborate unwinding movement pulled her hair down and shook it out. That was Zoe's cue to start removing her blouse. Abby pulled up her dress to show her heart-shaped ass framed in the roman aqueduct arches of thong and garter belt. Zoe squeezed it gently. Over several songs they stripped down to lingerie, all the while pawing Brent, who looked overheated. Then Abby turned down the music to make an announcement.

"Now we're going to play a little game called find the money," she said. "Brent here is going to lie down on the floor—lie down on the floor, sweetheart—and you are going to put money on him wherever you would like us to look for it. We will be very thorough."

"Find the money?" somebody asked. The guys muttered in surprise at first, but then they started affably reaching for their wallets. Zoe and Abby retreated to Darren's sandalwood-impregnated bedroom while the boys planted money all over Brent.

The men performed their task with the diligence of Boy Scouts. When Zoe and Abby came back up, Brent was lying on the floor with his sweater removed and rolled bills sticking out of both ears and his mouth. The music twanged softly. They straddled Brent and began their search. Zoe plucked the one in his mouth by squeezing her breasts together. They fished around in his socks, cuffs, and pockets, sometimes with their tongues, then undid his overalls and groped thoroughly around his boxer shorts. They pulled his T-shirt off to reveal a fleshy chest. On their knees, they faced each other, straddling his body and pausing their search to kiss each other. The game ended with all bills retrieved.

Next they played the tequila game. Zoe asked Brent to pick "two very reliable friends and one very thorough one." They gave one of the reliables a bottle of tequila and the other salt. Polite, brown-haired Joe, designated as thorough, was asked to fetch a towel dampened in warm water. Then they laid the bachelor on the floor and proceeded to perform what they called a two-girl tequila shot. Abby kneeled over soon-to-be-wed Brent's face, her pussy inches from his mouth. Zoe faced her and straddled his thighs. Darren, who had disappeared for a moment, walked back into the room just as Zoe removed her bra. "Oh, Claudia, oh, Claudia," he said when he saw her, and he leaped like a jackrabbit back into his spot on the sofa. Zoe instructed the man in charge of salt to put salt on her nipples. The tequila man handed Abby a full shot glass. Abby then reached down and, holding the crotch of her panties, appeared to pour the tequila over her pussy and into his mouth. Then she moved aside and with little prompting he sat bolt upright and dove into Zoe's chest, sucking off all the salt. Everyone laughed and clapped. Zoe stood up and simpered over to Joe, calling in her girlish voice, "Towel boy, oh towel boy." Ready with his damp cloth, Joe rubbed down her chest to remove any remaining tequila, salt, or saliva. His neck and face flared red.

"That was a two-girl shot," Abby explained. "It's twenty dollars for anyone else who wants one." Darren, the oldest and most enthusiastic, jumped to the floor almost before she had finished speaking. Most of the others still had bewildered smiles on their faces, as though they had found themselves in a very weird though not entirely unpleasant situation. They were polite to a fault. They took direction well.

Abby and Zoe traded places, and this time Zoe did the tequila pouring. They didn't actually pour the liquor on their vaginas or even their panties, though such was the illusion. Two more guys took to the floor in rapid succession. "Is there an ATM machine anywhere around here?" Joe asked while he looked in his wallet. The men traded tequila, salt, and towel responsibilities so that they could take their turn on the floor. The girls gently chided anyone who missed a cue.

After two-girl shots came whipped-cream eating. Zoe impressed the men by lying on her back, curling herself onto her shoulders and flipping her legs over her head so that her knees rested on the floor. They all gasped as, in her inverted position, she shook a can of whipped cream and applied a white stripe of it to either cheek of her ass. Standing beside Zoe like a circus barker, Abby invited someone to lick it off for a fee of twenty dollars. Zoe did this a couple of times. Then Abby doused cream on her nipples and fed the guests for the same price.

Abby announced "the grand finale before the grand finale," and they stripped off their panties. Abby shook hers down her legs, kicked them up with one foot, caught them in her hands, and twirled them around. She dangled them in front of Joe, who lifted his face up to meet them and nuzzled in the satin until she abruptly chucked them aside. Abby's pubic hair was sandy, the exact same color as the hair on her head. Zoe removed her shoes for what she called her "flip trick." One of the guests sat on the chair in the middle, and Zoe folded a solicited bill neatly lengthwise, then stuck it to his nose with a dollop of whipped cream. She made a production of carefully adjusting the position of his hands, feet, and lap. Abby stood behind him to hold the chair steady. Then Zoe dipped her head between his legs, rested her shoulders on his knees, and turned herself upside down, facing away from him. Arching her back she straddled his face, sparked a moment of general alarm by nearly kicking the stereo, and captured the creased bill before returning to standing position, legs squeezed together.

They asked for another bill, to be tightly rolled and placed in the bachelor's mouth. He was once more laid out on the floor without objection. Then, gyrating to the music—it was French hip-hop now—Zoe crouched over Brent's face and picked up the bill with her pussy. The men clapped and hooted. Another dancer at the Lusty had taught Zoe this trick, which wasn't very difficult if the bill was folded right.

They asked for quarters and had another guest lie on the floor. Abby placed one on his forehead, one on his nose and one on his chin. Then she squatted on him and in less than ten seconds picked them all up. She stood, turned around, jiggled her white ass and dropped them to the floor. The men cheered. That was the end of the penultimate act. Zoe and Abby instructed Darren to lay a blanket on the floor.

Back downstairs, Zoe put on a flimsy pink-and-purple slip with matching panties, and Abby put on a turquoise baby-doll dress. They left on their thigh-high stockings and neither wore shoes. They straightened their crumpled bills, many of them damp with tequila, whipped cream, and bodily fluids, and stored them in a jacket pocket to be counted and divided later. They discussed what to do after the basic lesbian show, which had already been paid for. They decided to ask for $100 extra for a toy show or $150 for toys plus a fisting. Then they washed all their toys with soap and water in the bathroom sink and wrapped them in a purple towel.

Upstairs they took their places on the blanket, which functioned as a sort of stage. They always asked for a blanket and instructed the audience to keep off. It was their space. They carefully laid out their toys along one edge: a hard plastic vibrator in pale pink; a sparkling purple dildo of flexible rubber ("the jelly one," Zoe called it); a curved glass dildo that looked like an elegant paper weight ("good for clit stimulation," Abby said); a double-ended black dildo; two bottles of lubricant (one strawberry-kiwi-flavored); and a string of five marble-size butt beads.

Abby explained the price structure, and the audience mumbled and fumbled. "I have this money I don't seem to need anymore," Joe said to no one in particular.

"Why don't we go ahead and get started, and you can decide," Abby said.

She and Zoe started kissing and hugging and fondling each other. Zoe went down on Abby, flipping her own dress up to give a good view of her thighs and legs while she was at it. They took each other's dresses off and ground their vulvas together. The audience stared with rapt attention. All the laughing and clapping and kidding from earlier subsided into intense quiet. No one moved a muscle except to tilt his head or shift position to fine-tune his viewing angle. Even the babbling paralegal fell silent.

After what seemed to the audience like only a few seconds, but which was, in fact, much longer, the fondling and kissing stopped. Abby said that now was the time to decide on toys. The men mustered up $100 quickly and quietly, opting to forgo the fisting. Zoe lay back on the floor while Abby picked up the pink vibrator and pushed it tenderly between her legs. The audience fell silent again.

The paralegal's voice rang out like an off-key horn. "Is that thing really vibrating?" he asked. "No," Abby said quietly, not turning to him. The next time he started to speak, every one of his friends told him to shut up before he could get a word out. Joe, without shifting his gaze, as though performing a mime exercise that required the upper body to stay perfectly still, slipped from his chair to the floor. He was as close as he could be without actually being on the blanket. Abby and Zoe moved methodically from toy to toy. They slipped the double-ended prong inside both of themselves and fucked each other. While they were doing it, Zoe giggled softly for a moment, and Abby furrowed her brow at her in exasperation. A tall guy, the actor housemate, danced in a corner while he watched.

Finally Abby slipped the pretty glass dildo inside herself and got on her hands and knees. Zoe lubricated Abby's asshole with kiwi-strawberry and started slipping the string of five beads inside. She inserted them slowly, one by one, while Abby moved lightly on the hard glass. At the end of the string of balls was a plastic hoop. Zoe tugged on the hoop and started pulling them back out, as though Abby were a doll with a pull string on its back to make it talk.

Then it was over. Abby and Zoe kneeled demurely on the blanket. The audience started breathing again. "Thank you very much," Zoe said. "Thank you," a couple of the men said hoarsely. The women gathered up their toys. As they left the room, Darren pulled them aside and said he would like a private show sometime soon.

They packed up quickly. Before leaving, Abby handed out her business card, which showed her phone number and a rose-tinted naked photograph of herself, legs spread. Giving out her own card was a slightly illegitimate move since the party had been booked through an agency. As soon as they stepped outside, a loud collective groan went up from the living room.

"Do you know how to get to the Best Western?" Abby asked Zoe on the porch. It was ten-forty-five, and they had a party booked for midnight in Bellingham. It was an hour and a half drive away.

Zoe counted the cash in the car. They had made a total of $274 in tips, mildly disappointing. At first it seemed like too little, but she went over the different games they had sold and concluded she had counted correctly. As parties went, these guys had not been big spenders. Split and added to their shares of the pickup, each of them walked away with $287 for about two hours of work.

Later, on reflection, Zoe decided the show at Darren's house had been a success. She would take making $287 at a couple of manageable Seattle parties, she thought, over making $600 while having a rougher time of it and driving halfway across the state. The party had been perfect in many ways. She and Abby did their routine, and everything went off as it was supposed to. The men participated and interacted. They showed appreciation for Abby and Zoe; they listened and followed directions. Essentially, they respected the women as professionals who knew what they were doing.

From Darren's they drove in separate cars straight to Bellingham. Zoe consumed chocolate and coffee on the way, and she arrived only a little late for their midnight appointment. Abby was already waiting for her in the hotel lobby, looking energetic. This was her show. She had performed for Bill and his friends at his bachelor party two weeks earlier, and he had called her again. He was throwing himself a second party for those who couldn't make it to the first one. Bill's wedding—his second—was set for the following day.

They knocked on the door of suite 215, and Bill let them into a pristinely generic hotel room appointed in shades of beige, overlooking the courtyard swimming pool. Cigarette smoke hung in the air, wafting up from the ten young men crowded into the living room. Bill, who greeted them at the door, was at least twenty years older than most of his guests. His khakis were neatly pressed, the tank top covering his beer belly bright white, and he wore a leather belt. He had thick gray hair, and his light brown skin looked polished. He escorted the girls into the bedroom, where two boys were passed out. "They're my cooks," he explained. "They've been up since real early." He roused them and kicked them out.

He was a storyteller, and within minutes he was telling the girls that for twenty-five years he had been the police officer and game warden on his tribal land.

"Lummi?" asked Abby. "No, Nooksack," he said. "East of here, in the foothills." He and his family had 110 acres, he said. Nearly all of the boys in the living room were his nephews.

"Okay, okay, let's see now," Abby said with authority, before he could launch any long-winded tales. "We're going to get changed here, we need to get paid, and, oh, do you have any of that nose candy like you did last time?"

"Yep," said Bill, and left the room for a minute. He came back and handed Abby an envelope, then opened a drawer and pulled out a tray with piles of white powder on it. Zoe went first, cutting and scraping herself a small pile then inhaling it through a rolled twenty. As Bill was leaving the room Abby checked to see how much money was in the envelope.

"Oh! Come here," she said to Bill, and gave him a hug and a kiss on the cheek. She turned to Zoe after he had slipped out. "Six hundred dollars," she said. "Six hundred dollars!"

It was a huge amount to receive on walking in the door, and it preempted any discussion of what the show would include. They would get toys, fisting, the works. When Bill came back to show them their

CD choices, he said the boys wanted to know if they could videotape the performance, to have something for them to remember it by.

"Though I just say 'use the Indian camera,'" he added, tapping his head with his finger.

Normally the girls would have said no, but because of the six-hundred-dollar initial payment, they said yes, provided that the camera was in a fixed position so they could keep their faces out of the frame, and that it would be turned off when they began the toy show.

"What are we doing?" Zoe asked Abby. They couldn't do their usual routine as they had at Darren's, because Bill and some of the guests had seen Abby's very similar one-woman show only a couple of weeks before.

"Just whatever. You know, lap dances, lots of attention," Abby said.

"I need an attitude adjustment," Zoe said.

Once out in the living room they started dancing around Bill, who sat in the middle with his nephews looking on. Absentmindedly, Zoe started to remove her blouse too early.

"No wait, I have more clothes on than you," said Abby, who had begun the show in a leather coat. Zoe pulled her blouse shut and waited a few more minutes to strip.

Once down to lingerie, they laid Bill out on the floor and asked for liquor. They did a two-girl shot on him, Abby sitting over his face and pulling her panties aside and pouring it into his mouth. Bill handed Abby a hundred-dollar bill.

"Who else wants one?" Abby asked.

Someone tried to push forward a ponytailed man named Carl. "No, he doesn't drink liquor," somebody said.

"How about beer? We can do it with beer," Zoe said. And so Carl was laid out on the floor and beer poured from between Zoe's legs into his mouth.

They didn't worry about charging for each act because Bill was proving to be a veritable money faucet. He handed them hundred-dollar bills at regular intervals, often for nothing in particular. More than once he just reached out and pressed a bill into Zoe or Abby's hand. The young men tucked ones, fives and occasional twenties into the girls' straps and stocking tops.

Once things got going, Bill removed himself from the center of attention and watched. The party wasn't for his benefit but for his boys. He leaned back and considered tomorrow's wedding and his family. He had been with the woman he was marrying for seventeen years. They probably wouldn't have bothered with the ceremony except that his elderly mother wished to see her son married again. He and his bride already had children to look after. He looked after his grandchildren, too, and he felt responsible for many of the kids in the room.

Before the lesbian show Zoe retreated to the bedroom with Bill for a break and another nose full. He had made his wealth logging his land, Zoe learned. He said he didn't believe in saving money. In the living room Abby knelt on the blanket, keeping everyone at bay with polite but firm answers to questions and her confident, unwavering presence.

"Just a moment. She'll be here. We just need to wait a moment."

Abby was accustomed to Zoe sometimes having these little retreats, and Zoe knew that Abby would wait patiently. A few times Zoe had had strange panicky moments, in the bedroom in the middle of a party, and thought to herself, What am I doing here? What am I doing with my life? A couple of times she had been so upset that Abby, who never had these freak-outs, had told her to stay put in the bedroom and that she would finish the show by herself. And to this Zoe had said no, that she just needed five minutes and would be back out. And she came out, not smiling, but carrying through on what she felt was her responsibility.

Zoe also sometimes got a vague feeling of squeamishness before or during toy shows. If it hit in the middle of their act, she giggled. Abby was always annoyed when she did this because it made what they were doing look less real.

But this time, at the Bellingham Best Western, it wasn't a freak-out or even a squeamish episode, it was just a moment of tired reluctance. The line of coke didn't perk her up the way it should have, but she came out anyway, and they started their toy show. As they began, Bill said quietly to his boys, "Watch this. This is real life."

They did the same toy routine as they had at Darren's house, only with the addition of a slow, careful, and well-lubed fisting, by Zoe to Abby. It went smoothly except for the moment when a drunken nephew lurched onto the girls' blanket. When rebuffed, he attempted to leave the suite, and Bill had to send several boys after him to keep him from getting into trouble.

When they counted their money from Bill's party, Zoe and Abby had made $742 each.

There was a postscript to the Friday night party at Darren's house. He called Abby for a private two-girl show, and they arranged a time on Sunday. It was the first time Abby and Zoe had ever done a private show together that was not booked through an agency. They discussed what to charge and settled on three hundred dollars, but when they told Darren he upped it to four hundred. They told him he could touch himself, they would touch each other, but he couldn't touch them.

They arrived to find that he had lit all the candles in his room and that he had just taken Ecstasy. Had Zoe been alone, she would have freaked out; but with Abby there, what would have been an uncomfortably romantic setting instead made a wonderfully cushy stage. He paid them, they talked for a while, and then Abby asked him what he expected. He said he hoped he could kiss them and go down on them—obviously there was some part of the phrase "no touching" that he didn't get. They said no, that wouldn't be possible.

Instead they asked him to take off his clothes and lie on his stomach, and they massaged him. Then they played with each other, going down on each other while he watched. Sometimes he had an erection, sometimes he didn't, and then his time was up.

Darren happened to have, through his work, a great many books on tape, which Abby liked to listen to on her drives to and from Seattle, so he said that he would give her some. While they got dressed, he left the room to go get them. Zoe went to the bathroom, and when she came back Abby was holding up something in her hand.

It was a video camera. There was a gap on the bookshelf where it had been tucked.

"Oh," Darren said as he walked back in. "I'm sorry."

They asked for the tape, and he immediately gave it to them. He kept apologizing, and Abby kept telling him that it was all right.

Zoe supposed Abby was saying that because they had the tape now, but she felt that it wasn't all right, it wasn't all right at all.

She shouldn't have been surprised, she told herself. But she was. Everything had been so nice at the Friday party, and so mellow today. He had seemed so respectful. It was surprising that someone like him had done it. They had been to plenty of bachelor parties where they had found cameras, where the guys had refused to hand over the tapes, and where they had gotten into arguments. But this was different, she wasn't mad the way she had been at those parties.

She was disappointed. She and Abby had not received the respect she felt they deserved.

Chapter 19

Matt had always said he wasn't bothered by stripping. When they first started dating, Zoe had invited him to come observe parties, and he had been impressed with her professionalism. But he often admonished her to think about her future. He had his investments. He had bought a second house now, two doors down from the first. What did she have? In fact, she had a healthy savings account, more than enough for a down payment on a house. But she also wanted to try to lay the groundwork for her next career. So after moving into the house on the hill with Matt, with his encouragement, Zoe increased her efforts to land writing jobs.

A small newspaper hired her to write a biweekly cycling column and reviews of bike books. Soon she submitted her small but growing clip file to Amazon.com for a chance to write freelance book reviews. She didn't get that job, but she was thrilled when she landed an internship at Seal Press, a small but respected Seattle publishing house. She had applied because Seal Press titles already occupied a disproportionate share of her bookshelf. Their list coincided neatly with her own interests, focusing on sexuality and feminism, with a sideline imprint on women in outdoor sports. She thought it would be perfect for her. At Seal Press she did data entry, put together press kits, and was eventually invited to read actual manuscripts.

Seal then offered her the chance to publish an essay in an anthology. A senior editor, knowing she was a stripper, asked Zoe to submit a piece for a book they would publish the following year called *Sex and Single Girls*. Zoe sat down to write about a private show she had done for a sixty-year-old quadriplegic. Patricia, a journalist friend of Matt's, agreed to edit the piece before Zoe submitted it. Patricia wrote

"Go Zoe, go!" at the top of the manuscript and returned it to her with three handwritten pages of thoughtful, encouraging criticism.

It was more criticism than Zoe was used to. She concluded that the piece was bad and lost interest in working on it. She also lost interest in Seal. She admired the integrity of the women who worked there. They published what they thought was meaningful, and what they saw as lacking in the book world. But the place operated on a meager budget, and no one seemed concerned with profits. The full-time employees made nine dollars an hour. Everyone was poor, and they all seemed too serious. Here they were, publishing books about women having great adventures, sexual and otherwise, but as far as she could tell none of them were having such adventures themselves. She tried to tell herself that just because they wore dumpy clothes and never mentioned sex didn't mean they weren't wild deep down, but she remained unconvinced. She turned down their offer of a paid job, quit the internship, and drifted into the summer bachelor party season.

She and Matt still had the same wonderful chemistry, but conflict began to arise more and more often. His personality was judgmental and quick to anger, while hers was mellow and accommodating, so he mostly criticized and she attempted to diffuse. He still said that he didn't object to stripping per se, but many of the things that came with it got on his nerves. The way she got ready for bachelor parties drove him crazy. Her cell phone rang, her pager buzzed, she turned her music to full volume and ran up and down stairs and from bedroom to bathroom while she dressed and made herself up. Between calls from Abby, other girls, agents, and customers, her schedule seemed to change fifty times before she got out the door. If he and Zoe were going to meet up on a night that she was working, he was left waiting for a call or appearance in the middle of the night. If she didn't show when she said she was going to, he felt helpless and worried. He didn't like it when she climbed into bed with her hair smelling like smoke. He didn't like the fact that she had once said she would never use toys at bachelor parties—that was a line she said she wouldn't cross—but that now she did. He didn't like the fact that she had to work with fucked-up people, be they drunk and aggressive men or druggie women who had sex with the customers. And he couldn't stand Abby.

In the spring of 2000 I received this note.

> Hi Elisabeth. I am still here on the hill with the expansive, ever-changing view, but only until July. After two years, Mr. Alaska and I are separating because I am a chronic "underachiever" and I don't provide enough "stimulating conversation." I am hurt, of course, because I have truly begun to realize the depth of my personal commitments to people, to relationships, and I almost cannot bear this "failure"—although I should recognize that I am a wonderful person with lots of quirky interesting viewpoints, I fell headlong into Matt's world of negativity and endless criticisms. On a daily basis I am "corrected" by him . . . on a daily basis I berate myself for making the same stupid mistakes, for not catching on fast enough, for not buying the right clothes. The decimation of my self-confidence has led me, surprise, onto the leather couch of a therapist every two weeks. Which is a very good thing, actually. Because I am 29 now, and I am terribly confused, feeling as though I've only been having fun and enjoying life, but not accomplishing anything. . . .

That summer of her twenty-ninth year, while working the party season, she did an internship with a major cycling club, helping to organize races and group rides. Zoe was aware that she had a hunger for immediate gratification. She had long worked in a field, after all, where she got money and praise right away. She had quit several of her other pursuits, ones that required long-range commitments and that caused a lot of self-doubt. But, she reminded herself, when it came to something that truly captivated her, she never quit. Her cycling trips took research, ingenuity, and determination, and she had never given up and gone home. Whether they lasted one grueling day or many months, she always persevered.

At the end of the summer she and Matt got back together amid the chaos of Burning Man, a weeklong amphetamine-fueled party in the Nevada desert. Zoe took heart when he told her that maybe he would come see her therapist with her. They rode back to Seattle together in Matt's old van, and she thought they might be starting something new. Matt was less hopeful. He saw signs that she hadn't changed in ways that he wished she had. They went to see a play at the theater where they held season tickets, and at the coffee bar she palmed a chocolate. She didn't tell him, but he saw her eating it after the intermission and knew she hadn't bought it. He was furious. In the past she had had an occasional habit of stealing small things, like candies or bottles of juice, but she had told him she didn't do it anymore.

Matt said to others, though not to Zoe, that he blamed their reuniting on the drugs. He sometimes made strange comments to her in bed. If she did something particularly special, which he knew was more to his liking than to hers, he would say to her, "If you don't like it and you do it for me, you could do it for money, couldn't you?" She didn't understand why he said these things. Maybe he wanted to hear her reassurances, that of course it was just for him, that he was special, that she would never have sex for money. He was two-faced, though. He said terribly harsh, critical things, both to her and about her. But he could also be thoughtful, baking her a strawberry short-cake, or buying her a book he knew she would love. Zoe hung on to the thoughtful moments.

She kept the rented place she had moved into when they split up, but she spent most of her time back at his house. The woman who had overseen her internship at the cycling club informed Zoe that she would soon be leaving her job, and she wanted to offer it to Zoe first. The club had only five full-time paid positions; here was an unusual opportunity that would suit her perfectly.

But Zoe didn't feel ready to tackle full-time work. She thought she could still squeeze a couple of profitable summers out of stripping. Plus, Matt would be traveling that winter, and Zoe wanted to travel too. She turned down the job and started planning a trip to India. She met with some initial resistance. Her family rarely talked to her about stripping anymore; they just waited, with controlled exasperation, for her to quit. Her mother, a travel agent, thought that going to Asia looked like running away instead of trying to start something new, but when Zoe insisted, her mom booked her tickets for her. Abby, who would be losing her main business partner for the winter, not to mention a close friend, was also skeptical at first, though eventually she gave Zoe her blessing.

One of Matt's favorite pastimes was inspecting new and remodeled houses in his neighborhood. Not long before he and Zoe left for the winter, they parked his van near a house he had been admiring. As they walked over to it, Zoe noticed that up on the deck of the house next door, a man who looked familiar to her was talking on the phone. It was David, she realized, a cantor from her childhood synagogue. He had been close to her family and had attended her bat mitzvah. She and Matt had run into him about a year previously in a bookshop he owned, and at that time he had asked her very intently how she was doing. He said that he remembered her as a smart, inquisitive girl with grand dreams. He had told her that he and his wife lived in Matt's neighborhood, but they hadn't known where his house was until now.

David motioned for her and Matt to come up onto the deck. It was a Jewish holiday, though Zoe wasn't sure exactly which one, and they had built a trellis and decorated it with evergreen boughs and hanging fruit. They had laid out a table and were expecting company. David's wife, Ruth, immediately invited them to stay for dinner.

"I have an appointment," Zoe said. She had to be at the Lusty Lady in an hour. David then looked at her and asked directly, "So what have you been doing?"

"Oh, a little bit of this, a little bit of that," she said.

He nodded and looked as if he wanted to ask her more, but he was scurrying around helping Ruth with the table.

Zoe looked at Matt. She wondered if he understood why she had responded the way she had, or if he was thinking, Why don't you just tell the truth. And then she thought, Why don't I just tell the truth? She sometimes didn't tell people from her childhood because she wanted to save her parents the embarrassment. But David probably didn't see them much anymore, and it wasn't as though he was going to pick up the phone and call them.

"Actually, I've been working as an exotic dancer," she blurted out.

"And she's going to Asia for four months!" Matt added. He was trying to help by showing off the advantages of Zoe's job. But in the exact same instant, both Zoe and Matt realized that David would think she was going to Asia to work. They started stumbling over each other to explain.

"As a break. As a holiday. I'm going cycling," Zoe said.

"She's going traveling," Matt said.

As David was nodding seriously, Matt started telling him about Zoe's planned itinerary.

"Did you hear about the young British woman?" David asked. A British woman working as a hostess in Japan had recently disappeared, and the story was in the news. "You should be careful."

The conversation was beyond salvation. Guests were about to arrive, and Zoe had to go to work. She and Matt retreated before David could react further.

Before leaving Zoe wanted to throw herself a thirtieth birthday party. She didn't want to hold it at Matt's. He would already be gone on his own travels, but he was touchy about potential damage to his carpets, and Zoe didn't want to upset him. Plus, his house was dark and drafty compared to the light-as-air venue she had in mind: Kim's house. Zoe thought Kim might welcome the chance to show off her beautiful space to their friends after so much work, and she was right. Zoe mailed out twenty invitations and swung into planning a four-course meal. Well into her preparations, she called Kim about a week before the party to talk about plans and decorations.

"It's going to look so pretty!" Zoe said, which turned out to be a mistake. Kim couldn't yet consider her house pretty. Certain molding wasn't done, the window frames weren't painted, and there were patches of plaster on the wall. As far as she was concerned it was all imperfect, and she panicked. Zoe didn't know what to do. She told Kim she would come over on Sunday morning at ten to talk about it.

Zoe woke up late, at 10:10, and called Kim right away, who told her she had just turned down a shift in view of their appointment. Zoe hurried over.

When she arrived, she told Kim that she had thought the party would be an opportunity to show everyone how beautiful the house was. Kim said she thought it looked shitty and incomplete, and everyone would think so.

"Are you worried about scratch marks from the rented tables?"

"No," Kim said. "I assume they'll have felt on the ends of the legs, and if they don't we can put tape on them."

"Do you want me to keep people out of the upstairs? We could do that."

"No, actually the upstairs is more finished than the downstairs."

Zoe asked Kim whether she wanted her to have the party there or not, thinking in the back of her mind that she could switch the location to Matt's. Kim said she was indifferent. Finally, Zoe took Kim by the shoulders. "Why are you so cold?" she asked. Knowing she wouldn't get a satisfactory answer, she simply told Kim that her house was beautiful and would be the envy of everyone, even without further touch-ups. She said she would undertake all the planning, furniture moving, cooking, and cleaning herself, and Kim wouldn't have to lift a finger. Eventually Kim softened. The party went ahead.

On the day of the party, Zoe's parents, who were visiting their daughters in Seattle, helped her pick up some of the food she needed, and she brought them to Kim's house to show them the decorations. She found Kim with red-rimmed eyes, and when Zoe's parents asked Kim how she was, she replied, "Medium."

Kim was worse than medium, though. She had been fighting with Shawn, her husband, all afternoon. Kim had spent much of the weekend sanding and painting things that Zoe had said she didn't need to sand or paint, and by the time Shawn rolled out of bed at midday, she was already fuming that he hadn't been helping. They fought, and in the middle of the argument she had given him a check for his share of the month's expenses and asked him to move out.

"So you don't have to worry about that twenty-first person for dinner," she told Zoe.

Somehow, though, Shawn was still there at six-thirty in the evening, just before the party started, helping Kim wash the dining room windows and string white fairy lights along the deck rail. They retreated upstairs, Kim started to get changed, and they argued some more.

"When you live by yourself, you can have a house with no toilet paper or toothpaste or shaving cream," Kim told him.

"Yeah, and you'll still be sticking your pussy in the mirror and being proud of it," he said. Kim didn't see the connection.

Shawn remained upstairs for most of the party. Kim descended from her bedroom in a long-sleeved, flowing purple dress with matching pantaloon trousers. She joined Zoe, who was wearing a see-through slip with a thong and bra underneath, as their guests started to arrive, all bearing champagne as requested. I had come early to help, and stood in a red satin dress in the kitchen spreading goat cheese on bread. Kim required everyone to go barefoot—she wasn't taking any chances on her polished hardwood floors. Zoe went around gluing colorful dots and teardrops that she called *bindi* to each person's forehead. She had started wearing *bindi* to bachelor parties around the same time she had begun planning her trip to India.

Other than some unpleasantness for Kim upstairs, dinner was a success. Zoe's friend Marshall, the chef from Ellensburg, blanched the asparagus, tossed the salad, and generally helped make all the food serving go smoothly. Most of the partygoers were dancers from the Lusty Lady. And to Zoe's surprise her sister Rachel, who worked for an insurance company, had accepted the invitation as well. Rachel and her boyfriend, Michael, kept mostly to themselves, but Zoe was pleased that she had come. Out of twenty people there were three men: Marshall, Michael, and Abby's boyfriend, Peter. I thought that was remarkably few, and it occurred to me that her lack of male friends was job related. Her coworkers were all women, and it wasn't often that dancers became friends with customers. Maybe it was inevitable that strippers would end up in a mostly female world.

It was also apparent that many of the guests thought of party entertainment in terms of the strip tease. After dinner, cake, and much champagne, Marilyn decided she was going to do a dance for Zoe. She seated her in front of the wide window facing the street and requested a specific k.d. lang song about "a big boned girl from southern Alberta." Marilyn was dressed in homage to picture-perfect 1950s femininity, wearing a checkered circle skirt and a snug black sweater over conelike breasts. She even had on genuine vintage 1950s underwear, layers of frilly, waist-cinching and tummy-flattening devices, and she exposed these to Zoe in a burlesque dance.

After everyone clapped for Marilyn, someone asked who was next. Someone else shouted "We need a boy! A two-boy show!"

"I will do a dance," Peter announced, "if"—here he paused—"you have 'If You Want My Body' by Rod Stewart."

"Why actually, I do," said Kim, and ran, catlike, upstairs to find it.

"What have you gotten us into?" Marshall asked. There was no question of Rachel's boyfriend, Michael, joining in.

And away they went, dancing in front of the window, though fortunately for Kim no neighbors seemed to notice. Peter started to undo his shirt. Marshall took off his pullover, exposing two pierced nipples and a washboard stomach. Peter wore a stack of leather necklaces and was taller and lankier. A few people shouted, "Take it off," but they didn't need much encouragement. Marshall wriggled out of his leather pants and Peter, not to be outdone, dropped his trousers to the floor; neither wore anything underneath, unless you counted the metal pin through the head of Marshall's cock. They bounced around, shaking their hips, until the end of the song.

After the guests left, Zoe, Abby, Peter, and Marshall went back to Matt's with a bottle of champagne that Marshall had kept in reserve. Abby gave Zoe her birthday gifts: two scented candles, an enormous and cozy black shawl, and six glossy enlarged photographs of the two of them, naked, in yoga poses.

Zoe barely slept in the following forty-eight hours as she packed her bicycle and backpack, said good-bye, and earned last-minute cash from private shows. Then her ex-boyfriend Cameron, who had been petitioning for the task, drove her to the airport. She boarded the plane, took two Valiums, and woke up in Bangkok.

Leila—Part II

I said: "What do you think this thing is that makes people like us have to experience everything? We're driven by something to be as many different things or people as possible."

—Doris Lessing, *The Golden Notebook*

Chapter 20

I was in a luxuriously appointed room on the twenty-third floor of a Miami hotel. As I changed in front of the bathroom mirrors, I could hear Paul moving around the room. He put some music on and sat on a chair, as I had instructed, and that's where I found him when I came out. I wore tight bands of satin, lace, and elastic, all black: a push-up bra, a garter belt, stockings, a thong, and stiletto heels. He wore his khaki trousers but no shirt or shoes.

I began to dance. He wasn't allowed to touch me right away, he knew. That was the drill, because I wouldn't be ready for a while yet. I twisted and bent, using the furniture to prop myself up, resting a foot on the dresser, or kneeling briefly on the bed. I watched us— watched myself, mostly—in a tall mirror. He moved to the bed, hand to his groin, pants undone, eyes looking hypnotized and helpless. I drew out the dancing, and when we had sex I came quickly. Afterward we didn't have much time before he accompanied me in a taxi to the airport and said good-bye.

Paul, who had been my boyfriend for about six months, had flown me to Miami to visit him. Normally we both lived in London, where I had moved for a job as a reporter. Paul's work, though, had taken him temporarily to Florida. That long weekend was the first time I had seen him in a month and a half.

He was tall and angular, with chiseled features, pale skin, and black hair and eyes. He was an investment banker, and twelve years my senior. Shortly after meeting him, through friends in London, I made dating him a sort of goal, and I wondered if I could have him.

I told him early on about stripping. He was sitting on my bed and we were talking about stripping in abstract terms after walking through the part of London's Soho that was lined with adult businesses. A little apprehensive, I told him that I had been a dancer myself. As I said the words, I wondered how he would react. Would he be shocked? Impressed? Unfazed? It occurred to me that I might simply scare him away. My awareness of how others perceived me had changed since moving away from Seattle. There, my social universe had been reduced to other strippers and a few old friends. I was virtually guaranteed not to face people who would declare misgivings about my job, except for Erik, and I had discounted his doubts as jealous, confused, and barely credible. But now I was surrounded once again by new people, and I couldn't be sure what anyone would think, even the ones I liked and knew best. As I moved into a strange new phase of adulthood in which I wanted others to take me seriously, I was suddenly hit with the feeling that I should be discreet. My past was too easily open to misinterpretation.

Paul was almost never at a loss for words, but this new information caused him to pause and nod slowly. His eyes clouded for a few moments, and then a small, surprised smile dimpled his cheeks, unsure if it should turn into a full-fledged grin. Over the following weeks he was curious and asked questions, but he seemed more pleased than anything else. He didn't worry over what my former job might mean about me, or about our relationship. I didn't question that he found the idea of my past job entertaining, somewhat provocative, but basically harmless.

Weeks later, as we sprawled on the sofa in his loft, he told me that in the past, mostly while living in the States, he had been to see strippers. He told me about one who had brought her crotch so close to his face that he could smell it. He wondered aloud, as I had heard other men wonder, what the point was—of becoming aroused and then not following it with sex or even masturbation.

I asked him if he had ever used prostitutes. I thought the question flowed naturally from the conversation, but he was startled. He hesitated while I stared at him neutrally, and eventually he said that yes, he had. I asked him questions about when, where, and why. His voice became quiet and uncertain, but he resolutely answered me.

He hadn't been just once, it turned out. There had been a period of time when he had paid for sex regularly. During some of that time, he had also had a serious girlfriend.

He had never told anyone before, he said. No one had ever asked. He assumed the idea that he might have used hookers would have been unthinkable to any of his previous girlfriends. "Then I guess they didn't know you very well," I said. My manner remained amused and detached, but I was numb, not sure what I thought. Later, I felt vindicated and bleak, because I was the girlfriend who did guess this sort of thing; I had suspected and even presumed it, and I wished suddenly that I hadn't. I wondered if I had sought out Paul because I sensed that he would confirm my expectations.

I felt thrown suddenly back to the Lusty Lady, Playday, and friends like Zoe. That Seattle world had taught me that every sexual rule was relative, except for the rule about never judging others. I had welcomed that attitude because I had been so frustrated, for so long, by the idea that anyone would judge *me*. So what did I think of a man— an attractive, intelligent one, no less—who had preferred, for a time, to pay for sex? Something in me was resentful and judgmental toward him, but I felt voiceless. To judge him would have required me to also scrutinize my own choices.

Paul forced a reckoning because he was a new kind of boyfriend for me. At some point while working as a stripper, I had subconsciously begun to divide men into two types—those who wouldn't pay for sexual services and those who would. Previous boyfriends had fallen into the former category. I was fairly sure that Alex, for example, or Erik, would have regarded it as pointless and dishonest. For a man to pay for sex as a matter of course seemed to show a profound insecurity or worry about women—that women wouldn't want to sleep with him without payment, or that when they did they wouldn't be kind or acquiescent enough, or that a man's and a woman's sexual wishes simply couldn't coincide. I also thought paying for sex indicated a subtle sense of guilt—if a man was uncomfortable facing the women he had had sex with, he could pay for the promise that he wouldn't have to.

These worries had not plagued Alex or Erik, nor, as far as I could tell, any other man I had dated. On the other side of my artificial divide, in the category of men who would pay, I had only ever known peep-show customers. But I didn't really know them; they were strangers to me, whose personal lives I had no cause to consider. In the booth it had occasionally crossed my mind, when noting a man's wedding ring, that I wouldn't want my own husband or boyfriend paying another woman to bring his fantasy to life. But these were fleeting thoughts. The customers were like cardboard cutouts.

As long as the two categories of men remained separate in my mind, I wasn't forced to articulate, even to myself, what I really thought of the customers, and I wasn't forced to reconsider sex work.

But Paul fell into a new category: a man who would pay who was also my boyfriend. He tapped into a deep font of resentment that until then had been well contained. What angered me, specifically, was his easy acceptance of a buyer-seller relationship between men and women. In some ways I came to regard Paul as I would a customer: someone cynical, who didn't place a high value on sexual honesty, who was easily manipulated by female façades. I could never bring myself to trust him completely. And though I wasn't fully conscious of it, on some level I decided that he wasn't due the respect I would have accorded a different kind of man. For me, Paul symbolized men who preferred buying women to knowing them.

Of course, I had also accepted that men bought and women sold, and I had even embraced this relationship. So while anger bubbled under the surface, I was uneasily silent.

My vein of resentment didn't drive us apart, at least not at first. We were locked in a pact of mutual acceptance. I was flattered that he had been so honest with me. Our shared secrets had bound us together and given us a sense of complicity. We knew that we understood aspects of each other's sexual personalities that others had not. We both had strains of impulsive self-gratification; we both felt as if we were a little off of normal. We had both had countless mercenary sexual transactions with strangers, such as no one who had not had them could understand.

We had the best sex, I thought, when I danced for him. And those were perhaps our closest, most understanding moments. It was as though whatever else we kept guarded or distant, we had found one place where we could meet.

For all these undercurrents, Paul and I were a remarkably calm couple. We got into political debates, but they remained confined to specific subjects. We almost never got into the kind of fights I had had with Erik, which started over the minutiae of daily life but sprawled explosively. Paul was easygoing and never exhibited, or elicited in me, any wild emotions. At the beginning there never seemed to be anything for either of us to get upset about, and I enjoyed the tranquillity. We had our first heated argument shortly after I arrived for the weekend in Miami. It started over a political issue. In the past these discussions had always stayed contained, but somehow, unusually for us, this one turned into an angry personal battle. After he started crying, in his suite overlooking the harbor, he said, "There, are you happy now?" I didn't know what he meant. "You made me cry. I cried first," he said. In our six months I had never cried in front of him, though I hadn't consciously thought we were in a competition. But when he said it I realized that I was satisfied to have reduced him to tears. That he had articulated, and I had felt, this competition over tears should have highlighted a sickness in our relationship—we both wanted to see the other person weaker and more hurt than ourselves; we were playing power games. And maybe we both realized this, but also saw that it made us even more alike than we had thought, and it pulled our bonds a little tighter.

Paul took a greater interest in what I wore than my previous boyfriends ever had. He had strong, specific likes and dislikes, and at first it struck me as bizarre that he would tell me so. I wasn't used to catering to a boyfriend's aesthetic preferences, but I started to, gingerly, wondering what it would feel like. Paul's taste was influenced by fashion and porn to an extent I had never encountered in my personal life, though I had seen the porn effect all the time in peep-show customers. He loved straps and thongs, stockings and teddies, and his delight made wearing them more fun. In outerwear he had specific ideas about what he wanted to see me in—he liked sleek, neutral-toned outfits, and high heels when feasible. He disdained bright colors and pantsuits, and he hated suede. Whenever I went to cut my hair, which I had started keeping shoulder-length or shorter, he urged me not to cut too much. He disliked jewelry, including the small pieces of silver that I always wore. All of his commentary and opinion on what I wore was a novelty coming from a boyfriend. As soon as I started dressing for him, I felt as if I was stepping into a role. This feeling was so strong that often, in my mind's eye, rather than experiencing something directly I felt as if I was viewing a film. I would watch, voyeur-like: *She's getting dressed. She's wearing the teddy that he gave her under her skirt, which is tight. He thinks she looks sexy and feels her breasts, stopping her from putting her shirt on. She finishes dressing; they go out.*

Once I was hurrying to meet him on a warm fall day, after which we were planning to see a group of friends. I put on a black skirt and boots, and then, on a whim, a suede shirt. I had recently had it sent from home with a box of old clothes, and Paul had never seen it before. It crossed my mind, as I put it on, that he hated suede, but dressing for him was still more of a game to me than something to be taken seriously. I walked into the café where we were meeting and spotted him. For a split second he smiled, and then suddenly he looked crestfallen. I knew why right away, and by the time I reached his table I was almost laughing because I had never seen such a strong reaction to a shirt. "What is that?" he asked, in a tone of disappointment that a father might have used when confronted with a teenager's facial piercing.

"It's just a shirt," I said, not believing that his aggravation could be in earnest. He looked stern. I scanned his face for hints that he was teasing me, sure that he couldn't be seriously upset, but he kept shaking his head and asking me where I had gotten it. My laughter didn't jog him into laughing at himself as I hoped it might. He was somewhat relieved to learn that I hadn't bought the shirt recently—it was, at least, the choice of an immature, pre-Paul self—but he remained visibly dismayed. We started walking to the restaurant where we were going to meet our friends, but before we arrived, he suggested we detour into a clothing store, and once inside he volunteered to buy me a new top.

"Fine," I said, and chose one. The sheer style I chose also required a new bra to go under it, I told him, and he bought both. I put them on in the dressing room and folded my old shirt and carried it in the shopping bag. He joked about taking it away from me so that I wouldn't wear it again. Only then did we proceed to dinner. I felt cut loose from any frame of reference. Was this normal? Should I feel angry? I was split: I found the incident above all comical, but it also brought out a mercenary side in me. I said to myself, seriously, Why get bent out of shape? You got a new bra and top out of it. It occurred to me, at the cash register, to pay for them myself, but I quickly dismissed the thought. He was making the fuss; he could pay. I reminded myself, cynically, that dating a man who took such an interest in my appearance had at least expanded my wardrobe. Paul had bought me beautiful clothing many times. But this was a new kind of personal relationship for me. I had retreated into myself before, but never in so calculating a fashion.

For me our trip to the clothing store was a repeat of the peep show: I agreed to look a certain way for a man, and he compensated me. But the peep show had been a small, safe, squared-away corner, where people mostly knew that the fantasy didn't leave the premises. What had happened with Paul disturbed me because I saw how I let the role-playing and performing go on in my "real" life. I laughed as we left the store, for the same reason I had laughed the first time I was catcalled, or made a pass at by a married man, or watched a customer bend and peer to get a look inside. It was laughter at the absurd ways in which my appearance affected my life.

I think that, if I had loved Paul, the shirt episode would have been unbearable. Such a concern over appearance wasn't grounds for an honest relationship. But my attachment to Paul, while strong, had more to do with playing a role. His gifts, plane tickets, and hotel rooms, and his unqualified pleasure in watching me strip, all made me feel as though I was acting in a play about someone else. It was as though for the entire time that I dated Paul I was living one possible alternative to my own, real life. As I withdrew further, I became conscious that I was letting myself be bought. My conduct was different in the details to that of a stripper or prostitute, but similar in the underlying state of mind. It gave me a thrill to act as though I was for sale, but it also made me harden toward him. He seemed to take my behavior for granted.

I started to feel that Paul was trying to mold my personality as well as my appearance. He spoke frequently of what "most" women wanted, and he contrasted it with my desires, which, I had told him when we met, didn't include marriage or children. He told me repeatedly, in the controlled tones of someone trying to sound neutral about a shameful disease, that I was "ambitious." Ambition was normal among twenty-eight-year-olds in London, but he treated mine as an oddity. He held fast to the idea that modern men and women were programmed to have certain personality traits—men, for instance, were aggressive and promiscuous, while women were maternal and monogamous. He gave me books and articles that supported his theories. He always drew my attention to the latest thinker to advocate full-time child rearing for women, and he spoke highly of overeducated women who left their jobs for motherhood. He pointed out that if a banker and a journalist were to raise children, it would only make sense for the lower-earning journalist to leave her job. He was subtle, polite, and flawlessly logical on these subjects. But he was also relentless, worrying over them like a dog chewing on a bone, bringing them up on a daily basis. I began to feel that he wouldn't let the issue rest until I fit his idea of what a woman was supposed to be. I started to conform. Maybe I did want marriage and children, I said. It was the easiest thing to say, and maybe it held a grain of truth. It was another alternative life at which to play. I watched myself pretend to be what he wanted. By playing these different roles of sex symbol or kept woman or future traditional wife, I felt as if I was a puppet master, manipulating a marionette of myself from a safe height. Paul didn't mind my aloofness the way some men would have. He embraced my playacting at face value. He even praised my coolness, complimenting me for not being clinging or overexpressive. He thought emotional frigidity was admirable. That, at root, is why I think I chose Paul. He wanted the smoke and mirrors that I had to give.

I started to actively want to deceive him. With earlier boyfriends, I had felt the opposite. I had hated the thought of lying to them because it would have compromised a central tenet of the relationships—honesty. Until the very end with Erik, I had tried to tell the truth even when it was painful. But since I had come to recognize the dance I was doing for Paul, I wanted to see how far I could push it. I wanted to have several men and give each one a different version of myself. At first I just flirted with other men to whom I was attracted. Then, during a vacation without Paul, I had an affair with a man completely different from him in appearance and lifestyle. He was younger than me, an itinerant journalist who had probably never worn a suit. I was living a grander version of the booth, where I had adapted myself to the fantasy of each man who came in. And like working as a stripper, cheating was a way to stake my independence, because it meant no one would be able to know me or claim me completely.

I sublimated my annoyance with little things Paul said and did into vengefulness. The shirt incident fed it, and so did his vocal preferences about my appearance. The fact that he had been to see strippers and prostitutes—for his own pleasure, not dragged along by me—also fed my vindictiveness, as did his theorizing on what was "natural" for men and women. With my simmering hostility, the obvious choice would have been to break up. There came a point at which it would have made perfect sense, when his company promoted him and moved him to New York. I declined to follow, but we said we would continue our relationship. I was still deeply attached to him. He was the prize I had captured and didn't want to give up. I wanted to see how long I could carry on.

When he left it became easier to lead a double life. Keeping up my act was becoming stressful when I was around him all the time, but faking it would be easier with him out of town. We promised to see each other often, but even as I was giving assurances to him, I was surveying my bedroom and regarding it as a site for trysts. I didn't know with whom yet—just that there would be someone. I did find a man eventually and began an affair, but I continued to see Paul once a month. I saw the new man almost every day while Paul and I planned our holidays together. I compartmentalized meticulously, lying about my whereabouts and making sure to hide stray hairs or T-shirts when Paul came to town. I smiled when I watched myself change the sheets on my bed after midnight one night, in anticipation of his arrival the next morning. I was fascinated by my ability to practice deception on this level, because I had never known for sure if I could do it. The new man gave me a feeling of lighthearted excitement, in part because of his good looks and sweet nature, but also because of his role in the game. I took great satisfaction in the fact that I could do what I did—I enjoyed both men, they both belonged to me, and I belonged to neither.

However, the new man was not the kind to stand for emotional distance. He knew more of the facts than Paul, and he probably knew me better as well. I could find nothing to justify hurting him—he would never have told me what to wear or bought sex; he didn't stoke any angers. He became upset, for the second or third time, because I had not yet broken up with Paul after I had told him that I was going to. I gradually had to tell each of them more and more lies. I faced the increasing danger of one calling when the other was present, or of Paul paying me an unexpected visit. As the excitement and pleasure of the situation wore off, I realized I was only truly relaxed when I was with neither. I felt I was headed for a collision, and so I resolved to break it off with both of them. The new man, having only known me for a few months, and being better apprised of the situation, was understanding.

Paul was more complicated. Though I had been behaving in a way that was sure to destroy the relationship, I found it difficult to tell him face to face that I wanted to end it. I finally did while visiting him in New York one weekend. When faced with his tears, though, I let him persuade me that there was still hope for us. I had been locked in our fragile, schizophrenic structure for so long that it was difficult to give up. But there was no question that it had to end. I had known it at least since the afternoon when he had bought me the sheer top, when I had seen that I was living in a larger version of a peep show and had left the store laughing. And so, after vacillating wildly, I broke up with him again a month after the first attempt, and this time I was successful.

After I broke up with Paul I fell in love again, much to my surprise, as though this were the prize waiting for me after finally ending something broken and dishonest. I hadn't felt a similar way, I realized, since I had first fallen for Alex, nearly ten years earlier.

This man was interested in my past in the way one might be transfixed by a road wreck: even as he prodded me for information, he was apprehensive and dismayed. He asked me questions that I couldn't answer or that made me angry and defensive. He thought part of me must have hated men even to start working as a stripper. He told me my body was private. I told him that it wasn't: I would be looked at sexually whether I acquiesced or not. He said I was cynical and defeatist. I told him that dancing silently for strangers was easier than he might think. I tried to explain that I had felt a sense of camaraderie at the Lusty Lady, and that I had met women I admired because they were bold—bold about using their sexuality as they saw fit and about everything else. He remained unconvinced.

He made me think. I wasn't persuaded that working as a stripper had been a sign of antagonism toward men, but I had to consider my treatment of Paul, which was unquestionably cold. There had been no reason to date Paul for as long as I had, behaving the way that I had, that could be explained without anger.

I had never thought of myself as someone who hated men. I had spent much of my adult life with one boyfriend or another, and my relationships often looked, at least superficially, as though they were happy, stable, or both. But I remembered how with Erik I had chafed, almost from the beginning, against a feeling of being trapped. By agreeing to get married and by buying a house, I had accepted being tied down, but at the same time I hated him, as though he had forced me. When I finally left, I felt as though I had escaped a prison.

When I quit stripping, I remained a staunch defender of both the profession and the women I knew who did it. But while I didn't feel that anyone *should* quit, I half-consciously expected that the ones I liked best would. Three years later Zoe hadn't, nor had Kim. When I asked, Zoe always said that she would do it for another year or two. Sometimes when I read her effusive letters, I envied her. In one from Venezuela, where she was cycling, mountain climbing, and having affairs with a man and a woman, she wrote that she was having the most "intensely lived" time of her life. But I also wondered what had happened to her writing or to her idea of leading cycling tours. The women at the Lusty Lady glittered in my imagination, and I wondered what had happened to them all.

I began to think that stripping had influenced my relationship with Paul more than I had realized. Down the block from my apartment in London there was a strip club called Venus, in front of which a heavyset bouncer in an overcoat usually stood, flanked on either side by pseudo-Roman female figures made of white plaster. Between our first and second breakups, Paul told me that one night when he arrived at my place early, he had thought about going to Venus—to have a drink and wait, he said—but found it closed. I felt indignant. I asked him if, in theory, he would patronize a strip club again. He said that maybe under certain circumstances, like for a friend's bachelor party, he would. I became upset. "I can't promise you that I wouldn't," he said. I became disconsolate and hung up the phone and cried, dejected out of all proportion. Another time he told me about a mutual friend of ours, a business student, who was interviewing for jobs in finance. One of the banks had courted its recruits by taking them out to an expensive strip club and paying for their lap dances. This, too, upset me greatly. I felt the same surge of rage I had experienced when I discovered a sexual double standard as a teenager. Any of my male peers could casually mention that he had seen a stripper at a bachelor party, or that an employer had taken him to a strip club, without raising an eyebrow. But I had participated in the same relationship, one that men could talk about openly, and I felt silenced. I couldn't tell most of my friends or family, and I could never tell an employer. For a man to say he had paid a stripper was unremarkable, but for me to say that I had been one changed other people's perception of me permanently.

I tried to toughen up. I told myself that I was inordinately upset. Of all people, I should have by now accepted that this relationship between men and women was a part of life. I should have understood that paying to use women's bodies as a commodity or an entertainment was the normal course of events. Part of me wanted to forget this lesson, but at the same time I felt that if I did, I would lose a layer of protection. So long as I didn't forget, the facts would never catch me by surprise.

I loved finally being able to work as a reporter. I loved trying to get to the root of other people's motivations and shaping stories so that they said what I wanted them to. And I looked forward to the lifestyle journalism promised, one of mobility and autonomy. I felt as if I had finally transformed my selfish independence, as it had been called by Paul, Erik, and others, into a virtue. And just as stripping oozed into my personal life, a fascination with sex roles seeped into my work. When I could squeeze stories in between other assignments, I found ways to write about gay rights, women in the military, and prostitution. I could write about subjects that burned at me, yet present them as though I were neutral, helping others to take stands without taking any myself.

I began to see that stripping was going to chase me. It was going to affect my relationships, as it had with Paul. And it frustrated me that, after all this time, I still didn't know what I thought about it. I couldn't answer simple questions about whether I thought it was right or wrong. And I couldn't answer the one question that most people were bound to ask, which was: Why I had done it? I felt defensive toward those who couldn't understand and tended to dismiss them as close-minded. But I could see that being secretive, angry, and dismissive would only make me feel more isolated over time. One year of my past had taken on incommensurate significance. To try to understand, I decided to go back.

Going back, for me, meant going back to Seattle, as though by going there I could find an earlier self. Seattle was also where I would find women whom I had known as dancers over time, of whom I could make some assessment as to whether they had changed. Because, feeling now like more of a journalist than a stripper, I felt I had to get answers from others, and I was doubtful that I could find any on my own. Once I decided to go, I quit my job and bought a plane ticket within weeks.

While I wanted to find women I had known at the Lusty Lady, I didn't go back to work there. There were so many ways to strip, and I wanted to push myself into things I hadn't tried before—which meant clubs with stages and private dances. The Lusty had been safe and comfortable, but it had given me the sense that I was missing out on something because I was afraid to take a risk. The peep-show windows were a physical shield that kept me from having to wield a psychological shield that I thought must be necessary in clubs.

I knew, through Zoe, Kim, and others, the fates of some of my former coworkers. Of the seventy or so who had worked at the L in my time, a couple dozen still did. Some had decisively ended their affairs with the sex industry and moved into new careers—there was a graphic designer, several lawyers, a few mothers, an actress, a midwife, an architect—or so I heard. I identified with this group. Except for the fact that I was going back, they were like me—they had opened and closed the stripping chapter in their lives and then moved on. Others, I heard, were working in strip clubs or peep shows elsewhere—so-and-so had gone to Boston, someone else to Los Angeles, another to Alaska. And others seemed to have disappeared entirely. I would ask Zoe, for example, whatever happened to Winter? And she would make uncertain noises, ask whether I meant this Winter or that one, and finally say that she didn't know or that she wasn't sure who I meant.

I needed a place to live in Seattle and thought immediately of Matt. He still had his old wooden house on the hill, and he had bought that second one on the same street. He was renting out parts of both. When I called him, he and Zoe had just reunited at the party in the Nevada desert. She had not moved back in but was spending time there again. They both suggested right away that I move in with Matt and take the yellow-painted bedroom with the map-of-the-world desk that had belonged to Zoe. Matt was only going to be around for a couple of months anyway, he told me, because he planned to go traveling in Asia, and he wanted to have someone in his house while he was away.

Chapter 21

I went to a wood-shingled storefront hung with a black-and-white sign reading "Talents West." It sat across from a used-car lot, on a stretch of Lake City Way crowded with used-car lots and Chinese restaurants. A small sign in the window of the single-story building read, "Parking for Italians Only." I stepped inside onto a faded shag carpet patrolled by a moplike dog. When I entered, a ruddy middle-aged man sitting at a desk broke off his telephone conversation.

"What can I do for you, honey?"

"I want to work at Rick's," I said. He directed me to fill in an application form and produce some identification, then returned to his conversation. He told someone that he had bought a horse for his daughter. Above his desk hung a plaque reading, "Number one boss, Frank Colacurcio." The Colacurcio family ran several Seattle-area strip clubs.

The man at the desk hung up the phone, introduced himself as Billy, and asked me my name. When I told him, he said, "Elisabeth. That's a preppy name. Are you a preppy girl, Elisabeth?"

"I was," I said. He muttered to himself about preppy girls while photocopying my driver's license.

He took several more calls, saying, "Hi honey," to each caller, then disappeared down the shag-carpeted hallway. A man with a smooth face and a gray bouffant came out, introduced himself as Mike, and shook my hand. He ushered me into an office where we sat down facing each other across his desk. He had a real estate catalogue open in front of him.

"There are some very fine homes in there," he said. "All over the country. One in Florida here for twenty-nine million, you can have it today with all the furniture." I nodded politely and then he looked over my form, which had my age on it. "How old are you?"

"Twenty-nine."

"Are you a married or single young lady?"

"I'm single."

"Got any kids?"

"No."

He looked at me suspiciously. "You don't have any kids?"

"No."

"How d'you make it to your age with no kids?"

"Just didn't want any," I said.

"You're waiting for the right guy to come along, right?"

"I guess so."

"Well, don't wait too long. Thirty-five. Thirty-five is a good age to have kids."

I nodded.

"So you haven't worked in the club environment before?" he asked.

"No."

He then plunged into some questions about my background and ambitions, which I tried to answer as briefly as possible. I mentioned that I had lived in New York, and I said I was thinking about going back to school.

"There are some great strip clubs in New York," he said.

"I wouldn't know; I never worked in any of them."

"You never worked in New York? God, how could you resist? There are some great clubs there."

He asked again what my goals were. I stammered again about going back to school. "I like to be able to take time off," I added for good measure.

"The reason I ask you this, Elisabeth, is because I am a firm believer that the women who decide they are going to embrace this field, adult entertainment, as a career choice—they lose. There are women who make a lot of money every day and spend a lot of money every day. They have a great time, but they are spinning their wheels. Some girls, on the other hand, use this business to get the money they need to do the things they want. They get the money, then go on and do something else."

I asked him how many women he thought managed to do that.

"In my experience, twenty to twenty-five percent." He paused. "But it doesn't seem like it will be a problem for you. You seem to have other goals."

He launched into a long list of advice.

"The less you wear, within taste, of course, the more money you will make. A T-bar and a stripper's bra are the obvious choice. Nipples and crotch must be covered. You are only naked onstage; you are clothed when you are doing table dances. Heels should be at least three and a half inches high. Let's see. Makeup. If you wear the kind of makeup you wear on a daytime basis, during daylight hours, in that kind of lighting, well . . ."

"It won't show up," I finished.

"Right. Lots of lips, lots of eyes," he said.

"There is a costume lady," he went on. "Several costume ladies, actually, who come around and sell costumes in the dressing room. Some of the outfits are thirty-five dollars, some may be as much as two hundred dollars. Do not buy a two-hundred-dollar costume. You don't need it. If you get a thirty-five-dollar one and take care of it—you know, hand wash it and lay it flat to dry—it will last you a long time."

He leaned back in his chair and clasped his hands behind his head.

"In this business, here in the city of Seattle, we are selling two things: soda pop and the fantasy of sex," he said. "The guys who come into Rick's are not guys who enjoy dating in a normal sort of way. They are not comfortable in a normal dating environment. A normal guy would maybe go to a bar, strike up a conversation with a nice young lady like yourself, ask her out to dinner, and maybe, if he's lucky, he'll get laid. The men who come to strip clubs are not comfortable doing that. But they are men, and they do love to chase. That is the most important thing to keep in mind. Now, Elisabeth. Let's say I'm a customer. What do you say if I ask you out to breakfast?"

"No," I said with enthusiasm, partly because I couldn't imagine wanting to go, and partly because the Lusty managers had drilled into me that to say yes could get me busted.

"What do you say if I offer you a thousand dollars to have sex with me?" Mike asked.

"No," I said again, feeling like a clever child.

"Wrong on both counts," he said.

My eyebrows shot up.

"You don't say no. You don't say yes either. You see, these guys love to chase. If you said, 'Yes, okay, let's go right now,' I can bet you they would find a reason not to. Now ask me the same questions I just asked you."

"How about breakfast?" I asked.

Mike raised the pitch of his voice a couple of notches. "I'd love to, but this is a dangerous world we live in, and I would have to get to know you a lot better before I would consider going on a date with you."

I nodded.

"Now ask me the second question, and be careful, I might take you up on it. I could use the money."

"A thousand dollars for sex with me," I said.

"First of all, I'm not a prostitute. I love sex, and I love it far too much to do it for money. And second of all, I would have to know you a lot better before I would even consider that sort of thing."

Mike stared at me sagely.

"Where do you think he's going to get to know you better?"

"Doing table dances," I replied.

"You see, you don't say no and you don't say yes, because as soon as you do, the chase is over and you're not going to get any more money out of him. He'll keep asking you for a while, and buying dances from you, and then eventually he'll get bored and decide, 'I don't want her anymore,' and he'll pick so-and-so over there to chase for a while." He paused and stared dramatically.

The discourse over, he began to explain Seattle's table-dancing rules. A dancer can touch the customer above the waist, he said, but the customer can't touch the dancer.

"We are not a church, but we are not a house of ill repute either."
If a customer touched a girl on the leg, it was no big deal, "but he's
not allowed to *handle* her," he said.

"Only three things will get you kicked out." He held up three fingers and counted off: "Prostitution. Drugs—selling drugs—at work.
And stealing from a customer or another employee. Anything else, we
can work with," he said.

Dancers' rent—money paid to the house for the privilege of performing—was a flat fee of a hundred dollars a shift, though it was
expected that I would also tip out to the bartender, bouncer, and disc
jockey. He said he would waive rent for my first three shifts. I signed
up for two six-hour day shifts a week. I was going to work Tuesday
and Thursday, but Mike suggested I do Wednesday and Thursday
instead, because if I sparked a customer's interest one day, he would
likely be back at the same time the next. "You'll make most of your
money from your regular clientele," he told me.

"Oh, and one more thing Elisabeth," he said deliberately. "If you
have, say, a personal problem that is causing you to lose sleep at night" he
paused "—let us know. We solve personal problems here every day."

Before starting work I had to go shopping. My old shoes were worn,
and my old thongs frayed. While on the Lusty's stage I had been able
to get by on nudity and an assortment of leg wear; for clubs I would
need clothes that I could actually remove. One night when Zoe was
getting ready for a bachelor party, I looked over the costumes she was
packing into her duffel bag. I picked up a shimmery red vinyl top and
held it by the shoulder straps. I turned over a white shoe with a five-
inch heel, wondering if I had it in me to walk in it. A few nights later,
Zoe and I went to a strip club and sat in the audience. I looked at the
shoes and thought that they had grown higher and more improbable
in my absence. Some were more like ornate stilts, making their wear-
ers look poised to lift off into outer space.

Seattle had stores that sold sex-worker gear, clothing made of span-
dex, vinyl, and leather. It had the Castle Superstore, the Love Pantry,

and various fetish-wear emporiums on Capitol Hill that sold clothes alongside toys and porn. I rejected all of these, though, and went to a shopping mall.

Footwear, so often the only thing to stay on, came first. I needed a few pairs of sky-high heels. My feet had only occasionally seen the inside of a truly high heel while I was away. I had a pair of stilettos that I had sometimes worn to go out, provided I could take cabs and lean on others. They made me feel bound up and observed. High heels, like any tight, strappy undergarment, bore a direct connection to sex for me, because they made me notice them. They were uncomfortable enough that they were a constant reminder of their own presence.

I was astounded at the way high heels were so persistently in vogue. Of all the things women can do to look attractive to men, short of surgery, wearing high heels is the most physically painful. Aesthetically, the only reason to wear them is to make one's ass stick out. In high heels a woman sways her hips when she walks, whether she remembers to or not. Many of the most fashionable ones force her to give up her own powers of locomotion and submit to helpless hobbling. They are hard to balance in, they hurt, and if she wears them too much they can cause permanent physical damage, shortening the length of the tendon at the back of the leg. But none of this stops them from remaining relentlessly in style. Every season's offerings are more delicate and less practical than the last. Women call one another chic for clattering around in them like geishas, while wearing Band-Aids under the straps in a losing battle against blisters.

A good stripper shoe is more practical than the most fashionable high heel, because however improbable the height, the base is heftier. Even the four- and five-inch stilettos favored by some dancers provide more ballast than fashion heels, because they put more shoe under foot and offer better weight distribution. Stilettos are the most popular. They narrow to a point at the base of the heel and have a thick sole under the ball of the foot. There had been a particular style of stiletto sandal popular at the Lusty Lady that dancers called "the Barbie shoe." (Barbie's plastic foot is shaped like the inside of a high heel.) I doubted my ability to balance on a stiletto, so I went in for platforms, which are wide at the base of the heel. On both stilettos and platforms, while the heel might be four or five inches high, the ball of the foot is raised two or three inches off the ground so that the foot doesn't have to make too precipitous an arc. Open toes were essential so that my soon-to-be-painted toenails could show through.

I went to the discount branch of a major department store at an Eastside shopping center, which had a wide selection of stripper shoes. It had towering heels in red glitter, black patent leather, purple velvet, and pink satin. Bright shiny colors suitable for attracting magpies were essential to the game; my beloved black wouldn't cut it. I had once seen a stripper with battery-operated flashing lights in her bikini top and bottom. There may have been customers out there who liked sleek and subtle, but from an accounting standpoint, it was best to go for the lowest common denominator.

I grabbed handfuls of shoes by the straps and started trying them on. I put on a four-inch red heel and admired it in the low mirror. The bend in my foot echoed the S-curve from my waist to my hip. I chose my favorites and got in line at a counter to pick up their mates. The woman in front of me, who had a wrinkled face and wore pink lipstick, stared at the gaudy collection dangling from my right hand. I felt as if I owed her an explanation.

"Party shoes," I said.

She smiled. "Are you a dancer?"

"Uh, yes," I said slowly, as my mind rapidly formed preparatory lies. I decided that if she asked what kind of dancer I was, I would tell her ballroom. But she didn't.

"I saw you trying on those red ones. They sure are high," she said.

"They're not as bad as they look," I told her.

Defiantly, I handed my shoes to the young man behind the counter, daring him to challenge me. But he brought the matches with no questions asked.

It was good to have a mix of shoes, so that when one pair started to rub me raw I could switch to another. I ended up buying three pairs, including a set of strappy scarlet platforms with four-inch heels. I also bought a pair of knee-high boots. Boots were essential. They were relatively comfortable and looked sharp with anything, from gloves and jewelry to leather. I remembered Korina, from my first visit to the Lusty, in nothing but white boots and long brown hair. Boots were an entire outfit by themselves.

The boots cost $79.90. The shoes, all deeply discounted, cost $34.90, $14.90, and $9.98. I was pleased with the lineup.

Before I left the store I walked through the cosmetics section where there was a display of makeup for children. They sold a flavored lip gloss called the Lipsicle, which looked almost exactly like a lollipop and came in candy colors. In the same display they sold Blown Away Bubble Fragrance, which could be applied as a perfume or used to blow bubbles, and a set of six tiny nail polishes in sparkling blues and pinks, labeled Blue, Shy, Happy, Crazy, Flirty, and Sassy. I bought a tube of pink body-glitter gel that came in a test-tube-shaped pump.

My next destination was a drugstore for more makeup. For my toes I bought nail polish in Red Glamour to go with my new red shoes, and Peek-a-Boo Pink, for a more faux-innocent sort of look. I also bought a violet lip pencil and razor blades, wondering if any of it could now be considered a business expense for tax purposes. When I was checking out, the cover of a women's fashion magazine caught my eye. I was irresistibly drawn to the headline: "Peep Show—What Men Really Do When They're Not with You." For a moment I thought it must be a story about men going to peep shows, but of course it wasn't. The writer had found that when men were not with me they read, cleaned, painted, played drums, cooked, did yoga, watched romantic comedies, wrote poetry, and exfoliated their faces. Not only did it not mention peep shows, it didn't even mention masturbation, which I was pretty sure men did when they were alone. The voyeuristic, teasing headline failed to deliver. I wondered if I had completely drifted away from reality or if the magazine had. The publication's subtitle was: "The Magazine for Your Me Years." A diamond ring advertisement appeared on page four.

I concluded that I must be the sane one, but I bought the magazine anyway. My drugstore bill, including nail-polish remover and cotton balls, came to $33.01. I drove to a more upscale Eastside shopping center called Bellevue Square, which had a Victoria's Secret.

Victoria's Secret was the mass-market lingerie mecca on street corners and in shopping malls all over the country. It was the most prominent clothing chain in the United States specializing in lingerie, and its soft-core catalogs featuring sultry models littered suburban coffee tables everywhere. Before Victoria's Secret women had to go to little-known boutiques and the far corners of department stores just to find the tamest lingerie. For racier garments they had to resort to catalogues that came wrapped in brown paper. But with the arrival of Victoria's Secret any teenager in America could get garter belts and see-through push-up bras at her local mall. Vicky's Secret also had the distinction of having brought the thong panty to the masses. Formerly the territory of porn stars, the flimsy scraps of satin were now worn by young women in the millions.

The Victoria's Secret at Bellevue Square stretched back from the entrance in a cavernous expanse of soft fabrics. The walls were striped in the company's signature candy pink and white. The store was full of objects that to my skewed imagination seemed designed with the stripper in mind. There were silk thong panties held together with a bow on each hip for ease of removal. Who required ease of removal more than a stripper? There were see-through, ruffled, ass-length nighties, held together with string bows, far too pristine and uncomfortable to sleep in. There were tight, strappy undergarments, replete with buckles and clasps, the kind the wearer couldn't possibly be unconscious of, the kind designed explicitly to be looked at.

A mother and daughter were shopping together in the short nightie section. The mother said to the tall blond teenager, "These things would barely cover your bottom," and was ignored, though I have no doubt that in her head the girl said, "Yeah, Mom, that's the point." I felt for her, grappling with that insistent pretense that her sexuality didn't exist. An Asian couple, led by the female half, shopped together. She was short and pretty, and he was short and round. "This is cute," the woman told him, and he nodded silently. "What about this?" she asked him, and he grunted. She pulled nighties off the rack, asking his opinion on each one, but he never spoke.

I gathered a slippery pile of bras and slips to try on. The same couple was in the dressing room area when I stepped into my pink-striped booth. The woman came out of her cubicle in each new outfit and twirled in front of him.

"Mike, come in here," she said. "What do you think of this?" Mike, who had been lurking near the entrance, strolled toward her, trying to appear nonchalant but looking painfully out of his territory. "Just tell me if you don't like it," she said. "It's okay if he's in here, isn't it?" she asked a salesgirl. The chipper woman said that, actually, it was not okay, and Mike retreated sheepishly to the entranceway. His woman came out and modeled for him in a short nightie made of different dark red fabrics. It was too subtle for stripping, I thought. Unresponsive Mike nodded quietly when she asked, "Do you like it better than the other one?"

In my rosy-hued mirrored booth, over the course of an hour, I watched my body slide in and out of elastic and satin. The lighting was soft and flattering. I twirled and posed a few times, twisting this way and that to see how my body looked. I picked out a leopard-print bra and thong, a lime green satin bra and matching mesh thong, a black mesh thong, and two black lace G-strings. (A G-string is like a thong, but the piece dividing the ass is an elastic string instead of a strip of cloth, hence the nickname "butt floss.") The bras I tried on in my normal size didn't produce enough cleavage, so I dropped down a cup and they were tight enough to squeeze more flesh out of the top.

I also bought a stretchy black minidress, sold as a "slip," that was so tight it made me look like an inner tube, as well as a long satin number with a slit up the left leg. It looked like a gown but I made certain it was easily removed. In the dressing room mirror I undid the single tie across the back, did a quick shimmy, and made the thing fall to the ground.

My bill at Victoria's Secret came to $231.87. By the end of the day I had spent a total of $420.88 on supplies, more than I had usually made at the Lusty Lady in a week.

*   *   *

My next task was to get two separate licenses from the city. At the Lusty Lady I had been an employee, but now I was considered a contractor. Even the city insisted on being tipped out.

Downtown at the city's Department of Licenses and Consumer Affairs, I filled out two application forms. The entertain license form asked for height (five feet seven inches), weight (135 pounds), hair color (blond), and eye color (green), as well as my stage name. On the business license form, I listed my trade name as "Leila," and my type of business as "dancer/entertainer." Then the woman who took my forms dispatched me across the street to the police department, where I filled out another form, this one asking for place of birth, age, and race. A police officer stamped my application after checking that I had no record of convictions.

Back at the first office a hefty man with one earring punched my details into a computer.

"Does anyone other than strippers ever get an entertainment license?" I asked.

"Nope."

"So what's the point of it exactly?"

"I've been working here twelve years, and I still don't know the answer to that question," he said in a baritone. "Women come in and apply every day. They're always asking me what it's for."

He said that the city did a particularly brisk business at the beginning of the new year, when the license had to be renewed, and in the late spring, when students prepared for summer jobs.

A photograph, then fees to the city of $37.50 for each license—half price because we were more than halfway through the year—and I was legal. My green-rimmed, 8.5-by-11-inch entertainment license bore a large black-and-white photograph of me with "Leila" and the address of Rick's printed next to it. Green lettering on it read "Post Conspicuously," though I couldn't imagine where they meant.

Chapter 22

I had seen lap dancing at a distance, but it was Zoe who made me understand it. We went to Rick's one night before I started, and by telling the reluctant floor manager that we wanted to work there, we convinced her to let us watch. It was dark and busy, crowded with seated men, in normal clothes, and women walking around in bras, thongs, and heels. There were two stages. We sat down at a table and a waitress brought us water, and we watched the dancers rotate from one to the other. Some were young and firm, others bruised and sagging; none smiled. Zoe noticed that none of them wore stockings or boots, which she thought showed a strange lack of variation.

Zoe said she wanted to get a lap dance before we left. She told a waitress, and a few minutes later a petite young blonde in a white bra and thong appeared by our side and introduced herself as Lulu. Zoe exchanged a few words with Lulu, and then got up to go over to the cushioned bench against the wall, motioning me to follow her. She had tricked me. By the time we got to the bench she had already paid Lulu and instructed her that the lap dance was for me. Feeling exasperated, I resigned myself.

When the next song began, Lulu straddled me and began to grind as though it were a full-contact sport. She pressed hard into me—facing me, back to me, then facing me again. She had a few other moves, but for most of the song she was in my lap. Her skin smelled sweet and dusty, and her tits brushed my face a couple of times. I couldn't help thinking, as she rode me, that if I had a cock she would be sitting on it squarely. I checked myself for signs of arousal, but there were none; I was numb. Through most of the dance I faced her chest, and she didn't look at me once.

After my song Lulu sat between us for a few minutes. She said that she had a three-year-old daughter and that she was putting herself through university, majoring in psychology. She had worked at Rick's for about five months. On a bad night she made three hundred dollars but usually it was more. She tried to do at least five or six private dances every hour. And she didn't do dirty dances, she said, she only danced clean. I wasn't sure exactly what that meant at the time, but later I learned that the full rubdown she had just given me was "clean." "Dirty" dancing usually meant jerking people off.

"You can use this job to get what you want. You can save your money and get the things you want and just do it for a little while," she told us, which reminded me of Mike, the man who had interviewed me. I wondered if he gave everyone the same lecture. "But some women let it use them," Lulu continued, "and then they're still here five years later on."

I glanced up at Zoe, who had been in the business nearly ten years, but if this comment struck her at all, she didn't show it. She asked Lulu if there were many girls in her situation.

"Well, a lot of them have kids, but not many are going to school."

A lot of the girls did have kids, I found out as soon as I set foot in Rick's dressing room. I arrived at midday on a Wednesday, and as I stepped inside the club, it was so dark in contrast to the daylight that I had to wait a full ten seconds for my eyes to adjust. Then I found the fluorescent-lit dressing room, which was never locked, and let myself in. It was a small rectangle of lockers, with a padded bench in the middle and a mirror at one end. Dancers had to bring their own locks, and I had brought the same one I used at the gym. There were girls scattered around the room in conversations with one another, but no one paid me any notice when I walked in. I looked down, kept quiet, and changed into bra, thong, and heels. From the talk around me, it sounded as if they all had children. The room was dominated by discussions of customers, children, and drugs. One dancer, who had a nipple that had slipped its moorings and was creeping down her ample breast, sold pills and pot. Girls smoked from a pipe that looked exactly like a lipstick tube.

When I came out to the floor, the elderly daytime manager took me over to a sign near the bar and pointed sternly at it. It read, "No lap dancing, no bumping and grinding." It gave me a moment of relief, but only a moment, since it obviously had no bearing on what went on here; presumably it existed just to protect the club's liability. All it did was further scramble any notion of what I could expect.

I did my stage dances—one song on each—and found that it still wasn't difficult for me to perform naked, for strangers, on a mirror-backed platform with a pole in the middle. In some ways it was easier than at the Lusty Lady because I had more space and the audience was a short distance away. Yet it lacked the private, protected feeling of the Lusty's stage. The dark club seemed to stretch away in the distance with only pinpricks of light marking the bar and the exit, and it gave me the vulnerable feeling of being in wide-open space.

My mind was not on the moment, though, but on the task ahead, which was to sell a lap dance. I still wondered if I could do it. It required going up to any likely looking man not already in use and offering him one. I had been hurtling toward this moment since my interview with Mike, but now I was faced with it. There were about a dozen customers and double the number of dancers, so just convincing someone to let me shake my breasts in his face for twenty dollars was going to be difficult.

When I did sell one, I was both pleased and dismayed. After he said yes I waited for the next song to begin, as Lulu had, sitting beside him and asking banal questions. And then I danced. I started about a foot from him, then straddled his legs and moved closer. I danced as though I was carrying a dirty rag at arm's length and looking the other way—as though I was trying to both do it and not to do it at the same time. My body resisted his physical closeness, holding back while I made myself move forward. He looked to the side and down at my breasts, studiously avoiding my face. The part of me that hadn't thought this possible stood by in disbelief. I had an urge to laugh. It was the nervous laugh of my self splitting, of my failure to reconcile what was going on in my head with my outer reality.

He paid me silently, and I tried another one. This time I was hit middance with an abrupt realization. The man had his hand on his crotch and could have easily opened his fly. It would have been so simple, I suddenly saw, to fuck him right there and then. It would barely have taken more physical effort than I was already exerting, just the slightest squirm and push. I was surprised that it would be possible but more surprised that I was thinking it. Following fast on this insight was the observation that if I did fuck him, I could charge him. A bunch of notions suddenly reshuffled themselves in my head, giving me a swift bout of vertigo. Talk about slippery slopes, about getting more to do more. I understood the pillars at Déjà Vu now. I had heard that people had sex in strip clubs, but I had never really grasped the logistics. Now I did. I felt dumb. Prostitution was suddenly not an abstract label but a sticky, tangible choice.

After the second dance I sat down on an empty bench and watched the stage. I couldn't lap dance. It was a physical action too intimate to do with anyone but a lover. I was violating my own ethic about sex, namely, that I should only ever do it because I had the desire. It was the flip side of my long-ago determination that I must have sex in the first place. I had a right to it, but I also had to be honest with myself. I had worked hard over the years to maintain this principle; never to undertake sex manipulatively, always to check and double check that I did, honestly, physically, emotionally, want to. I had never mentally disengaged during sex, never once checked out or focused on something else. If I continued to lap dance, I would have to disengage. I would have to keep my mind on the money, unhook body from thought. Through all my stripping, my boyfriends, my role-playing, and my different lives, I had never lost hold of the person at the center of it all. But lap dancing, if I continued, would force a split. I had found my edge.

*   *   *

To say that Rick's was not a church, as Mike had, was wild understatement. At Rick's, one quick glance around the back bench, which was in the area that was darkest and farthest from the door, revealed women giving hand jobs. Some girls did it on their knees, between the men's legs; others straddled the men, and I could see their forearms pumping up and down. Others "breast-fed," as I heard one dancer call it, and some had devised a sort of backward hand job, in which the dancer straddled the man with her back to him and reached around behind. Later I met a former bouncer who told me he had seen a woman have anal sex with a customer on the back bench. Another ex-employee said that condoms were often found between the cracks in the bench cushions. A dancer at Rick's named Lara told me that not all shifts were the same—at night there were more customers, and the girls could make money dancing clean. She called the day shift women "the cream team."

The women did worry about cops, who sometimes came in and handed out tickets. Usually, a male cop came in and requested a dance. Since nearly all lap dances were technically illegal, he often gave her the citation as soon as she started. Some dancers, though, had received tickets in the mail, which meant that the cop had come in, bought a dance, found the woman's license in the manager's file, and sent the ticket to her home address. In such cases a woman didn't even know which dance had gotten her charged.

Clubs everywhere were netted in a tangle of regulations, usually ill enforced, around which the more-for-more impetus flowed unabated. The laws varied not just by state, but from county to county and town to town. Some states, like Washington, forbade alcohol in strip clubs. In other areas, like Las Vegas, alcohol was permitted in topless lap-dancing clubs but not fully nude ones. Certain districts north of Seattle had a four-foot rule on the books, meaning private dances were supposed to be performed at least that far from the customer, but it was not widely enforced.

The whole country was a patchwork of different regimes, each one a combination of rules on modesty, proximity, and alcohol. Some states had laws about covering nipples—but a dancer who worked in

Oklahoma told me that there, clear latex was a legal nipple covering. In parts of Texas and Florida, dancers did fully nude lap dances in clubs that served booze. Oregon allowed alcohol in strip clubs but also required them to serve food, which meant that many clubs had busy sports-bar type environments. Oregon clubs were the sorts of places where men could say they weren't just there for the naked women, which couldn't be said with any plausibility in Seattle.

As far as dancers were concerned, serving alcohol was preferable in one important respect: the guys spent more money. It also meant that a club didn't need to make as much money off dancers' rent since they could make far more selling drinks. The no-contact rules in many of these clubs were vigorously enforced because they didn't dare risk losing their liquor licenses. By contrast, in Seattle the clubs themselves were almost never penalized.

Lara, the dancer from Rick's, had an idea for stopping lap dances. Instead of ticketing dancers, she thought the police should charge the men who bought them. But that, she believed, would never happen.

I would have left Rick's then and there, in the middle of my first shift, but a peculiar thing happened. There was a genus of strip-club customer whom I thought of as the rescue man, and one of his ilk turned up. They go to strip clubs and peep shows with the intent to save dancers from themselves so that they can feel like heroes. I had seen a few at the Lusty Lady. One was very young, perhaps twenty, and he approached my window on the hallway while I was waiting for booth customers. He tried to say something to me, and I gestured for him to step into the customer booth. He refused and continued to look plaintively at me, gesticulating and speaking. I urged him into the booth again, he refused, and so I cupped my ear and mouthed, "I can't hear you."

He raised his voice and his words came through. "Why are you doing this?" he asked. I gestured for him to enter the booth again. It seemed obvious: he wanted to talk to me; my job was to talk to people. I would have tried to answer him if he had stepped into the booth and slipped in a five or ten, instead of standing in the hallway and scaring away other customers. But he refused.

"Why are you doing this?" he asked, louder this time. When I pointed at the booth again, he looked exasperated.

"No, why are you doing this? You don't have to."

I laughed. "Of course I don't have to," I yelled across the glass.

He threw up his hands, paced around in a little circle, looked at me again, and disappeared down the hallway. A few minutes later he was back, staring at me with pleading eyes. "I just want to know why you're doing this," he said.

I pointed to the customer booth. He stood there, and at that moment an older man peeked politely at me from over the boy's shoulder. I motioned for the man to step into the booth, which he did, and shut the curtain on the boy, whom I never saw again.

Rescue men seemed to think that they stood a better chance with a stripper, by posing as her savior, than they would if they tried to pick up a cashier or waitress at her work, when, in fact, the opposite was probably true. They didn't understand that it was presumptuous and offensive to advise strangers on what to do with their lives. One customer at the Lusty Lady told me that he was a Christian, that in the Christian scheme of things what I did was wrong, and that I should quit. He came to the stage several times to watch us. Of all the customers I tried to fathom, rescue men were the ones I sympathized with the least.

The boy in the hallway at the Lusty Lady belonged to a rescue man subgenus, the penniless naif, but many rescue men were quite willing to spend money on strippers. When the FBI agent Robert Hanssen was arrested in 2001 on charges of spying, a side story ran in newspapers that over a period of years he had lavished hundreds of thousands of dollars' worth of gifts and cash on a particular stripper, and that he had asked for nothing in return. She theorized to a reporter that perhaps he was grooming her to be a spy, but I thought the truth was simpler. He just wanted to inject some hero worship into his life. He was a rescue man. In his eyes a stripper was a fallen woman, but not so fallen that she couldn't be saved.

At Rick's I approached a man at a bench near the main seating area—the back bench already seemed impossible to me—and offered him a dance for twenty dollars. He gave me a fifty and told me to do a couple. I gingerly began, hovering a few inches above him, and he made no move to grab me or pull me down. After the first dance I sat down beside him and started talking, and he told me not to do another. He was from Pennsylvania, had moved to Seattle a year previously, and hadn't yet gotten to know many people. He asked me a few questions about myself that I deflected, trying to turn the attention back to him. His name was Ken, and he had been married once but was divorced, with no children. He looked about forty. He seemed kind and intelligent.

As we spoke, he asked me if I wanted an orange juice. They were ten dollars; he gave me a fifty and wouldn't let me give him forty back. When I tried to tip the waitress out of what he had given me, he instead tipped her himself. Then he periodically handed me fifty and one-hundred-dollar bills for sitting with him. "Well, I'm taking up your time," he said.

When I asked him what he did, he rolled his head around like a bashful schoolboy. A few minutes later he alluded to the secrecy of his job. He said it was one of the reasons he had split with his wife. He was obviously inviting me to drag it out of him, so I complied. He told me he was an FBI investigator and, without saying so directly, hinted that he was working on a well-known case in the Northwest.

So this is your shtick, I thought. I barely believed him, but his credibility was hardly the point. I understood what he needed. I widened my eyes and injected some excitement into my voice. Had he uncovered anything? Was his job very dangerous? I had to go do my stage dances, but I came back afterward, and he was still eager to have me sit beside him.

I liked Ken. If any of what he said was true, he was interesting—certainly interesting enough that he shouldn't have to pay people to listen to him. He wasn't bad-looking either. He asked me out to dinner, and I said no, telling him that it wouldn't be appropriate and that

I didn't know him well enough. Over the course of our conversation, it came out that he had once dated a stripper—she was in medical school now—whom he had met in the course of an investigation. Aha, I thought. A repeat offender. But despite my skepticism about his motives, I found him genuinely pleasant.

When he left, he said he would be back at the same time the next day. I left right after he did. At Rick's dancers could leave any time they chose so long as they paid their rent. (Though if they stayed more than six hours they had to pay extra rent.) I didn't owe anything since I was within my first three days. The bright fall sun dazzled me as I walked to my car. When I counted my money, I found I had made $615 in three hours, $575 of it from Ken. Even as I looked at it, I couldn't quite understand how it had gotten there. I felt as though I had found it on the sidewalk.

Ken was back the next day, and we talked for about two hours. He spoke wistfully about wishing he had met me in a bar or restaurant. He even mentioned the name of his favorite restaurant, several times, either to hint that that's where he would take me if I said yes, or in the hope that if I knew he went there, he might run into me sometime. But he didn't push it. He seemed to understand that it wouldn't happen and even savor the impossibility of it. When he left, he said he wouldn't be back, and I agreed that that was probably wise.

On the second day he paid me $534, my entire income for that day. So he had given me $1,109 over about four hours while I talked, clothed, about an assortment of things that did not include sex. I could barely make sense of it. I put the money in an envelope on my desk, not wanting to spend a penny. I knew it wouldn't happen again, and it seemed that a windfall should be stretched as far as possible. A few days later, I carefully removed $30 for groceries, and that was how I drew it down: groceries, gas, rent.

I went back a third day, to see if Rick's was as I remembered it before Ken, and it was. I sat on one of the benches, staring into the dark with a row of other underemployed lap dancers. I listened to two girls standing behind me talking about a customer.

"Charisse said that guy's a cop."

"No way."

"She said she'd seen him before."

"He better not be a cop. He just came all over my hand."

I left having made nothing, and the next day I quit.

Satire

Physical eroticism has in any case a heavy, sinister quality. It holds on to the separateness of the individual in a rather selfish and cynical fashion.

—Georges Bataille, *Eroticism*

Chapter 23

Though we both worked, at different times, at the Lusty Lady and at Rick's, I didn't meet Lara in either place. We were introduced to each other by her friend Megan, a dancer at Déjà Vu, whom I in turn met through a former bouncer at the club. Megan had been dancing for about eight years, had nearly finished a bachelor's degree in women's studies, and wanted to design clothes. She wanted me to meet Lara because she thought I would find her different from the other dancers I knew.

Lara was the sinuous, gravity-defying pole dancer who had inspired Stephanie to take up stripping with her performance at the Fallen Women Follies. She had started dancing in 1989 when she was twenty-two, when she was a business major at the University of Washington, paying out-of-state tuition and working two jobs. By day she was a secretary in a law firm and at night she telemarketed, but she was still broke most of the time. She ate peanut butter and jelly sandwiches for supper and skipped off buses without paying the thirty-five-cent fare.

Much to her surprise, a woman she had known for an entire year told her that she was a stripper. The things people can hide, Lara thought. The woman told Lara that she should try it, too. Then she could stop living hand to mouth and maybe even have time to study.

Lara was a dancer by both training and disposition, a girl who had taken tap, jazz, modern, and ballet from the age of four and who had been a cheerleader in high school. She was also reckless in a number of ways, particularly when it came to sex and drugs. She was a lesbian, so she figured stripping wouldn't interfere with her love life. And she needed to pay tuition. She went to work. She was blond and flat-chested, a little slip of a thing. When she first started, she performed barefoot.

She wanted to quit that very year. Still twenty-two, she was onstage one night and suddenly felt clear, as though she had just woken up. She ran offstage crying and swore she would never come back. But it turned out to be just the first of many resolutions to quit.

The money was the lure. She could work just a few nights a week and make three thousand dollars a month. She could justify stripping every which way. It let her travel, go to school, and pay for her growing interest in photography—all without having to have a nine-to-five job. When she worked straight jobs, she found that she was calculating all the time, thinking "It just took me eight hours to make eighty-four dollars, and I could have made that in twenty or even ten minutes."

Lara left the university but later returned as a photography major. She was passionate about taking pictures in a way she realized she would never be about business. She earned her bachelor's degree in fine arts. She spent money on film and equipment and tried to get work as a photographer's assistant, but she always resorted to stripping when she needed cash, which seemed to be all the time. She had rent to pay, and student loans. She acquired more debt by way of her credit cards and a thirty-thousand-dollar car. Dancing became like a festering sore that only material things could soothe. A big-ticket item somehow proved that it was worth it. But while stripping enabled her to buy things, the more she bought the more she had to strip.

When Lara started getting hired as a photographer's assistant, shooting her own work, and exhibiting in gallery shows, she came to regard stripping as a strange sort of crutch. She would not have been able to get as far in photography as she had without the money. And yet she had the creeping, unexplainable feeling that she would have been further along as a photographer if she had stopped falling back on her less-reputable career.

At one point she felt as if it was truly going to make her crack, so she quit and got a job in the film industry. Her income was immediately cut by two-thirds, and she couldn't pay her bills. Lara soon declared bankruptcy, which erased most of her debt, but that meant she could no longer get any credit. She managed to stay away from stripping for two years before going back. Before, she had to dance on Valium, but when she returned she tried not to. She wanted to be present and connected. At most she had a drink or two before a shift. But it was so much more difficult to work sober.

Over time her appearance morphed. As a teenager kids had made fun of her stick figure, and their ridicule still stung. So when, in her first year as a stripper, she made enough to pay the $3,300 price tag, she went out and had her tits done. The silicone boosted her cup size from an A to a C. She later missed her little breasts and thought maybe she had enlarged them for the wrong reasons, but at least she had good fakes. They were proportionate to her body and hung well, and people could rarely even tell. Not like the helium balloons everyone started getting later. Lara dyed her hair black, got black tattoos, and started wearing stacked, menacing boots. Her blue eyes remained clear and piercing. When she danced, she was serpentine.

Lara fled often. Some might say she just moved, but she saw it as fleeing. She stripped in Washington, Oregon, California, Arizona, New Mexico, Nevada, Texas, Florida, New York, Alaska, and Guam, as well as Taiwan, Japan, and Iceland. She liked to travel, but also she was always trying to get away from where she was and find somewhere better. When she went abroad, she told her parents, who almost never left their home state of Florida, that she was teaching English.

Within the United States, Oregon had been the best place to strip, and Washington, her home base, the worst; overall, Taiwan was the best, and one horrific week in Iceland the most awful. All the girls in Tokyo had been saying that Iceland was really good, so she and her friend Chris sent their photos to a club manager and got themselves hired. Lara asked the manager in e-mails what the structure of the club was—were dances out in the open or in little rooms? He said he didn't run a whorehouse; they were out in the open. But he had lied. They did dances in small rooms with curtains across the door, fully nude, to music so loud that no one could hear you scream. When Lara left for Iceland she had been planning to

stay for months, but in the middle of her first week she had a dance
so bad that she knew she had to get out. He was huge, and when he
grabbed her, she screamed but no one came. She went straight for
his throat and squeezed it and said she would fucking kill him that
very second if he didn't sit down and get his hands off of her.
Somehow it worked, but there were others that were even worse.
She and Chris didn't have enough money to leave Iceland, and the
club only doled out what it owed them at the end of the week. That
was the way it had worked in Guam, too—they kept you captive by
keeping your cash. So she and Chris started going into the rooms
together—one dancing while the other watched. They split the
money, but it didn't matter because there wasn't a lot of money
going around anyway. At the end of the week, as soon as they were
paid, Lara and Chris got out of the country.

Taiwan, on the other hand, had been wonderful. The first time
she went was with Jessica, which wasn't the only reason she enjoyed
it, though it had certainly helped. They had met and fallen in love
in Seattle, and both changed their last name to Venezia. Fed up
with the city, the Venezias first fled to Texas. They were working in
a high-class Dallas club, not making any money, when an agent
and another dancer came up to Lara and said she should work in
Taiwan. They didn't know where Taiwan was, but they knew they
wanted to get away from where they were, so they said okay.

They and about a hundred other people were the only foreign-
ers in Taichung. Lara learned Mandarin. She immediately connected to the culture, the crowds, and even the pollution. She
loved that it was different than anywhere she had ever been. And
the club was about as good as a club can be. They had to dance
onstage. They didn't take their underwear off. After dancing they
walked around the room and collected tips, but there were no
table dances or lap dances. The customers bought them drinks.
Each night Lara danced three times and made five or six hundred
dollars. The men were polite and seemed to show respect. Maybe
they just saw her as a cute, white commodity, but she didn't care.
It felt like respect.

Lara went back to Taiwan on and off for five years. She entered the country each time as a tourist, worked illegally, and could stay only until her visa expired. All the strippers in the club were foreign. Taiwanese girls promoted the place, going out and bringing in customers, but they never danced. The club also had a group of very young Koreans whom they pimped out. Lara never talked to the Korean girls, who were a tightly closed bunch, but she had a feeling they were not the decision makers in whatever course of events had made them hookers in Taiwan. For the dancers, however, the club was wonderful. The audience was appreciative, she made money, and no one touched her.

But it got harder over time to work with Jessica. Working with a lover, Lara eventually decided, was about the worst idea in the world. It was bad enough working with a friend. Lara and Megan, the woman who had introduced us, had met outside of work. When Lara started working at Déjà Vu, she saw Megan give a lap dance for the first time. She watched her grind him crotch to crotch for several seconds, then looked away and tried never to watch her again. It had caused a storm of unpleasant feelings. She had thought to herself, How can Megan do that?, knowing she was being ridiculous, since she did it, too. But Lara used denial to help herself move through shifts like an efficient machine. Watching someone whom she knew as a friend was like looking in a mirror and being forced to acknowledge what she did.

But if it was difficult for Lara to work with a friend, it was a thousand times worse with Jessica. Jessica was a competitor—Lara couldn't help comparing their bodies or the money they made. Jessica was a mirror in the same way that Megan was, and watching her dance was a reminder that she did the same thing. But worst of all, Lara was in love with Jessica. She wanted Jessica to herself. Instead she had to watch her touch strangers night after night. It didn't matter that they both knew it was all fake. When Lara saw Jessica with a guy, trying to look sexy with her lips apart and her eyes closed, grabbing his hard-on through the fabric of his pants, she burned.

The jealousy started to flow both ways. One time Lara found herself physically pulling Jessica off a customer. Jessica had been on her knees in a red dress, grinding his dick with her breasts, and Lara flipped. Afterward she burned the dress so that she wouldn't be reminded. When Jessica made six hundred dollars in an hour, Lara demanded to know what she had done for it, and Jessica did the same back to her. Japan had been especially difficult for them. When Jessica walked around to ask for money, she would sit on the customers' laps and look submissive while they grabbed her breasts. It was awful to watch her beg. But then Lara would go around and do the same thing herself.

Other than watching Jesse extract money from men, Japan had been okay. Not as good as Taiwan, but okay. The men were less confused than American men in their attitude toward strippers. Japanese men had never messed with her when she asked if they wanted dances. They never said, "Is it going to be good?" or "But I don't know you," or "What, is it all about the money?" or any of the other stupid things they said in Seattle clubs. Of course it was all about the money. She didn't go to work for her own pleasure. In Japan they didn't seem to want to torment the women. They didn't try to force her into charming them, like some kind of caged monkey, before they bought a dance. They never tried to negotiate down the price. They bought their dances, paid, and usually said, "Keep the change," as if it would be beneath them even to touch it. The men *got* it. They understood the buyer-seller relationship. She hadn't been happy in Japan. But the customers were all right.

Many times Lara and Jessica had a variation on the following discussion:

"Jesse, you should quit."

"If I quit, then you have to quit."

"I can't. I have twenty thousand in student loans, plus car payments and insurance. You have nothing to pay but rent. Quit."

"How can you ask me to quit when you won't?"

And around and around it went. Like two junkies, they watched their relationship sink.

Lara and Jessica turned up at the Lusty Lady in the late autumn of 1998. Lara was principally a club girl, a lap dancer; she had never worked in a peep show. But she was trying to get away from being manhandled, and though the Lusty couldn't match the money from a good club night, at least it was predictable, and sometimes it was better than a bad club night. You would never have such a bad night at the Lusty that you would leave owing rent. Lara took the stage name Satire. Soon it would be a decade since she had started stripping, and "Satire" reflected how she felt—like part of a bitter joke. She wanted Jesse to use the name Irony, but she wouldn't; Jesse went by Nikki instead. They worked late shifts, arranging their schedules so that they nearly always worked at the same time. Whoever finished first waited for the other, and they walked home together, up First Avenue to Belltown, at two or three in the morning.

Some dancers would rather see than touch. Others, like Megan, would rather touch than see. Lap dancing, Megan liked to say, was like riding a bicycle. Lara quickly found out that she sided with Megan. Watching men jack off made her want to vomit, and she filled the Lusty Lady's toilet bowl with puke more than once. She couldn't and wouldn't smile, even though the show directors kept telling her to. But if she was disgusted by the men, some of the women were worse. She would see Georgia on her hands and knees, ass to the window, with a big smile on her face, and wonder how the hell she could grin like that. Either Georgia loved it, or Georgia was completely checked out. Maybe someone else was in her body at that moment. Who knew?

At the Lusty Lady Lara was a black hole of negativity in a galaxy of peppy feminists. She bickered with Jessica. She wore black onstage regardless of what others were wearing, flouting the rules. She scowled at the customers, if she could bring herself to look at them at all. Suffocated by the smell of glass cleaner, baby wipes, and bodies, Lara constantly felt as if the stage were closing in on her. The mirrors made it impossible to get away from herself, and she would pace like a caged animal, thinking, Small room, can't get out, no escape, until other dancers would have to try to soothe her.

One time at the Lusty a man started following Jesse from window to window. Jesse asked him to leave her alone, but every time she moved he popped up again in a demented game of cat and mouse. An irate Lara finally went up to his window and told him that if he didn't stop she was going to come through that door behind him and stop him herself. When Lara, with her raven hair and stabbing eyes, funneled all her anger in one direction, the result could be threatening, even across glass, even from naked person to clothed person. The man left and never came back.

Lara would not consider doing double troubles with her girlfriend. Just the suggestion made her sputter. She felt it would be like turning her relationship into a commercial product. She didn't ever want to have a moment with her partner, in bed, and have it occur to her that people had given them money to watch what they were doing. Her relationship with Jesse was a part of who she was, and she didn't want to sell who she was. She wanted to keep it entirely separate from work.

Lara and Jessica didn't last more than two months at the Lusty Lady. They left, not taking a leave but actually quitting, and therefore burning their bridges. The Lusty wasn't like clubs in Seattle, where you could quit one day and come back the next, show up late or not at all, owe weeks of back rent, argue with the managers, take drugs, jerk men off, assault people, whatever, and still not get fired. No, Lara couldn't go back to the Lusty. Despite the smells and the cummy windows, it was a decision she sometimes regretted.

Lara and Jessica went back to working in clubs, which Lara considered almost an entirely different industry. She summed up the difference thus: "Strippers think that peep-show dancers are whores and peep-show dancers think strippers are whores, and we all think whores are whores. But then whores would say, 'Well, at least I only fuck two guys a night and you're practically fucking fifty.'"

Lara and Jessica broke up after three years together. Jessica lent Lara thousands of dollars to help her get out of her other debts, and Lara wanted dearly to do right by her and pay her back. Jessica left the business for good and returned to school. Lara went to work at Rick's, known among Seattle strippers as the low-downest, dirtiest club in town. At thirty-three, eleven years after she started, she still fantasized about the day she would get out.

Chapter 24

Lara's apartment was monastic: wood floors, stark white walls with dark wood trim, leaded-glass windows, crosses on the walls. On a cold December afternoon, the radiator hissed while she showed me her portfolio. All the photos were in black-and-white. She explained how she blurred the images with rice paper as she developed them to create a dark, dreamy effect. A few showed old stone buildings that were now crumbling and overgrown. Most, though, were of naked women trapped in moments of violent movement. Their bodies were contorted into twisting, arching coils; sometimes they posed with crosses or chains so that they looked like creatures from a medieval vision of hell.

Lara worked to stop working. But she had stopped saying when she was going to leave. Whenever she made the promise to herself that she would quit after a specific amount of time, or dollar figure, she failed. She finally told herself that when it happened it would be cold turkey. She would decide, then leave, just like that.

When Megan arrived at Lara's place that afternoon, she said, "Tell Elisabeth about our plan for the night that we retire." Lara was reluctant at first. She wanted it to be a surprise, and they had already told several people. Megan joked that no one would remember because it would be years until they quit. "Don't say that," Lara said, "please don't say that." But after some discussion, together they went ahead and told me the plan. They wanted to do something insulting, memorable, and outrageous enough to ensure that no Seattle club would let them work again, so that they couldn't go back even if they wanted to.

Lara had an enormous black strap-on dildo that she called Leroy. It had a special feature, which was that its balls could be filled with liquid, which could then, by squeezing, be shot out of the shaft. On their last night Lara planned to fill it with yogurt. Stealthily, so as not to draw attention, she would dress up as a priest and Megan as a nun. When one of them had her stage turn, they would both go up before the audience. Megan would give Lara a blow job, Lara would shoot her yogurt as far and wide as possible, and then they would grab their things and leave.

I stared at them. I wasn't sure what I had expected after the buildup of their discussion, but I felt vaguely disappointed. I was surprised at both the childishness of the prank and the violent anger behind it.

Lara couldn't quit, she felt, until she got out of debt. She wouldn't leave until she had paid back Jessica. But she couldn't seem to scrape together the money. With Megan's encouragement, she started working at the Déjà Vu on Denny Way, and she went back and forth between it and Rick's. She disliked them both but in different ways. Rick's was darker and seedier, but Déjà Vu, which had a fluorescent pattern of women's legs on the carpet, and more stages, more mirrors, and more pop music, was worse in some ways. It was too social. Guys wandered around and tried to talk to the dancers as though it were a party. This repulsed Lara. She wanted them to sit down, shut up, get their dance, and pay her. To her, the men were marks. No pretense of amiability was required. She could barely tolerate a shift at Déjà Vu without at least a drink beforehand. Rick's was dark; she thought of Déjà Vu as neon dark. She and Megan resolved to go to work sober one night, but they quickly concluded that it had been a mistake. The time crawled.

Female customers had started coming into Déjà Vu with their boyfriends. Strip clubs, it seemed, were trendy. Lara didn't know why. There must be a video out, she figured, or a television show with strippers in it. Sometimes the women condescended to the dancers, which Lara didn't get. She tolerated, even expected, condescension from the men, but not from the women. Lara could think of few things she wanted to do less than a private dance for a woman. She tried now and then but couldn't. She couldn't objectify women.

The perfect stripper, Lara thought, had to be a lesbian. At least then the work wasn't personal. She couldn't understand how straight women did this job when they had to go home and deal with men intimately. Some 80 percent of her customers wore wedding bands. How could a dancer trust her own husband after seeing that? "I don't understand," she told me, as though I could somehow explain it.

I tried to think of dancers I knew in solid relationships with men. Certainly, they existed—or did they? I had seen glimpses. I had heard strippers speak highly of their male partners, and I had been to homes where they lived in apparent peace with their husbands or boyfriends. But the relationships I had gotten close to had crumbled before my eyes. When I returned to Seattle, I didn't date or sleep with anyone; I was in a long-distance affair with the man I had met in London— the one I had fallen for who had challenged me on stripping. I reflected that in three of my earlier relationships—Alex, Erik, and Paul—I had found myself at some point corresponding across thousands of miles. I thought I was weary of long-distance romance, and yet here I was again. I missed him terribly, and yet on some level I must have been comfortable experiencing closeness at a great remove. In any case, the solitary celibacy of a long-distance relationship suited a return to stripping. There was no one around to make jealous, to compare to my customers, or to question me every day on what I was doing.

I looked to the other dancers I knew for some example of happy, monogamous heterosexuality. Kim was considering divorce. Zoe and Matt were tenuous at best. Megan lived in a studio apartment with her ex-boyfriend, with whom she said she was "just friends," and they shared a bed but didn't have sex. Many dancers told me that their boyfriends didn't mind their work in the slightest. They told me, "I don't date the jealous type," or that both they and their partners knew that it was "just a job." But I remembered that I had reflexively said similar things when I lived with Erik. It was more dismissal than explanation: "Of course he doesn't mind; he isn't allowed to." A boyfriend, I had thought back then, shouldn't dare to challenge my independence. Stripping, like promiscuity, was independence. It was the refusal to allow oneself to be the sexual property of one man. With

Erik I had been willing to accept that promiscuity was unacceptable, but I could still strip and say that it was "just a job."

Abby, as far as I could tell, had the best romantic relationship with a man of any stripper I knew. But while she would openly talk about her work with me, she was private about Peter. She said this was because he didn't want his future as a lawyer compromised. So I knew only the broad outlines of their relationship. They had met in high school. She had followed him to Bellingham, where he went to college. By the time she was twenty-three they had been together for four years, and they still appeared to be going strong. She regarded him as her best friend. She never lied to him and, in fact, had difficulty even surprising him because she was no good at keeping secrets. She said that she knew what his boundaries were for her with clients, and that she never violated them—she was completely faithful to him within their definition of the term.

But I knew relatively little about Abby and Peter, and much more about Zoe, Kim, and their partners. And I knew that Erik, long after we broke up, told me frankly that stripping had "made him crazy." I knew, too, that after leaving the Lusty Lady I had chosen, almost deliberately, a man I could keep at a distance, and that I had treated him badly. So when Lara asked me how straight strippers dealt with boyfriends, all I could do was shrug.

Lara said that sometimes when she saw a new girl on the floor, she would tell her "Run. Go. Get out of here." They never listened. When you were twenty years old and making eighty thousand a year and driving an SUV, Lara figured, nothing else mattered. If you were twenty years old and thought that having a thirty-thousand-dollar car was some kind of great achievement, you were already in trouble. Something had already gone wrong. Consumption, status, society—the whole picture looked out of focus to Lara.

It was getting harder to make money at both Rick's and Déjà Vu. Rents had gone up steadily in the last ten years. She could barely believe it now, but when she started, the standard house fee in Seattle had been thirty-five dollars. Now, depending on the club, it was usually three times that. Strippers' incomes had not kept pace. The clubs charged the dancers more and more but failed to bring in more or higher-spending customers so that the girls could make more money. When Lara started, there had been such a thing as a table dance—where you just danced for a customer at his table, in the middle of the floor. Table dances were obsolete now. It was all lap dancing on the couches. Lara remembered a time when, if a guy looked as if he was going to touch her foot, she would say, "Don't even *think* about touching my foot." Now she was grateful if *all* they touched was her foot. At least then she knew where the hand was. There had been a time when she never grabbed crotches; now she did. In retrospect, Lara felt that her boundaries had never been very solid. But a decade into dancing, she was now trying to establish some. She rarely took her bottoms off onstage anymore. It felt defiant to keep them on, as if she was reserving, or regaining, something of herself.

Rick's didn't limit the number of girls they would put on the floor. And why would they? They got a hundred dollars in rent from each girl whether she made money or not. In the afternoons they often had thirty girls working and fewer than a dozen customers. And almost every man was a regular; there was little new blood. That meant they all knew exactly what Satire would and wouldn't do, and how much she charged. She had decided that if she was going to jerk men off—outside the pants—she would only do it for thirty or forty dollars. But she couldn't even get that anymore. At Rick's some girls were doing outside the pants for twenty, and other girls were doing inside the pants, saying they were charging thirty or forty, but Lara didn't believe them. It was a circle jerk, and there was no way to break in.

She couldn't make ends meet at Déjà Vu either. Their base rent was lower, seventy dollars or less, depending on the day and time. But the club charged the women for each dance they did, which added up. One night Lara ended up paying the club $165 and leaving with only eighty. It seemed as if she was having three bad nights for every good one. She was averaging about four hundred dollars a week.

She knew that her own lack of motivation was part of the problem. Often she just couldn't drag herself in to work. It was too depressing. Or she arrived, worked for a few hours, felt aggravated, and left early.

But even when she only worked two or three shifts a week, she found it hard to get anything else accomplished. Dancing paralyzed her. She stopped working on her portfolio. She never got around to advertising herself as a photographer's assistant. The day after a shift she always felt dazed. And if she was working in the evening, the day leading up to it was shot. She spent the whole time anticipating. Then she got angry with herself for not getting anything done.

She needed a plan to make a lot of money in a short period of time. One final burst, and then she would get out. The trouble with Seattle was that she didn't have the self-discipline to go in six nights a week. She needed a structure, someone making her work. She considered going back to Japan. She got some photos together and called an agent who rounded up American girls. Between the money she owed Jessica, and the amount she wanted to put toward her student loans, she needed twenty thousand dollars. That was her goal. She would work until she could pay back twenty grand, then quit. She didn't care if that left her with zero.

The Japanese, though, were slow to book her, so she started casting around for another plan. She had worked in Las Vegas before and had hated it, but a dancer at Rick's told her about a new club called Spearmint Rhino that was supposed to be good. So she went there for a week in January 2001, to see what she was getting herself into. It went well, and by the end of April she had been there three more times and was planning to go again. It turned out she could fly down, stay in a hotel, pay the house fee, and still make more than she would per week in Seattle. She stayed for two to four weeks each time, working five or six nights a week. On her very worst nights she made three hundred dollars, but on quite a few she made over a thousand. On her best night she made seventeen hundred dollars. Because she was working all the time, she hardly spent anything. It did burn her out, and she got sick of having the same conversation over and over with different men. But suddenly she was no longer eight months behind in paying off three different loans. And, more important, she paid Jessica back four-fifths of what she owed her. She would work the summer in Seattle—summers were best in Seattle, and Las Vegas was dead—go back to Vegas for the fall, and maybe, just maybe, be out by Christmas.

Even when she didn't shoot for months on end, Lara carried around in her head ideas for photography projects. One in particular kept coming back to her. "I want to build a box and illuminate the inside red," she said. "And it's furry. It's a tiny tiny tiny tiny box with a window, and a girl is crushed in it. It's lifted up off the floor and everything else is in darkness. So it's this little box stuck in the middle of nowhere, aloneness, like how they always describe hell—separation from God and everything else. That's how I'd want to do it. There would be screaming, everyone screaming, just always screaming, with anguish on their face. Losing their mind. Coming undone. I think of dancing as coming undone. The slow unraveling of yourself."

Megan had been right that I would find Lara different from other strippers. I had never met anyone who articulated as clearly as Lara a feeling of being destroyed by her work. She spoke about it as someone might talk about a drug addiction. When she said she had forced herself to stop taking Valium before work, and later, to stop drinking, it struck me that without them she suffered from hyperawareness. She had compelled herself to be clear-eyed and sober, but this made her painfully conscious of her own compromises. She was acutely aware of every pledge she had made to herself and broken, whether it had been to get out of the business by a certain time, or pay off a debt, or refrain from giving customers hand jobs for an extra ten or twenty bucks. She could come across as intimidating, with her throaty voice, black-on-black attire, and piercing eyes, but at the same time she was painfully sensitive to every slight and indignity that her work entailed.

Though both had traveled the world on their gains from erotic dancing, Zoe and Lara were opposites. Whereas Zoe was convinced that she had made the sex industry work for her, Lara was sure that the equation was reversed. Lara felt exploited every time she went to work, and it made each shift an endurance test. She hated the men she lived off of. They might leave the clubs with empty wallets, but she still felt as if she had been robbed at the end of the night. Zoe's attitude toward customers, in contrast, seemed to be one of amused tolerance. One night when I went to a movie with both of them, I was struck by how little they had to say to each other. They remembered each other from the Lusty, and they were cordial. But their entire understanding of their working lives was different, and I thought that if they talked at length, each one might knock out vital parts of the other's worldview. Zoe's identity as a stripper was precipitated on the belief that she was winning a game, while Lara's on the belief that she was losing.

I couldn't understand why, if Lara thought stripping was so destructive and loathsome, she couldn't bring herself to leave. But I realized that I found her more believable than Zoe, whom I had known more closely and for much longer. Though Zoe would not have said so herself, I was starting to think she was trapped. It frustrated me. I knew the things she said she had wanted, and what she was capable of. I couldn't understand why she clung to Matt, despite his fits of anger and his insults. I thought her confidence had eroded in the three years I had been away. I noticed this one night when we were with friends of mine who were not sex workers, but men and women in their twenties and thirties of various professions. It suddenly hit me that if Zoe wasn't talking about stripping or sex, she was shy. I knew she had opinions, that she was thoughtful and well read. Zoe, in my mind, was bold—she would go anywhere by herself, and she wasn't afraid of what people thought—but she would not have given this impression to a stranger.

I looked at her, standing with a small, boisterous group, and I noticed the way her shoulders hunched forward. I watched her giggle softly and cock her head so that her hair hid her face. When she stood, she bent one leg inward and ground her toe into the floor, practically a caricature of reluctance. She became animated, once, when telling a stripping story, and her voice was as sugary as ever, but otherwise she barely spoke. Her entire posture was one of diffidence. I wondered how long she had had these mannerisms and why I had never noticed them. I thought about the fact that many of her "social" interactions were with customers. She was out of her element with new people when the context wasn't sex.

I knew now that I didn't believe her anymore. I couldn't make the connection explicitly, but I associated with stripping the loss in confidence that I saw in her. She could still convincingly list the benefits of her "ideal" job—free time, money, feeling sexy. But I was skeptical when she said that she was happy. Although Lara was an extreme case—I didn't think that everyone who told themselves the truth would be as unhappy as Lara was—I thought she was more honest with herself. I wanted Zoe to think more about the consequences of her job.

Delilah

. . . The "life model" was the erotic sensation of the 19th century and the precursor of the erotic dancing of the 20th century. . . . The static nude bore a likeness to a work of art and was therefore deemed legitimate as an object of contemplation. Nudes that moved were arousing and therefore pornographic.

—Lucinda Jarrett, *Stripping in Time: A History of Erotic Dancing*

Chapter 25

Abby had been voted the most liberal student in her high school. To her, "liberal" meant someone who always did what she wanted to, and that was how she tried to live.

When she graduated, she hoped that being a track athlete would get her a free ride to college so that she could go without the help of her parents. She was offered only partial scholarships, though, and her parents, who already had one daughter in an ROTC program, strongly encouraged her to go to West Point Military Academy in New York. It offered a free education in exchange for serving in the army afterward. To Abby, it seemed like a radical idea. She wanted to make a difference in the world, and she thought maybe she could become one of the first female generals. In June 1995, she finished high school, turned eighteen, and enrolled at West Point.

On her first day of basic training she knew she had made a mistake. But she didn't have a backup plan and didn't want to go home, so she tried to stick it out, rising at four-thirty every morning to a strictly ordered day. She thought the way the academy treated cadets was hypocritical. In her psychology class she had to memorize a definition of discipline that said better soldiers were made with respect than with fear, yet she underwent relentless verbal abuse from her upperclassmen. Four months into her training she was about to leave for her first long weekend at home. On Friday morning, her superior grilled her on the contents of the day's newspaper, which cadets had to memorize every day. Abby answered incorrectly and was commanded to have the entire paper copied by hand before she returned from vacation. It was the last straw for her, and she left the cold gray corridors that afternoon knowing that she wouldn't be back.

She moved to Bellingham, where Peter was, and enrolled at a local college. She became a stripper and started modeling for magazines and websites. She still wanted to make a difference in the world, and she decided that it was going to be in porn.

The first time I thought about being photographed sexually, I was seven or eight years old. It was part of a game I played with a girl who lived down the street, my memory of which has persisted but grown softer in focus over the years. I can only date it because it had to be after my family moved to that street and I became friends with Violet, but before she and I became too old and self-conscious to play. I remember it as being her idea. We were on Violet's high, enormous bed, shut in her bedroom. She explained that one of us had to remove all her clothing, while the other had to pretend to take pictures. I remember her saying that the girl being photographed could leave her socks on, but nothing else, and how, when it was her turn, she lay coquettishly on her side with her head propped on one hand. We played the game more than once, and I became annoyed because she always tried to make me be the photographer.

Perhaps it's not right to call what we were doing sexual, but we knew that our game was illicit and that it had to remain a secret. We knew that there was a difference between being naked in the bathtub, or in a changing room, and what we had in mind with our pretend photographs. We consciously wished to be pretty for the camera, and we had the idea that we were posing for a magazine. We knew, some-how, that there were magazines full of naked women, and we pretend-ed to be those grown-up women, much as some girls pretend to be the mothers of baby dolls. Where we had learned about those magazines, I don't know. I don't remember ever seeing one as a child, and so I imagine that Violet had found one somewhere and told me about it.

Some two decades later I was acquainted with many women who posed naked for pictures. Abby was the most enthusiastic of them. She sought out more ways than I had known existed to sell the viewing of her body. When she first moved out to Bellingham after leaving West Point she worked as a model for drawing and painting classes. Then she started doing bachelor parties and met Zoe, who introduced her to the Lusty Lady, and she began to work in Vancouver clubs in the winters. She started scanning the back of the *Seattle Weekly* and *The Stranger* newspapers for "models wanted" ads, and she posed nude for magazines as well as Seattle's proliferation of new websites. But she had an entrepreneurial mind that was always looking for ways to increase her cut from the fifty dollars an hour she was usually paid as a model. She saw that others in Seattle were making money in Internet pornography and decided that she could, too. Teaming up with photographers and Web designers, she hatched a series of business plans. One involved shooting collections of still images and selling them on CD-ROMs as content for websites. She took courses in accounting and business management, and as a class project launched nakedcascades.com, a site intended to sell her CD-ROMs. As co-owner with a photographer she also launched abbyinbabeland.com, a membership site with a monthly fee of $21.95, which was regularly supplied with new photos of Abby with various women.

She was an inspired manager and negotiator. She recruited the models, usually from the Lusty Lady, and paid them at the going rate of fifty dollars an hour or with some sort of trade. Often the model wanted prints of herself, but in one case a model, Victoria, agreed to pose in exchange for photography lessons. Zoe posed for Abby for free, doing the sort of graphic pictures Abby considered salable, but in exchange she insisted on doing a less-marketable shoot of the two of them in yoga poses. Even when Abby wasn't modeling herself, she organized and directed every shoot, coming up with most of the ideas for costumes and settings. She decided, for example, to shoot petite black Victoria as a bejeweled, bewigged, mostly naked Cleopatra, and a six-foot blond dancer as a half-dressed cancan girl, surrounded by black ostrich feathers. She decided when to do toy shoots, lesbian shoots, and male-female couple shoots, and once she did a speculum shoot with Zoe, recording their cervixes for posterity. Abby, as much as the photographer, directed the women from pose to pose, and most of her models said she was good at making them feel comfortable.

When Abby told me she wanted to revolutionize the porn industry I asked her what she meant. An instinctive public relations operator, she would only respond to questions like this in writing. She said that many porn purveyors tried to cheat and underpay their models, and that they didn't care whether the women felt beautiful or had any emotion behind their expressions. She wanted to do things differently, to get women involved in her projects so that they took a personal pride in it. Her photographer Lenny, she wrote, "has a tremendous respect for women. Taking pictures of women without portraying them in their most beautiful form is almost an insult to women, and a form of degradation in his eyes." I thought this had an unsettling implication: that appearance is central to every woman's self-worth.

Abby said she wanted to make art: "I want to produce photographs with a picture quality that could just as easily be called art. I think that sex is beautiful and porn is no different, and there is no reason that art and porn can't be combined."

I found it impossible to define the difference between pornography and art. It wasn't a simple question of what body parts were exposed, as plenty of images of nudity and sex were widely considered art. It seemed to be more a question of intent—if the creator's main intention was sexual arousal, I was probably looking at porn. But what about the times when intent and interpretation didn't coincide? If a piece wasn't intended to turn me on but did, was the creator responsible for potential pornography? Abby thought porn and art could be the same thing. I thought she was as qualified as any lawmaker or art critic to decide.

Abby agreed to let me watch a special photo shoot she had planned. In exchange she asked me to pose for one of her photographers, and I agreed, with some caveats: no toys, no pussy shots, no one else. She said okay, I could do "mild erotic" pictures. The difference between "mild erotic" and "porn" for her boiled down to salability, which in turn boiled down to the vagina. The vagina, preferably up close and spread, was the lowest common denominator of porn. It also happened to be exactly what I didn't want photographed. I would let the rest of me be visually recorded, but the idea of my labia in the viewfinder made me cringe. If I hadn't quite internalized the lesson that my pussy was private, I had at least absorbed that it was too private to put on film.

Abby had a long-standing plan to have herself photographed naked in a field of tulips, and in the spring of 2001 she was finally about to put it into effect. Every time she drove between Seattle and her home in Bellingham, she passed through the Skagit Valley, an area with world-renowned tulip farms. For a few brief weeks every spring the flowers burst into rainbow-colored bloom, blanketing whole fields in sunny yellow or velvety red. Before they were cut and shipped to market, thousands of tourists came to walk between the rows and gaze at the snow-capped Cascades.

She planned carefully. She looked for available photographers. On her way to and from Seattle, she exited the freeway and drove up and down country roads, trying to decide which field was best. She realized that she would have to shoot in the late afternoon because too many tourists and farmers milled around in the morning. The weather in western Washington was, as always, unreliable, so she had to be prepared when a sunny day struck.

Four photographers had tentatively agreed to shoot Abby in the tulips, but on the day when she decided to go for it, Mary was the only one available. Abby asked me to pick up Mary in front of Seattle Central Community College and drive her up to the fields. When I asked Abby to describe Mary so that I could find her, she said that she was a busty brunette. Mary turned out to be a soft-spoken twenty-one-year-old, wearing a black tank top, green corduroys cut off at the calf, and flip-flops. She wore a nose ring and sunglasses and carried a gray camera case. On the drive up, she told me that she had worked at the Lusty Lady, as Camille, for about a year, but that she was planning to quit in two months, as soon as she finished her degree in photography. Watching men masturbate, she said, was frying her mind.

Mary was the sixth or seventh stripper I had met who was either already a professional photographer or was studying to become one. I had been fascinated with cameras myself—I had taken photography classes in college and would still often shoot whole rolls of just one scene to make sure I captured what I wanted. I may have come across stripper-photographers simply because it was a competitive job that required expensive equipment, and was therefore likely to require a high-earning part-time job. But my own interest made me wonder if there was something else: both stripping and photography were about the relationship between seeing and being seen. Strippers and photographers create an image detached from the underlying person. With a wink and a smirk, they both hand over to the viewer something that might represent reality, or might not. Perhaps a person who was drawn to one was likely to be drawn to the other.

As well as being a photographer and a stripper, Mary had been one of Abby's early recruits into porn modeling and had posed with her often. A few weeks earlier, Mary told me in the car, Abby had called and said she wanted to do a Betty Crocker shoot. They would wear plaid aprons and smear chocolate frosting all over each other with wooden spoons. "I don't know where she comes up with this stuff," Mary said. She had gone ahead and done it. The Lusty and Web porn had paid for her degree.

We met Abby in a gas station parking lot at exit 230, then set off in her station wagon to look for tulips. Abby told Mary that the frosting photos had come out well. They talked about the photographer and agreed that he was good. "It wasn't that amateur shit that pisses me off," Abby said. Few things annoyed her as much as the fuzzy, poorly lit nude pictures, usually shot by men of their girlfriends or wives, that littered the Internet.

We passed fields of chopped green stalks, then a field of singed-looking daffodils. "Don't worry, I know there are some good ones. These aren't the ones I scouted," Abby said.

"Are those tulips?" Mary asked.

"Yeah, those are fucking tulips," Abby said, getting excited. "The predominant color is yellow. This may be a good place to park and shoot as many pictures as we can until someone comes and arrests us." She turned the car right, toward the sinking sun.

"When I went out there this morning there were migrant workers all over the place. This is tulip town. Look at that shit." She turned again. Fields of red, white, and yellow spread out in front of us. But many of the fields were dotted with "No Trespassing" and "No Parking" signs along the edges. We arrived at a field that looked spectacular, only to find that it was charging admission. We continued past the cluster of people waiting to buy tickets. I was surprised that people would pay to look at a farmer's field, and at the owner who had thought to charge.

"Peter told me to pee on a tulip for him. Isn't that sweet? Dirty little pervert," Abby said.

"Great," Mary said without enthusiasm. "We can put it on a golden showers website." We were still driving around, and Mary was staring out the window. "Oh! I want the red!" she burst out.

"Yeah, the red ones are good, and definitely more sexual," Abby said.

We pulled into a dirt parking space where fields of red stretched away in front of us like a brilliant carpet, fringed by a stripe of yellow in the distance. Tourists milled around the parking area, but there was no entry fee. Sitting in the driver's seat, Abby changed into a sundress that was long, loose, and easy to get on and off, in case we got chased out of a field midshoot. Two migrant workers tried to watch her change from their beat-up car. Mary and I got out of the station wagon and waited while Abby dug through a box of clothes and accessories. The two men from the beat-up car got out and hovered.

"I brought my Daisy Dukes, and I brought my chaps," Abby said.

"I'm not feeling the chaps today," Mary said, gazing out across the tulips. She had a slow, pensive way of speaking. Abby brushed her hair and put on a brown suede cowboy hat. Mary, worried about the fading light, hurried her. Mount Baker's peak gleamed in the east, and the two women briefly discussed going snowboarding on the following Saturday. The two men finally found an excuse to speak to us, and they asked Mary to take their photo, with their camera, in front of the tulips.

We set off into the field, walking down a long dirt track that ran between two oceans of red, putting as much distance as possible between ourselves and the other visitors. Abby took long, determined strides and her sheer green dress caught the breeze, outlining her body. Mary snapped pictures to test the light. Signs said not to walk between the rows, but we disobeyed and plunged between two yellow stripes. The two workers had started out following us but had given up and turned the other way. We walked until we were far from the entrance and there was no one else around.

Mary, who wanted some photos with the hat and dress on, started shooting, directing Abby to stand, turn, crouch, and toss her hair. Abby straddled a row of tulips, lifted the edge of her dress above her knee, and pushed her hip out suggestively.

"Look more natural," Mary said. She would repeat these words several times in the next hour, because Abby tended to put on her porn-star glamour girl expression for the camera—parted lips, lowered eyelids.

After a half roll Abby took off her dress and handed it to me, and they continued. Though tall and muscular, when she crouched between the rows she looked small and white, like an overgrown lily. Mary was thrilled when a perfect, tulip-shaped shadow fell across Abby's belly, and she had her hold that position while she shot off several frames.

Abby wasn't very interested in doing clothed shots and had posed stoically for them, and she was patient while Mary tried to capture the shadows on her skin. She urged, though, that they get to the pussy shots. She also mentioned again that she wished to be photographed peeing on a tulip. "I don't need to be a part of that," Mary said. But Abby insisted, and they set it up, Abby straddling a row and bending over. "I want my pussy to face the light. Which way is the light?"

Abby peed and Mary shot grudgingly. Then Abby wanted several shots of her spread lips over a tulip. "I've envisioned this for ages," she said. Mary bent and took two frames, then straightened and said, "Okay," refusing to continue.

They discussed what to do next. Abby suggested naked poses shot from a distance. "Gesture poses," she called them. She said it was a term used in art modeling.

"I guess I'm not into the whole porn-tulip thing," Mary said slowly but firmly, as though she had been thinking about it and now reached a conclusion.

"When I say gesture poses, I don't mean porn," Abby said. "There were just a few porn shots I had in mind. I wanted to do them and now I've done them." The two women stood in the field, each considering her own vision and wondering what she could convince the other to do. Mary started making suggestions, and they did shots of Abby walking, of her face just over the tulips, and of her calves and feet sticking straight up from between two rows as though they had grown there. Then Mary asked Abby to put her dress back on.

"I feel like my freedom of choice is being curtailed," Abby muttered while Mary loaded a roll of film.

Ready to shoot again, Mary reached out to tweak Abby's dress strap. "I want innocent farm girl," she said. The strap slid down and exposed Abby's nipple ring.

When they moved over to a rutted dirt road running alongside the field, their artistic ideas finally seemed to coincide. Mary was excited about the texture of the cracked earth and tire tracks, and Abby wanted pictures of herself in the mud. Abby grabbed clods of dirt and wet them with a spray bottle that she had brought along just for the purpose. She smeared stark brown streaks across her breasts and thighs and sat on the road in front of the tulips.

"Oh stay right there, that's really nice," Mary said, and started clicking her shutter. They shot happily for several minutes, and then Abby, who was sitting on one hip, shifted slightly and parted her legs.

"Will you do me a favor and take, like, a pussy shot? It'll sell."

Mary complied and shot one frame.

As the sun faded, Mary shot Abby crawling along the tire tracks and lying in the shape of a crucifix. The mud on her body dried and cracked.

"I like being naked in general, but being naked and getting dirty is even more fun," Abby told us. "I like being outside."

When they were done, Abby slipped her dress back on and we walked back to the car, Abby hugging herself now as the evening chill set in. On the ride back to my car, Mary proudly showed me the portfolio she had prepared for prospective employers. It was full of pictures of bright-colored shoes and sports equipment, none of which would have been out of place in a glossy catalog.

In the car back at the gas station they discussed who would get what. Abby wanted Mary to burn her a compact disk of the images, but Mary refused; she offered, instead, a contact sheet, which was less reproducible. They discussed photographers' rights, models' rights, film, and money. They didn't come to an agreement, but when she was getting out of the car, Mary said, "I had fun. We'll talk more."

"I had fun, too," Abby said.

Mary sighed deeply after we left Abby and got back on the interstate. The sun was going down.

"I do porn, but for me it's just a way to pay for school," she said. "Abby is devoted to it. She's my close friend but artistically we're coming from different places."

She said she wished she hadn't done the peeing shot or the pussy shots over the tulips. They disgusted her.

"I feel bad," she said, staring out the window. "I don't want to be responsible for putting that stuff out there in the world. Even if it doesn't have my name on it, I still put it out there," she said. "Abby doesn't want to leave anything to the imagination. I don't think you need to show everything. Suggestiveness is better."

"But don't you feel the same way about dancing?" I asked. The Lusty Lady left little to the imagination.

"The person who comes into a peep show has chosen to come in there," she said, "but with an image like that photograph, probably fifty percent of the people who see it won't have chosen to." And at the Lusty, she said, someone might see her pussy, but it was in the context of her whole body. It was just a flash as she moved around. "It's not a photograph. It's not still and it can't be taken away and spread to the world on the Internet."

I asked her: Didn't she worry about having her image all over the Web, where anyone could see it? What if it was used against her? These were my own anxieties, after having agreed to pose for Abby. A photo would be taken and then it would be out of my hands. I thought I had a uniquely female fear, this ever-present sense that my sexuality could be used against me. I didn't know what I was afraid of exactly. Blackmail, I supposed, if I someday had the stature or money to warrant it. Stripping was nothing but a moment in time, but photos were permanent. This vague alarm that photographic evidence would haunt us had permeated the Lusty Lady. It was never articulated, but there had been a general loathing of any man who tried to take a picture. In San Francisco, the dancers had fought bitterly to have the one-way windows removed, just so would-be photographers would have no place to hide. And I knew that Zoe and other bachelor-party girls discouraged photo and video taking. They felt that allowing photography was giving far more than the men had paid for. If they did allow it, they tried to make sure that the images were cut off at the neck. Even those of us who bared our bodies associated doing so with punishment, and we saw photos as the proof needed to hang us.

This, at least, was my feeling. Mary was relatively unfazed by naked pictures of herself. They bothered her far less than having shot the tulip photos of Abby. For one thing, she said, in most professions naked photographs weren't going to do you any harm, and they might even help. I wasn't so sure about this, and I thought our difference in opinion had to do with nine years in age. Second, Mary said, the Internet was vast; she didn't use her real name; and it seemed unlikely that anyone could ever find her out there. She was comfortably detached from pictures of herself rolling around in chocolate frosting, as though they were impersonal products that she had merely helped to produce. They had nothing to do with her, Mary, the person.

True to her word, Mary quit the Lusty Lady as soon as she graduated. When I heard through Abby that she had been hired as a commercial photographer, I felt a sense of relief. She had been launched in a career that was safely removed from porn. I had a growing feeling that this was the best way to handle stripping, to get in and get out, and I was cheered to know she had done so.

*   *   *

I arrived early at Lenny's studio, which was an enormous airy room built on top of a house. The edges of the room looked like the backstage of a theater, filled with props, portable backdrops, and lighting equipment. Neither he nor Abby had arrived, and while I waited I looked through a stack of hundreds of large black-and-white prints. They mostly showed nude or seminude women, and occasional male-female couples. In many of them he had draped the bodies with richly textured fabric or had used water and light to make the skin look luminous. I thought some were superb and some overly soft and dreamy. The women were not professional models—they had small breasts, or short, ordinary hairstyles, or plain faces, and they weren't all youthful. Most of them looked beautiful, perfectly set off by some exotic combination of lighting, costume, and backdrop.

Abby arrived, in her glasses, overalls, and sneakers, wearing a newsboy's cap backward over her long, sandy hair. As part of her greater business plan she had been taking classes in makeup artistry, and she sat down to paint my face. Between Lenny's supply and her own, Abby had an excess of makeup to use, and she started on me with products I wasn't well versed in. I hadn't known, for instance, that there was a difference between concealer and foundation, both of which are creamy, come in skin tones, and cover the face, but one of which is thicker than the other. She told me I needed both.

While Abby worked she complained about the difficulty of finding men to do couple pictures. Her boyfriend, Peter, would pose with her but wouldn't do penis shots because he wanted to be a lawyer someday. That put an end to my theory that a fear of naked photographs was uniquely female.

"I'm the only person who doesn't care about that stuff," she said.

"What, you don't want to run for president?" I asked.

"No, and if I did, I would tell everybody, like La Cicciolina," she said. She was referring to Illona Staller, the Italian porn star who became a member of parliament.

Lenny arrived, a slim, gravelly-voiced man in black jeans and shirt. Together he and Abby directed me through a series of poses in different clothing and with different props. In the most outlandish one I stood on a wooden cross in the shape of a giant X, spread-eagle, while Abby draped me in sheer, wet fabric. I felt the way I had posing for drawing classes: as though I were merely a point of inspiration on the way to a final image. Lenny was polite and professional. When he gave me precise directions, such as to adjust my chin or shoulder by a quarter inch, I was reminded of childhood portrait sittings in department-store studios.

The shoot was pleasant, with light and air pouring in the windows. The three of us talked and joked, though Lenny sometimes went silent, concentrating on his work. I could see how even if I was doing proper porn, it would be easier in this environment to detach myself from the end user. I wasn't faced with the man who would be getting off on my image. I was in comfortable, professional surroundings and could remain willfully ignorant of what happened after I was paid. Being photographed was like buying a cleaned, packaged chicken in the supermarket, while live stripping was like wringing its neck myself. Live, I saw what I did.

Lenny had several lines of business, I found out—his thus-far unprofitable porn collaboration with Abby was just one. His main photographic income came from what might be called boudoir photography: he took erotic photos of people, mostly women, for their own private use. He rattled off the professions of women who had come to him for photos: doctors, lawyers, politicians. They paid him to make them look like *Playboy* models. "What do they do with the pictures?" I asked.

"A few people, like a couple I had last week, put them up on their walls. But mostly women want them for their boyfriends."

To prove that they can look that way, I thought to myself. To prove that they can be a sex object, in the soft-focus, arched back, parted lips, lingerie-bound commercial style of a porn model. Lenny had been making an adjustment to his camera, and when he looked up, he saw that I was still staring at him. He said, with a shrug, "Everybody wants to look sexy."

Leila—Part III

Chapter 26

There was only one strip club in the Seattle area that forbade lap dancing, and I went there after I gave up on Rick's. It was called Extasy and was on Highway 99, in SeaTac, a city created out of all the hotels and car rental agencies that had sprung up around the Seattle-Tacoma International Airport. When I spoke to Robin, one of the managers at Extasy, he asked me: "So, you want to work somewhere where you don't have to grind dick?" I said, "Yes, please."

Extasy had a mirror-backed stage with a pole, a seating area scattered with tables and chairs, and a bar serving enormous, overpriced glasses of soda pop, all standard arrangements. The city of SeaTac had been determined, unlike apathetic Seattle, to stop prostitution in strip clubs, and it had come to an arrangement with Extasy resulting in some unique architecture. The main stage and seating area were to the left as one walked in, and off to the right, screened from the door, were two private-dance platforms. They were high, up to my neck, and big enough to comfortably accommodate about six dancers each. A series of wide nooks were cut into the sides of the platforms, and in each nook was a bench facing the stage. A customer sitting on one of these benches faced a countertop, for drinks or elbows, that separated him from the platform. Above him it looked like a playground. As well as floor-to-ceiling poles there were hanging manacles, a rope, a trapeze, a fake bearskin, and a zebra-striped blanket. Girls climbed skinny stairways to get up, and on top of the stage, if they were standing, their calves were at the height of the customer's face. It was impossible to touch a customer while performing, and, in fact, Robin reprimanded girls if an elbow or knee even strayed out over the edge of the platform. So the women did a two-song dance on the main stage, then pitched private dances to the men in the audience. When they had a taker, they brought him over to one of the platforms.

Extasy's policy dictated that dancers strip only to their thong on the main stage, which effectively encouraged customers to buy fully nude private dances. And dancers were not allowed to wear just their bra and thong on the floor, among the audience. They were required to cover their bottoms with a sarong or shorts or whatever they liked.

Extasy didn't have the sinister vibe of Rick's, but it was run some-what haphazardly. Rent was between forty and seventy dollars, depending on the day and time, plus two dollars for every private dance. Robin and the other managers sometimes got in magnanimous moods and gave girls a break. Robin was a loquacious armchair philosopher in Harley-Davidson tattoos, who had worked at every strip club in the greater Seattle area, including Rick's and Déjà Vu. For a while, a boa constrictor in a glass cage was in residence just inside Extasy's front door; Robin claimed that someone had left it on the doorstep like an orphan. Sometimes in the early evening he burned incense at the bar. He spoke with no inhibitions, and odd pronouncements often tumbled out. "Everyone in this business has a split personality, one for work and one for outside. That includes males and females. That includes me," he told me. When he wasn't working, he went fishing or visited his mom in Idaho.

When I arrived in the dressing room for my first shift, the other women smiled and introduced themselves. The eighteen-year-old bar-tender made benign, inept passes at me and many of the other dancers, all of which were ignored. I picked out my list of mass-appeal sex songs—Prince, the Police, the Rolling Stones—and the soft-spoken disc jockey punched them into his computer. He said he was just working at Extasy until he could land a job at the local classic-rock station.

"Please welcome a very sexy lady to the stage; this is Leila!" he growled into the microphone before I expected him to. The first pounding bars of my music played, and I strode up the steps to the mirror-backed stage. I strutted across the stage several times, trying to look intimidating, while I got my bearings. (Edge of stage—there;

pole—there; audience members—there.) I wore black hot pants, high black heels, and my lime green bra.

I grabbed the pole in both hands. I had never mastered any serious acrobatics, but I was flexible and could do things that looked good without being very difficult. I could hold on to it and arch way back, for example, or swing around it in a downward spiral, or, my favorite, kick one leg straight up and catch my heel on it like a grappling hook. I worried about getting stuck in this last position, but I never had.

At the end of the first song I slowly unzipped my shorts, held the fly open while turning and shifting my weight from hip to hip, then made them fall to the floor by shaking my knees. I had a black thong on underneath.

I was startled when the first wadded bill landed onstage. Getting tipped at the stage was completely new to me. I smiled at the man who threw it.

During the second song I unclasped my bra and shook my shoulders, not quite letting it slip off, pacing for a few bars before letting the straps slide down to my wrists. My nipples puckered in the cool air. I whipped the bra away, swung it around, then threw it stage right, the same direction in which I had kicked my shorts. Landing them in the same spot made regathering easier.

More bills, all crumpled or folded compactly to lengthen their trajectory, hit the stage. They were probably all ones, I thought, but still, they would add up. I was flattered. I felt encouraged. Robin came up, put a bill on the stage, then gave me a nod and wink of reassurance. I remembered Megan telling me that she hated it when bills were thrown. She thought it was degrading and preferred that they be placed onstage or handed to her. I didn't see much difference.

I lowered myself to the floor by leaning against the mirror, kicking a leg above my head and sliding down. With my ass on the floor I scissored my legs open and shut, then swung them sideways and rolled forward. Facing the ceiling, I bent my knees and arched my back, making a lopsided M with my body. I stayed there, resting, for a verse. Then I rose to my knees, faced the audience, opened my knees and leaned back. I was thinking: The more kneeling the more bruises. I wish I could wear knee pads. Don't tire too early.

I jumped lightly to standing, and more bills landed. I noticed one skitter out of view and made a mental note to find it. I scanned the audience, wondering who would be the best prospect for a private dance.

After a couple of more turns around the pole, I was finished. As the song ended the DJ growled a barely comprehensible patter: "Say thank you, gentlemen, to the very sexy Leila, and buy a fully nude private dance. . . ." He trailed off into the music. I felt energized.

I walked around and gathered the bills, not exactly sure how to go about it, carefully keeping my back straight, picking them up with quick, fluid crouches, as though I were in a Miss America Pageant, trying to appear ladylike. Then I stepped down and stood in a dark corner slightly shielded from the audience, where I put my shorts and bra back on. I straightened the crumpled bills and folded them neatly lengthwise, then held them between my fingers the way I had seen other dancers do. Eleven dollars wasn't much. On the other hand, I counseled myself, it had been only about six minutes. The next dancer was climbing the steps. As she tucked her own sheaf of folded bills next to the mirror, she leaned toward me and whispered, "I like the way you dance."

I had not grown out of the dancing part of it. There remained, first of all, the sheer pleasure of movement. Then there was the thrill of being the sexual center of attention. While I danced nearly naked onstage, all I saw were eyes in the darkness watching me in my pool of light. I felt desired, and it was desire unaccompanied by threat. Danger and coercion so often came along with being wanted. Here, I was in control, making their eyes follow me, making them clap or wink or throw money. Sometimes dancing was exquisite. Even at Rick's there had been moments onstage that felt like time suspended.

Unfortunately, there was nowhere in Seattle where I could earn a living this way. In effect, I paid the club for the privilege. Stage dances were so nonessential to one's income that at Spearmint Rhino, Lara had told me, many dancers paid the club to exempt themselves. Money didn't come from the stage, it came from shaking down the marks.

It was so easy to fall into picking and choosing. At Extasy I would approach men because they looked nice, or smart, or rich, and I would be rejected. Then I'd see that someone else had just sold four dances to the surly guy in the corner. The best way to make money was to troll the room systematically, as if I were on a search-and-rescue operation, traveling back and forth in a grid, over and over, hitting up every man, then going back and hitting him up again, until somebody said yes. I found it hard to make myself do this.

Extasy encouraged us to sell soft drinks. They had good waitresses, and as soon as one saw me sitting with a customer, she would descend like a vulture and ask if he would like to buy the lady a drink. He could buy me a ten- or twenty-dollar vat, and I always chose Coke to help me stay awake. Half the price of each drink sold went toward my rent, which I could often work off this way. But it was an inefficient method for making money. I might sit with a customer for thirty minutes and get only five dollars out of him, when I could have been selling dances. And the sitting and chatting and being charming to strangers wore me out far more than the dancing. I found all sorts of stupid things coming out of my mouth.

"Do you know what Dante's definition of hell is?" I asked Clarence from Cleveland. Being so near the airport, Extasy got a lot of business travelers. He wore shiny loafers and a pressed shirt.

"Proximity without intimacy," I said. Clarence nodded politely but vaguely. He was game to talk to me. Both of us chipper and friendly, we had gone over names, cities of origin, his job, the weather, that day's football game. He looked unsure of whether he should pick up my new conversational strain or change the subject entirely.

I knew almost nothing about Dante. I had read a reference to him in a novel that day, and it was floating around in my head. I wanted to kick myself as soon as I had said it. It was absurd. I was absurd, Clarence was absurd. This place was absurd, and the *Divine Comedy* was an absurd thing to bring up. I didn't want to appear well read because it made me feel like a talking monkey. I had been show-offy and self-indulgent, which suggested that I cared what Clarence thought, and I didn't want to start caring, or appearing to care, what any of them thought. I wanted to give them only my façade.

Selling drinks and private dances was fatiguing. It was like being in the private pleasures booth all the time, having continuously to present a fake personality. And the booth had been two hours long at the most, whereas a club shift was at least six. Dancing onstage was the easy part, but the hustle of the floor wore me down. As I got tired and bored, it became harder and harder not to let down my guard.

It wasn't that I disliked Clarence. In fact, he was pleasant, which only made it more ridiculous that I should think of him in terms of how much he spent. But it felt wrong to like or dislike any customer. I didn't think anything that began in this kind of house of mirrors could survive outside. Other dancers sometimes tried to cross the bridge, and I could see how, the more time one spent at work, the more tempting it would become. If the only men you ever met were customers, the desire to connect with someone, or anyone, might become overwhelming.

I was never tempted. As far as I was concerned, the fact that strip clubs were unreal was part of the appeal. We had all come here for illusions. I had come to play the role of sex object. The disc jockey fantasized about his future at a radio station, while the bartender fantasized that a dancer would someday ask him for more than a Coke. The booth customers had come to the Lusty Lady to act out their erotic dramas. Ken, my rescue man, had come to Rick's to have his secret-agent fantasies flattered, even though he had been wise to the game. He knew that it ended at the door, and that was why he looked only a little wistful when I turned him down for a date—if I had said yes, I would have shattered the fantasy, and we would have had to begin as real people.

Illusion offered no basis for connecting with others. This was true in a strip club, and it was true in my relationship with Paul in London. In Paul I hadn't found someone who thrilled me, or whom I, as myself, would have thrilled. Rather, I had created a persona that

I thought would seduce him, simply so that I could say to myself, Look what I caught. That imaginary world with Paul had been doomed to splinter when I became exhausted by the charade. Similarly, when I became weary of selling dances, cracks started to show in my mask, and I behaved as I had with Clarence. Instead of asking him another question about his job, or the weather in Cleveland, or complimenting him on his cuff links, I told him, like a machine gone haywire, that proximity without intimacy summed up Dante's vision of hell.

On a good night I could make $300 at Extasy. One night I came home after making $180 in six hours, and I ran into Zoe as we both washed off our makeup in the bathroom at Matt's. She had just arrived home after two short parties, both nearby, at which she had made a total of $540. When I heard this, I felt deflated because she had made so much more than me. And when I told her about my night, I imagined that she was silently judging me. I imagined that she was thinking how silly I was not to do parties, and saying to herself that now, after hearing about her brief, profitable evening, I would understand.

In the morning I chastised myself for comparing my night to hers. It suggested that money had become my score card, too, and I didn't want it to. I didn't have to be here, I told myself. I was just trying to find something out. But I still found it impossible not to compare earnings.

Stripping had turned Zoe into a strange hybrid of ascetic and materialist, and I wondered if it could do the same to me. I felt that at heart Zoe was not an acquisitive person. She had no desire for expensive goods, no interest in getting a television, a stereo, or high-priced clothing. She didn't want any car other than her paid-for, secondhand, ordinary little sedan. She called expensive sports like skiing "decadent." She had once said to me of someone she admired greatly, "He has a lot of beautiful things, but isn't attached to any of them." Yet comparing money was a relentless part of her job. A "good night" was one in which she made a lot of money and a low-earning night was always a disappointment; these assessments tended to hold fast no matter what had occurred at the parties. She judged how her season was going exclusively in terms of how much she made.

I thought her attitude toward the sweat- and food-stained bills she earned stripping had rippled out into her perspective on money in general. She tended to judge others based on what they made. She wondered out loud to me how the people who worked at one of her favorite stores maintained their self-respect when they earned only eight dollars an hour. One of her reasons for turning down the job that Seal Press had offered her was that it paid too little, at nine dollars an hour. I didn't understand her reasoning, since one of the points of stripping, I had thought, was to finance the pursuit of more creative, satisfying jobs.

Zoe remained unmaterialistic in some ways, and I tried not to let my job be only about the money, but there was no escaping the competitive, comparative, dollar-counting side of stripping. The dollar figures of a particular hour or night were as symbolic as they were utilitarian. The money told us what we were worth.

Chapter 27

I had moved out of Matt's house by the time he and Zoe planned to be back. Zoe arrived in Seattle on an April Friday, and she worked a party the very next night. She was nervous about it at first. She had lost her cherished washboard stomach from eating delicious Thai and Indian food and exercising less than usual. Her hair, which she had dyed bright red in Bangkok, had bleached out to an orangeish color, and her back was burnt and peeling. Her appearance was not up to her usual work standards. But the men were sweet, nerdy types, the bachelor had actually been to India, and they thought it was cute when she giggled because she had forgotten her routine.

Zoe felt invigorated for the season ahead. Her plan to continue working for one, two, maybe three more summers, had not wavered. She decided to wring as much as she could out of stripping, working as many seasons and making as much money as possible. The future, she had finally concluded, would take care of itself.

But she worried about how much work she would be able to get. Abby had been doing lesbian shows with Tami through the winter. Now that her original partner was back, Abby didn't want to just drop Tami, especially since Zoe was already talking about going away again the following autumn. The Lusty Lady didn't look promising either. Zoe's leave had been for under six months, which meant that, according to policy, management would rehire her—but only if there were fewer than sixty-five dancers on the schedule. It turned out that there were more than sixty-five dancers working, so Zoe was put on the on-call list. She wouldn't be scheduled, but she could pick up work from dancers giving away their shifts. Three dancers would have to quit or be fired before she could move onto the schedule. Zoe worried that she might not be able to pick up any work at all. If she couldn't get back in to the Lusty she would lose a reliable two hundred bucks a week.

She asked Abby, who was on the schedule, if they could work something out. Zoe asked Abby to request two shifts a week instead of her usual one—then she could give the extra one away to Zoe. Abby resisted at first, because she thought management would be on to them in a second. When she relented and requested two shifts, it didn't work. They gave her only one, and not on the day she had wanted but on the day she had been planning to give away to Zoe. She had to make a special trip down from Bellingham just to work it. Zoe didn't ask her again.

Then came worse news. Management called an all-staff meeting the Sunday after Zoe's return. She herself missed it, but Abby called her with the news: All dancers were being given a dollar-an-hour pay cut. They had also cut pay for prep time again, so that now it stood at seven dollars an hour, which translated to a meager $1.75 per shift. Support staff were also taking cuts, and the show directors said that the San Francisco Lusty Lady was in bad financial shape, which might put both outfits out of business.

It all served as another reminder to those who were too dependent that they should think about life after the L. Zoe understood management's decision, and on the whole it seemed that most dancers understood, because the cuts prompted very little complaint. They could all see that business was down. There had been constant construction around First Avenue and University, and amid it all the city had taken away the street parking in front of the Lusty. Zoe thought the whole neighborhood seemed to be waiting for the L to disappear.

But in the end Zoe found she was able to pick up a shift a week at the Lusty, and often more. Bachelor-party business started booming again. Wanting to save at least ten thousand dollars over the summer, she resolved not to turn down a single party if she could help it. She also cultivated repeat customers who wanted private shows.

It felt like a privilege to be able to walk back into her job and be afforded the money, the free time, and the independence that it gave her. She had been to see the dancing girls at a club in Bangkok. They were all friendly, positive girls, all eighteen or nineteen years old; they all wore numbers and were prostitutes. Many of them were probably supporting their families—that was good, Zoe thought—but it was unlikely that any had gone into their jobs because they wanted to, the way she had. It was unlikely that they were buying themselves free time for their own pleasures. They made Zoe feel overwhelmingly fortunate. She thought she was lucky to be able to do this job when other women had inhibitions that prevented them. She thought it was fortuitous that she had discovered bachelor parties. She might get chaotic, stressful shows, but when she did, even if she had three in a row, she knew a good show was waiting just around the corner. The ill feeling never had a chance to linger. Most of all, she was happy that she could spend four months in Asia, come back, work twenty hours a week, ride her bike and go to movies, and then go back to Asia again. She thought she would take an English-teaching course when she returned to Thailand. She knew it was simple and not very ambitious, but it was enough for now.

Meanwhile, she wasn't sure where to live during the half year until she left. In her first months back she stayed at Matt's. His mood vacillated, and he would be angry and standoffish toward her one day, then affectionate the next. Zoe went to great lengths not to anger him. He told her that he didn't want to see her stuff mixed up with his, so she kept all her belongings in the yellow room. She asked permission to keep her slippers under his bed, where they both slept, which he granted. She tried to keep the one thing he had always hated, the way she got ready for parties, out of his sight. She took all her calls upstairs, dressed in her room, and kept the music down. She hoped for a rapprochement between them, or at least some sort of peace. None was forthcoming, so eventually she set a date, the first of July, by which time she would move out.

*   *   *

Kim worried about the pay cut, too. She could absorb it, but it made her evaluate her options. She and Shawn had finalized their divorce, and she had been hard up for money since he had moved out. Despite the size of her three-bedroom, two-bathroom house, she hated the idea of having roommates. She did allow her ex-boyfriend Allan to move into one of the spare bedrooms, but they didn't get along and she ended up asking him to move out after only two months.

She and a group of other Lusty Ladies then tried to organize a naked maid service, and they held several meetings at which they discussed advertising, pricing, and cleaning supplies. They all agreed that the Seattle market was ripe for exploitation. But while many expressed a desire to work for an up-and-running naked maid service, no one proved up to the task of getting one off the ground. Kim really wanted to get it going because it was better than her Plan B—she started seriously to consider going to work in an Alaska club for the summer. If she did, it would be a major departure for her, from the clean, glass-enclosed Lusty to a full-contact club.

Kim started thinking again about longer-term plans. She took a training course to become an emergency medical technician, and she was reminded, with some surprise, just how much she enjoyed medicine. She hadn't given much thought to that career in nearly five years, since she had been working in the abortion clinic and planning to apply to Bastyre. Now, she started looking into naturopathic school again. She filled out a federal financial-aid form and mailed it in.

She came up against obstacles. Tuition was $25,000 a year and it was a five-year program. She could get it financed, but because Seattle was saturated with naturopaths, most Bastyre graduates in the area only made about $60,000 a year after graduation. She feared it would put her in debt forever.

Kim revised her thinking. Registered nurses also made about $60,000 a year. On top of their salaries they received signing bonuses—employers wooed them because there weren't enough around. An RN certificate could be earned in under two years. Kim was still training so that, sooner or later, she would be able to pass the fire department's physical exam. Perhaps she could even be a firefighter and a nurse at the same time. She needed to pass three prerequisite courses before she could get into the nursing program at a local college. She signed up for physiology, nutrition, and developmental psychology and proceeded to earn 4.0s in all three, guaranteeing her admission.

She did not, in the end, become a naked maid, go to Alaska, or work at ExoticTan, the whack shack on Capitol Hill. She continued to max out at the Lusty, and eventually Zoe offered some temporary financial relief. She needed a place to stay for four months and asked Kim several times if she could move in with her for that period. Kim was hesitant. She thought that she herself was too uptight to live with Zoe, and Zoe too unaware to live with her. Zoe was a free spirit, and in Kim's experience free spirits were too caught up in their own world to notice if anything upset other people. The rentable room—she kept the other one as a guest room—had the sleeping porch off of it, which Kim liked to use in the summer. Also, Zoe was a lapsed vegetarian and might bring meat into the house. Worst of all, she might be messy.

Zoe promised that it wouldn't be what Kim thought. She was a clean freak now. She swore that not a whiff of meat would enter Kim's kitchen. She assured Kim that she could use the sleeping porch any time she wanted, day or night. Kim relented, and was amazed. Along with paying her rent, Zoe bought groceries, cooked, cleaned, did all the laundry, and worked in the yard. She took care of Kim. Kim started telling people that Zoe was her "mama-girlfriend-wife." Zoe, meanwhile, was so delighted to live in such an inspirational house, and to have her efforts so appreciated, that none of it felt like work. And she relaxed, knowing that she could get ready for parties, or have Abby sleep over, without complaint.

Zoe offered to take Kim to a bachelor party or two, with the idea that Kim might need or want to start working them. The first one started well. Kim, Zoe, and Abby met some of the party guests downtown at the very fashionable W Hotel. But then the men took them to a nearby dive, to a room so small that a bed had been tipped up on its side to make space. Several of the twenty-odd guests were extraordinarily drunk: one kept falling down and hitting his head; one started slugging his friends; one unzipped his pants and offered to piss on the bachelor, saying "Here, I'll give you a golden shower; it'll save you twenty bucks." During Zoe and Abby's dyke show, one guest was so rude that they had him thrown out; when someone else offered a comment a few minutes later, they ended the show abruptly and packed up. They would have left immediately except that Zoe's skirt had disappeared, presumably stolen, though no one would produce it. On top of all this, they were cheap.

Kim was appalled. She concluded she would never be able to handle the level of physical contact or rudeness she had just seen. Had she been performing, she was pretty sure she would have hauled off and smacked somebody, which was no way to make money. She scratched the idea of bachelor parties.

Zoe invited Kim to come for one more bachelor party, but for a different reason. Zoe and Abby had a party scheduled for a group of firefighters, and Zoe hoped that she might launch Kim on a summer romance. Shawn had been gone for six months, and in the end Kim had never had an affair with Nice Guy Bri. She had continued to see him, as a friend, while she wavered on her divorce, which had upset Shawn greatly. But around the time Shawn moved out for good, she realized that she simply wasn't attracted to Brian anymore. With the sexual tension gone, she began to ask herself what the purpose of the friendship was, and she found she had no answer.

Kim, Zoe, and Abby arrived at a handsome Craftsman bungalow in south Seattle and introduced themselves to the hosts, Doug and Nick, who were both fit, broad-shouldered men with short dark hair. The three girls were about to enter the bedroom when Zoe asked Kim to get her hair products from the car.

"Where are you going?" Doug asked Kim on her way out.

She told him; he offered to help, and for the rest of the evening they were inseparable. He gave her a tour of the house, which was his pride and joy, taking care to point out the sections he had refurbished himself. He showed her the garden and described the summer projects he had planned for it. The party was a disaster—two of the guests got into a brawl—but Kim and Doug remained oblivious to everyone and everything else. The fight gave Doug the opportunity to tell Kim that he wanted to get out of his house, and he asked if she would go with him.

Kim and Zoe ended up inviting both Doug and Nick over, and while Zoe and Nick made out, Kim and Doug stayed up all night talking. Kim was flying to her grandmother's birthday party in Connecticut the next day, and he offered to pick her up at the airport when she got back. He asked her to go to his friend's wedding with him the following weekend, and she agreed. In the following month he undertook sanding and painting jobs around her house and promised to help her train for the firefighting exam.

As well as Zoe's rent money, Kim found another way to ease her financial straits. At the very back of *The Stranger* every week, following all the personals and the hundreds of ads selling sex services, there appeared a page of miscellaneous blurbs. One back page from the summer of 2001 carried sixteen ads for therapy and counseling, five seeking paid subjects for medical studies, two for divorce lawyers, one offering "permanent, safe" penis enlargement, one selling a booklet on how to change one's identity, and four seeking women to sell—or in the advertisers' words "donate"—their eggs. These last ones had caught Kim's attention. She knew two dancers at the L who had done it, one of them three times—the clinic-imposed maximum—and the other one twice.

She called a clinic, then went and applied. Attributes like a college education and bright green-blue eyes tended to be in high demand in the egg market, and before Kim had even left the premises, the woman who read her application said, "I know exactly who will want you." They offered to pay her $2,500 for one harvest. Normally the fertility doctors collected about twenty eggs from a vendor, then attempted to implant them in the recipient with the hope that at least one would take hold successfully.

The notion of having eggs removed from my body made me cringe. I had always been squeamish about medical procedures, especially anything that involved puncturing my skin. I had descended into a panic the last time blood had been taken from me, an activity I avoided, whether for charity or medical checkups, as if it were torture. I couldn't have sold my eggs because of physical revulsion at the process. Psychologically, I was less sure, but I was troubled by the idea of selling body parts. I was starting to feel overwhelmed by the idea that everything was for sale—nudity, sex, tulip viewing, and now eggs.

I tried to account for my discomfort. In an abstract legal sense, I thought that everyone should have jurisdiction over her own body. But viscerally, it disturbed me that people were faced with the choice of whether to sell a body part at all. It reminded me of something that Kim had once said about the booth: that while she had never felt that anyone was making her do anything, she had seen herself give up her own boundaries for money. Perhaps, I thought, when money was at stake, no one's choices were real.

But Kim and I had different boundaries. She was enthusiastic about the idea of selling eggs, and the lively way she spoke about it made me think it wasn't strictly because of the $2,500. She had looked into it once years earlier but had not gone through with it. She was fascinated with medicine even when she herself was the subject, and she told me that she hoped she could watch her insides on a video monitor when they did the extraction. She said she liked the idea that she could "have babies without having babies"—as though fulfilling primal reproductive urges by rational choice. The doctors put her on birth control pills to get her cycle in sync with the recipient. They gave her a hormone nasal spray and a schedule for taking it. When her procedure was about a week away, she started injecting herself with hormones every day and then going into the clinic, where they drew her blood and examined it. Based on the hormones in her blood, they then picked a precise day. It was a relatively simple, outpatient procedure. They pushed a needle through her vaginal wall to her ovaries, and harvested a total of thirty-six eggs.

*   *   *

Zoe needn't have worried about not getting work on her return from Asia. From the day after she arrived home until the end of the summer her schedule was busy and lucrative. She got so many parties and private shows that when the Lusty Lady did put her back on the schedule, she sometimes gave her shifts away. Part of this was thanks to Abby, who had gained the trust of one of their party-booking agents over the winter. The agent now had Abby handle the occasional phone call, and when she did Abby always scheduled herself and Zoe first. There were enough parties to go around to keep the two of them busy and to give parties to Tami, Abby's winter partner, as well.

Abby and Zoe also launched their own website and put an ad for it in the back of *The Stranger*. They listed both of their mobile phone numbers on the site so that they could take party bookings at any time. The calls poured in, effectively making them their own agents and saving them the fees they would have had to pay. By the end of the summer they had hired Tami and another dancer to work for them.

Zoe had set a goal of banking ten thousand dollars over the summer, but by August, working as many as six parties a weekend and almost never turning down a show, her balance was already above fifteen thousand dollars. She bought her plane ticket for the coming winter. She would go to teaching school in Bangkok, then visit her ex-boyfriend Cameron, who now ran a business in Bali and said that she still made his blood boil. Then she would cycle around Australia and New Zealand.

Following her breakup with Matt, she looked for a summer fling, but though she started a few, they all fizzled. After she moved out of Matt's they continued to have sex regularly, and sometimes they even hung out like a couple, going to movies and shopping together. She had four other affairs over the summer. The first was Rick, whom she met cycling while she was still living with Matt, but she quickly decided she wasn't very interested and broke it off. She met the second, Caleb, at a music festival. He seemed promising but suffered a family tragedy shortly after they met and withdrew. The third was Doug's housemate Nick, but while Kim and Doug took off, Zoe dated Nick for only about a week. And finally, there was Mark.

Zoe had met Mark in Rome three years earlier and, though not overly impressed, had kept up an e-mail correspondence with him. He lived in California, and they agreed to meet at Burning Man, the sprawling annual party in the Nevada wilderness, at which Zoe and Matt had reunited the year before. All year Zoe and Matt had both said that they wanted to return. They became exuberant when talking about the weeklong carnival and the costumed revelers in self-sufficient trucks, who convened in the middle of the Black Rock Desert, where they set up a minicity of fabulous tents and effigies. They both made the three-day drive again in 2001, separately, but they ended up seeing a lot of each other during the week. Like the majority of attendees, Zoe spent most of her waking hours during the week on Ecstasy and other drugs. She and Matt talked warmly to each other and promised that they would spend some time together as friends.

Zoe met up with Mark, whom she had not seen since Rome, and, to her surprise, found that this time she was attracted to him. He told her that he had saved all their correspondence and that she was the only girl on whom he had ever kept an e-mail file. He treated her with effusive kindness in front of her friends, tidied the camp when it was messy, and, getting into the carnival spirit, wore dresses. She was impressed, and they quickly fell into a romance. Matt was disconcerted when she ditched their plan to spend time together. He felt as if he was witnessing a repeat of the year before—when they had been broken up for only a few months, and Zoe had brought a new man to hang out in Matt's camp, with Matt's friends. That time he had become furious and they had fought, reconciled, and gotten back together. This time he tried, successfully, not to become angry. He was more detached from Zoe now than he had been the year before.

Zoe was smitten with Mark. If she had made a list of the things she wanted in a man he would have fit it perfectly: He was responsible, smart, adventurous, and spontaneous. It occurred to her that she didn't want to take her next journey alone—she wanted him to come with her. She encouraged him to follow her to Thailand; he said he would come. Toward the end of the week he proposed to her, publicly, on his knees. In a fanciful ceremony they pledged themselves to each other in front of all their friends, including Matt. When they separated, she promised to visit him in San Francisco the following weekend. He said he would come up to Seattle for the costume party she and Kim were planning to throw. She left Nevada full of passion. She felt that Mark saw her as a whole person.

After sending her several warm and touching e-mails, he dropped out of contact. On the Friday of the weekend she was to have visited San Francisco, she couldn't reach him. He resurfaced on Sunday, calling her to say that he had forgotten. The next day he suggested they break off what Zoe had thought was a budding relationship. Zoe was terribly hurt and mystified. Later she found out through a friend that he spent the night after they parted ways with another woman. She went to Matt, told him what had happened, and cried; he listened quietly. They started sleeping together again.

Because of the way Zoe spoke, I often felt that she put emphasis on the wrong things. She would describe a meal, for example, with so many breathy stops and starts that anyone hearing the tone and not the words would think she was talking about skydiving. Similarly, when she told me about Burning Man and Mark, I thought she emphasized all the wrong things. She kept repeating that Mark had treated her kindly in public, in front of her friends—a reminder that Matt had not done so in a long time. She said the reason it hurt so much when he broke it off was that Mark had seen her as a whole person—an indicator that other than Matt, there were few men who she felt saw her this way.

She said that being dumped by Mark was ten times more painful than being blown off, as she felt she had been, by Caleb, from the music festival, or Nick, the fireman. I was troubled that she felt so much anguish over Mark, but I thought her overall view of the situation was extraordinary. She had told me, after all, how many chemicals she and Mark had consumed that week. But she didn't seem to consider them when she said she was "mystified" by his behavior. I had watched how Ecstasy made my own emotions pour forth unnaturally, and how it had clouded my judgment. I had often wondered to what extent the fact that Erik and I had been on the drug when we met accounted for our relationship. I didn't credit the whole four years to it, but there was no denying its influence in the way we felt at our first meeting. We had opened up to each other instantaneously. Warmth and trust flowed right away. It disturbed me that the relationship might have unfolded differently if we hadn't been high that one night, and that I would never know how it could have been.

Since then I had used Ecstasy only occasionally, perhaps five times in my twenties. But it was enough to have seen myself and others, because of it, feel too much too soon for people who were essentially strangers. Ecstasy was ersatz feeling. It bought an unearned, illusory closeness with other people, much as stripping produced an instant, illusory sexual closeness. Ecstasy provided connection—but not a connection from the luck of meeting someone empathetic, or the slow buildup of getting to know him. Zoe, a user who had been around other users, presumably knew all this. I suggested to her that perhaps the drug was the source of her confusion over Mark. Perhaps he had looked back at the week and said to himself that it was a party, they were high, and that none of it should be taken too seriously. This was the reaction I would have expected from any adult, especially one who knew enough to know better. To all this she said, "Yeah, probably."

Bachelor parties started to wear on Zoe. It wasn't that they had changed recently. It had been several summers since she had started using toys and doing dyke shows. Parties had always required a lot of driving and rushing around, and there had always been some men, and some groups of men, who harassed, spoke rudely, slapped, and groped. There had always been parties where no one asked her name. But now it bothered her that they didn't ask, which was perverse, because she would only ever tell them she was Cassandra. Now, after nearly a decade, she wanted the men to want to know her as more than a naked girl.

The parties were made more difficult by the fact that her love life was in turmoil. She hadn't realized it, but having someone to come home to at the end of a night was a solace. She needed attention focused on her, both sexual and otherwise, after expending so much energy over an evening. She needed to be with someone who saw her as a whole person. This was why, she realized, she kept retreating to Matt, even after he had ejected her from his house and despite the way he sometimes treated her. He knew her better than anyone else.

Zoe started preferring the private shows to the heavy, staring, swaying chaos of parties. But even private shows had their hazards. One of her agents, a woman named Ginny who lived in an Eastside suburb with her husband and two yapping dogs, booked Zoe for a show with Deena. Ginny, who specialized in private shows rather than parties, and didn't ask her girls too many questions, had built a studio in her basement. When Ginny called, Zoe felt a stab of doubt. Deena, she knew, sometimes had sex with customers as part of the show.

But, Zoe reasoned, Ginny and Deena both knew that she was adamant about not having sex. Ginny wouldn't have booked her if that was what was expected. So she agreed, and on a sunny weekend afternoon, she drove out to Ginny's studio. When she arrived, Zoe found that Ginny was having a yard sale on her front lawn. She picked her way among neighbors combing through tables of old clothes. The two Yorkshire terriers greeted her with piercing yelps and hounded her all the way to the studio's back door, where Deena waited.

When the customer arrived, Deena greeted him by name, and they embraced. Zoe had a sinking feeling because they had obviously met before. He gave them the money, the usual amount for a two-girl show, and the two women began to touch each other and undress. He watched them, from a close distance, and after a while he started to stroke himself, all three of them lying roughly side by side. And then, somehow, Deena escaped Zoe and was with him, and he was asking her to have sex with him, and she was saying no, and he was asking her again, and she was saying no, no, no, and offering to suck his cock instead, but he said no, and then Zoe watched, frozen, while they fucked.

After he left and they split the money, Deena must have sensed some reproach because she said, "I don't always. Only if they're pushy."

Zoe fled, past the dogs and the garage sale, and once she was in her car she burst into tears. She cried all the way back through the Eastside, over the long, low bridge across the lake and into Seattle, and all the way home.

Over the summer, during parties and private shows, Zoe found that she was distancing herself from her performance. It happened especially when she was doing toy shows in front of big audiences. She felt as if she was watching herself from a distance, as if it wasn't really her in front of all the people. So she came to a decision. She would no longer use toys at parties. She told Abby and explained why, worried that she might turn back to Tami and do more shows with her instead. But Abby was an amazingly good sport about it, just as she had been the times when Zoe freaked out midshow and retreated to the bedroom. Abby agreed to take all the inserting herself. Their first night after Zoe's pronouncement they had two dyke shows. At both of them, the guys asked why only Abby was being fucked with toys; at both of them, they said they took turns from party to party.

Why toys? Why, for that matter, would Lara give a hand job from outside the trousers but not in? And why did Deena want to give a blow job rather than have sex? It wasn't the act itself, it was a matter of setting up boundaries *somewhere* so that one didn't feel like one's entire sense of self was oozing away. Zoe had resolved once before not to use toys at parties, and she had told Matt she wouldn't. She had let the decision slide to the pressures of the market. It relieved me to hear that she had decided to set this limit again, partly for her sake and partly for selfish reasons. I wanted to know that she had sexual boundaries because I felt uneasy when I suspected that she neither had them nor respected those of others. That was why I had been disturbed that time when she made a casual pass at me, and annoyed more recently when she had sprung Lulu's lap dance on me. Now, at least, Zoe was indicating that however sexually malleable she might seem, the divisions between herself and others mattered. I felt reassured.

As soon as she told me about her resolution, though, she described a private show in which she had used a toy. It turned out that her new border was a fuzzy one. She explained that she still felt comfortable in front of a single customer, just not a crowd.

Toward the end of the summer Zoe started to see a regular private client, Gene. He often had her meet him in an expensive hotel room. He paid Zoe by the hour, and on each occasion they talked for a while first. Then she began to undress, and she would use a toy on herself while he watched and masturbated. Zoe felt comfortable with Gene, and Gene made her feel good about herself. He was appreciative, not just of her body but of her personality, she thought. He seemed genuinely interested in the things she did, and he asked dozens of questions about her trips. Seeing Gene was a calm and almost pleasant experience, in drastic contrast to so many of the parties she had worked at over the summer. He told her that his wife of twenty-two years was clinically frigid, and Zoe felt as if she was doing him a kindness, or even something therapeutic. She began to disapprove of Gene's marriage; the way he described it, he stayed with his wife for the sake of keeping up appearances. The fifth time Zoe and Gene saw each other he made her an offer. He wanted to have sex with her, and he would pay.

The amount he offered her was enticing: six hundred dollars for each occasion, and he wanted to see her once a week.

She enjoyed the idea that because of the state of his marriage and sex life, she could be a sort of healer to him.

She felt at ease with Gene. It wouldn't be as though she were streetwalking, taking just anyone. She would be choosing. And parties had started to distress her so much that the idea of having sex with Gene, who struck her as a decent guy, was more appealing. He was good for her, she felt, a positive influence, because he treated her with more kindness and respect than any man she had been with recently.

One thing, or rather four things, stood out in her mind persuasively: Rick, Caleb, Nick, and Mark. Especially Mark. Rick had been kind, but the sex had been terrible, and she had felt used by the other three. She had given herself to them, and they hadn't shown appreciation. On the whole, the sex she had had over the summer—excluding that with Matt—had been unrewarding. This would have made some people conclude that they should choose their sex partners more carefully. Zoe, though, saw an opportunity for profit. If she wasn't going to enjoy it, she reasoned, perhaps she should be paid. She talked it over with Matt, though not with Abby, who she believed wouldn't understand. As summer came to an end, she began to seriously think about taking Gene up on his offer.

Chapter 28

My last dance was at Extasy. The customer, a young man in a cowboy hat, politely put a tip onstage while I danced, placing it rather than throwing it. I watched him watch me with his chin on his hand. Afterward I bent over him and said, "Thank you for the tip. Would you like to buy a private dance?"

He didn't just yet, and so I sat down beside him; when the waitress came around, he bought me a twenty-dollar Coke. We watched a tiny, agile dancer scale the pole to the ceiling, as though she could escape that way. He said he was from Texas and that he worked in the oil business. Texans were one of the groups—like the Japanese, like older men—that could be said, on the whole, to have a better understanding of the stripper-customer relationship than other groups, such as Washingtonians or younger men. When he was ready, I led him over to the platforms and chose the most private corner, farthest from the bar and the rest of the club. I told him it was twenty-five dollars a dance and climbed the narrow stairway to the platform so that I stood above him. He leaned back and tilted up the brim of his hat. I took hold of the pole and swung, coiling my body into S-shapes and spirals. I removed my miniskirt and bra and just before the song ended I pulled my thong to one side and let it snap back into place. He looked flushed. Without a word he held up his left hand and circled his index finger.

"You want me to keep going?" I asked, and he nodded. As the next song began I took off my thong and lowered myself to the floor so that my body was level with his face. I rolled, arched, licked my lips—at this he shook his head slowly—did the splits, stood up, and twirled. As the second song ended he circled his finger in the air again, languidly. I was surprised. Easy money, I thought—no hustling on the

floor, just continuous dancing. I reminded myself to move slowly. He
was quiet and intent, and I tried to match his mood, to keep him in
his state. If only they could all be like this, I thought. He raised his finger one more time, for a fourth dance. Now I was the one lulled into
a trance, hypnotized by my own movements, locked in his gaze. I lost
my sense of time. At the end I wished he would ask for more.

He didn't. I picked up my clothes, put them on, and descended the
stairs. He handed me a hundred. "Worth every penny," he said. I
thanked him and told him to have a nice night.

I pushed open the dressing room door and stepped from darkness
into bright light. At my locker I stripped absentmindedly, dropping
things into my bag one by one. Thong. Heels. Skirt. Bra. Then I went
through the process in reverse, reassembling myself in jeans and a
sweater. I tied my hair into a ponytail and wiped off my lipstick with
the back of my hand. I hoisted my bag onto my shoulder, walked past
the mirror, and left.

Looking back, it seemed as if the Lusty Lady's mirrored boxes had contained me like a chemical reaction in a test tube. There had been no
place else to put the volatile mix I had inside: desire and vanity, seduc-
tiveness and anger, exhibitionism and self-consciousness. Stripping, in
retrospect, looked like a much-needed outlet, and I wondered what
would have happened to all that energy if I had never taken the job.

Stripping had also diffused my love-hate relationship with being a
sex object—I had less of a need to be one now, and I minded less if I
was one. I was simply more dissociated from the way others saw me
than I had been before. Stripping had given me a sense of control over
being looked at and had taught me where some of my own boundaries were. It had also taught me about sexual power: how to use it as
a blunt instrument and what happened when I did. And stripping,
finally, was sometimes simply fun. My last dance, for the man in the
cowboy hat, was an example. It was thrilling to dance, to be adulated, to control his eyes with my body, all while feeling distant and
untouchable. Once the dance was over and the money paid, there was

no expectation from either of us. There were no consequences, no emotional debts. It was perfect freedom.

But most dances weren't like that one. Before the man in the hat it had been a long time since I could have said that I was having fun, which was why I knew right away that dance had to be the last. I had also, by then, started to think that stripping did more harm than good.

At the annual Sex Workers' Art Show in Olympia, Washington, I met a writer and performance artist named Penny Arcade. "Erotic dancing is the only feminist art form," she had said. "It's the only thing designed by women that controls men, unlike the millions of things designed by men to control women." I thought part of the statement was correct. In a crude way erotic dancing did control men, at least those men who chose to subject themselves to it, but I didn't think this made erotic dancing feminist—unless feminism was about control rather than coexistence.

To some the term "feminist stripper" is ironic, but it's not an oxymoron—it's just that one has to become a very extreme feminist to remain a stripper. When men don't matter at all, stripping makes perfect sense. It's the natural result of combining sexual freedom with a hostile, anti-male feminism. If men are seen as something to control or ignore, what they think of women is beside the point. This is why there are so many lesbian strippers—men are simply less relevant to a lesbian's personal and sexual world than they are to a straight woman's. A stripper can be a feminist, if she is one who wants either revenge on men or their total exclusion from her life.

In the long run hostility and exclusion were not what I wanted. So I had to consider the effects of stripping, not just on me but on men and women in general. Stripping reinforces the stereotype of women that came to bother me the most: that they can be bought. For a price, a stripper will pretend to be a kind of woman that doesn't exist outside the imagination—the naked, adoring, one-dimensional sex object. She creates the idea that a woman's appearance, behavior, and sexuality are for sale. For a few dollars, for a few minutes, she will be nothing but tall, busty, and blond.

I knew I had internalized this buyer-seller relationship when a friend said to me that while he liked the idea of naked women dancing around, he didn't like the idea of paying for it. My immediate reaction was disdainful. Of course you don't want to pay, I thought, you want it for free. This was a sex worker's reaction. I had accepted a lesson that I wished I hadn't—namely that a woman's appearance should have a price tag. I had submitted to the idea that a woman was *worth* looking at. I didn't want to think this way anymore. I wanted to think that a woman should wear, or not wear, whatever she liked— but that it shouldn't be a matter of money.

I had once been offended when a professor told me that I "got out" of stripping. I resented the implication that it was something I wanted-ed to escape. I had left the Lusty Lady several months earlier, and, far from swearing never to return, I looked back at it fondly.

Some three years later I related what my professor had said to Megan, a long-time dancer. I was still rankled by the presumption that all strippers must want out.

"No, he's right," Megan said. "You're lucky. You did get out."

Within months of returning to Seattle I had come to agree with her. I now thought of dancers in terms of when they would leave their jobs. And I had a disturbing realization: If I had escaped, as Megan suggested, did that mean that if I hadn't I might have ended up like Zoe? I had identified so strongly with her when we first met. I tried to imagine what would have happened if I had done things a little differently, if I had made some of the same decisions she had made. Suppose I had stayed in Seattle, not gone back to school, and continued to work at the L in the name of pursuing other goals. And suppose my other goals didn't pan out and I became more reliant on stripping, then found that it wasn't enough to live on. What if I found that there were other ways I could make money more easily than getting a straight job? The longer I stayed in, the more cynical I would become about men and sex, and the more I would push, then breach, my own boundaries.

I rejected this idea; I would not have taken Zoe's path. But I no longer believed that Zoe had chosen it, even though she said she had.

She still claimed to have selected her "ideal" lifestyle, for money, fun, and freedom. She said that she still told "other smart women" that they should get into parties. When they didn't take her up on it, she noted pityingly that they must have moral issues, or a lack of self-esteem, that prevented them from doing so. Because some women couldn't do what she did, she said she felt lucky, and she spoke of her abilities as a gift.

I just wanted her to quit. But who was I to have desires for her when she claimed to be pleased with her choices? There had been so many times when she had confounded me that I wasn't even sure who I was dealing with, as though I, like a customer, had had an idea of "Zoe" or "Cassandra" in my head that had not turned out to be real. After returning to Seattle, the feeling that I was getting to know her better was often punctuated with the disconcerting suspicion that I knew her less and less. This suspicion ballooned one night when my phone rang as I was getting into bed.

"I'm a friend of Cassandra's," a man's voice said. "She says you're really hot."

"Who is this?"

"I'm a friend of Cassandra's."

My first thought was that someone had stolen Zoe's address book and was calling numbers at random. The second was that someone had kidnapped her. He kept saying that he was with her, though, and finally I asked him to put her on the line.

Zoe was there, sort of. She was in the private pleasures booth, and he was in the customer compartment, across the glass. They had been calling people on his mobile. As soon as I confirmed that she was okay, I said good-bye and hung up. I couldn't believe she had given away my phone number. The next morning I was still trying to think of some motive or unusual circumstance that would have prompted her to do it.

"So what was last night all about?" I asked her when we met that day for coffee. At first she acted as if she didn't understand what I was referring to, then she brushed it off. There was nothing special about the customer, she said, except that he was into phone sex. She had met him just then when he walked into her booth. They had called me so that I would talk dirty with them.

Zoe frequently rocked my sense of normality, making me suddenly doubt my own instincts about what was right and wrong. Surely it wasn't right to give a friend's phone number to a peep-show customer. Or was it? I was so dizzied that I called other friends, explained the situation, and asked if I was right to be disturbed.

On an earlier occasion, when we were both living at Matt's after he had left for India, I found a note slipped under my bedroom door. "Hey Elisabeth," it read. "It's 12:45 A.M. and I'm headed to see Terry at the above address. If for some strange reason I don't turn up in the next 24 hours, start the search there."

Terry, I knew, was a private customer whom she had seen several times that week. I didn't know how I was supposed to react to the note, and questions were still running through my head when she turned up safe and sound the next day. Should I worry? Am I worrying *too* much? If it's really so dangerous, why does she keep doing it? And, suspiciously: Was she just trying to get my attention? After all, seeing customers was a part of her daily life, and she didn't slip a note under my door every day.

I had thought that her giving my phone number to a customer was a sort of last straw, and that she couldn't unsettle me more. But the final, disturbing surprise had come when she revealed that she was genuinely considering Gene's proposal to have sex for money. While the phone call had angered me, this idea left me sad and bewildered. She had been in the business a long time without taking this turn.

It would be a positive development, she said. Gene was very kind. He treated her much better than Caleb, Nick, and Mark had, or than Matt still did—for she and Matt were still having sex. I realized that I was upset because I thought something had been finally lost to her. I had always believed that sex should be chosen freely for itself. I had tried to stick to this principle since I was fifteen, and it was what I thought of now when I thought of Zoe. Any notion of sex being purely for herself was gone, and I realized that it must have been ebbing away for years.

Of course, I had sold my sexuality, my nakedness, and my words, but I hadn't seen this as the same as selling sex. Everyone had their boundaries, and the reasons behind them were as varied as personalities. For me the main division was between looking and touching, which was why I had recoiled from lap dancing and could never have worked parties. But I could be looked at, because I didn't necessarily connect looking sexual to having sex. Being looked at sexually was something that just happened, something I had learned to live with. It was removed from me as a person, which was why I could exploit and play with it. Having sex, though, was about me. I chose it.

Zoe, like me, had started out selling the right to look. And before that, we had both begun by wanting to make our own rules about how we would handle our sexuality. The problem was that breaking rules should have only been a first step: something had to be created to take their place. The sexual morality I grew up with was rife with inconsistency. It had words to insult promiscuous women but not men, it ticketed strippers but not their customers. It imposed on women, far more than on men, an intricate code of modesty that came down to a few inches of fabric, and then read a woman's clothing or lack thereof as an indication of character. I didn't want the morality that said I must cover my body, and that if I didn't I was responsible for whatever came my way. I didn't want the morality that said I should be coy and shameful about sex.

But while the rules I had inherited didn't serve me well, they still served me. I needed to have boundaries, and have them respected, and respect those of others. This was what I found so unsettling about Zoe—she wanted to wipe all the rules away. She had taken the process of breaking down boundaries to the extreme. At first she had willfully led a life unencumbered by the expectations of others. She had bought freedom in her life at large—freedom from a nine-to-five job, and freedom from having to choose one single role to play. But she had done it by conforming over and over again to an exacting, specific role—the sex object that says, in appearance and words, Pay me and I'll be what you want. Sometimes she struggled to pull herself back—she questioned what she was doing in the middle of a show, she decided not to use toys at parties, she burst into tears after watching Deena have sex with a customer. For a couple of years, she had shown energetic interest in finding other jobs. But, ultimately, I thought she had stopped choosing. She was earning a living that made choices for her. Honest decisions about boundaries and sexuality were impossible, because they had both become subservient to cash.

The money was corrupting. The part of stripping that I had found the most difficult had not been working the booth, or even lap dancing. It was working the floor of a club and providing all the false kindness that the customers expected in exchange for cash. Flattering a man with looks and words while I calculated what I could make off of him had made me palpably more cynical. Even more sinister, however, was the way the customers treated these exchanges as normal. They wanted fawning, illusive female charm, and they knew that it was for sale along with everything else.

In the end I decided that all sexuality for profit was insidious. Sooner or later, the effect of money would turn sex into something dishonest, and I didn't want that to happen to me. I realized I didn't want to live in a world where women's bodies, images, or characters were treated as something to buy. And so I quit.

But that was the easy part. To try to avoid the commercialization of sexuality altogether would be harder. Would it be possible, for example, never to use pornography? Never to take a job where flirtatiousness and a tight T-shirt would earn me more tips? To avoid buying things advertised with a woman's body? Or any of the millions of products that were supposed to make me look better? Would I never let a man bore me because he was buying me dinner and drinks? Would I dissent the next time a woman asked me to admire the conspicuous diamond that announced to the world she had been claimed? And could I be sure that I would never subtly cater, for my own gain, to the way a man wished I would look or behave?

Could I, once and for all, escape the idea that a woman's worth was in her looks?

I wasn't sure, but I could try.

*   *   *

Zoe cut the Thailand portion out of her winter travel plans. She had failed to register for teaching school in time and the program had filled up. She left Seattle in December of 2001 for Bali, where she traveled by bicycle and learned to scuba dive. From there she planned to move on to New Zealand and Australia. Zoe planned to continue working as a stripper for as long as she made money.

At the end of 2001 Abby finished a two-year degree in accounting and general business. The website she and Zoe had set up to advertise their party services continued to bring her a steady stream of customers, and she continued to work at the Lusty Lady once a week. She still had high hopes for abbyinbabeland.com, her monthly membership site, though it had not yet turned a profit. Nakedcascades.com hadn't either, and she was less optimistic about it. It turned out that websites could buy mass-produced pornography so cheaply that it was difficult to sell her higher-priced erotic art.

Abby didn't know when she would quit the sex industry, but she believed that stripping had improved her skills as a businesswoman, and that she would be the better for it when she left. She remained with her boyfriend Peter, and she fantasized sometimes about having many children and frolicking naked on the beach with her family.

Lara continued to work as a lap dancer at Déjà Vu, and occasionally as a photographer's assistant. She and Megan hadn't yet staged their no-holds-barred quitting day. Thanks to her lucrative months in Las Vegas, Lara was almost entirely out of debt with Jessica, and she felt closer to leaving stripping for good.

Kim started nursing school at the beginning of 2002. She expected to finish her studies in eighteen months—unless in that time she passed the fire department's physical test and was invited to train as a firefighter. She planned to quit the L when she graduated, but if it closed before then, which looked increasingly likely, she didn't plan to strip anywhere else.

While taking a full course load, Kim continued to max out at work. She stopped acquiring new debt and was able to just meet all her bill payments. Four months after she sold her eggs, the buyer had still not been successfully implanted. If the final attempt didn't work, she wanted to know if Kim would sell to her again. Kim told her that she was still game.

I went to Kim's airy blue-green palace on a sunny morning at ten o'clock. She let me in with the telephone receiver pressed to her shoulder, mimed apologies, and disappeared to finish her conversation. When I heard someone else coming down the stairs I assumed it was Zoe and turned to say hello, but instead found a strapping, smiling man in bare feet, sweatpants, and a T-shirt that stretched over his taut chest and arms. It was Doug, the firefighter. He shook my hand, introduced himself, and said he already knew who I was. By the time Kim got off the phone, Doug had told me in excited detail how they had met. She cut up fresh fruit and put it in a plastic container, which she insisted he take as he kissed her good-bye. I spent the next hour with her, and she was more animated than I had ever seen her. Between her money problems and her agonizing divorce, I had grown accustomed to seeing her in a state of stoic resignation. Now she was bursting with excitement, and it was a pleasure to watch.

I went back to the Lusty Lady one night after leaving friends in a nearby restaurant. A young man I didn't recognize sat behind the front desk in a "Have an erotic day!" T-shirt. I changed a five-dollar bill for quarters in the machine next to the desk and let myself into a customer booth. It was a two-way booth at the short end of the rectangular stage. To my immediate right was the one-way where I had first watched the show with Catharine, before my audition.

The stage looked smaller than I remembered. I had looked at it only rarely from the customer's point of view, and I always forgot how dark it appeared from down in the cubicles. The window was a dim red square framed in black, crossed by floating naked bodies. I thought about how the stage was when I was on it: the vivid red, the shining mirrored walls, and the closeness of the other women. I didn't recognize anyone onstage, but two dancers smiled at me, and one waved. I was special—a female customer. The stage entrance was at the far end from me, and I watched one dancer arrive while another one left. The one exiting spoke to the one entering as she passed, making her smile. The new dancer took the old one's place.

A woman came over and started dancing for me. She was slim, pale, and pretty, with straight brown locks hanging down her back and tufts of hair under her arms. She brought her face close to the window and asked me how I was. We couldn't hear each other very well.

"You should come work here," she said. For a moment I imagined myself stepping across the glass, as though I could enter my own reflection in a mirror. I felt that she was reaching out her hand and offering to pull me in.

"I already did," I said with a smile.

She nodded. I felt understood. A few seconds later she sauntered to another window and fixed her gaze on a man.

I stepped out into the gloomy hallway where two rows of black doors stretched away from me. A man in the hall jingled the change in his pocket. I could see crumpled trousers below the doors. The music, muffled by the windows, sounded faint and tinny. The stage still operated to the same mechanical rhythms of coin-operated windows and "on the zero" scheduling. *Hammering Man* still pounded away outside, blind and relentless. It was a static world. The Lusty Lady made me feel as if I could visit a former self, and I knew I would be sad if it closed.

But I no longer had any desire to go back. That was the reason, I realized while standing in the hall, that I had gone in—to test myself. When the woman onstage had crouched conspiratorially and smiled at me, an image of myself flashed briefly through my head. Glittering. High heeled. Naked. It lasted only for a second. I didn't feel the need to cross that artificial divide anymore. I didn't have to be the naked girl.

Acknowledgments

I would like to thank Samuel G. Freedman, Betsy Lerner, Peter Gethers, and Leyla Aker for helping to shape this book.

I am especially grateful to all the women and men who appear in these pages. Many of them opened their lives to me and trusted that I would tell their stories fairly, which I have tried to do.

And finally, I thank my parents for teaching me to explore, think, and work.

About the Author

SAFIA FATIMI

Elisabeth Eaves was born and raised in Vancouver. She has a master's degree in international affairs from Columbia University and has worked as a journalist for Reuters. She lives in Washington, D.C.

SELECTED TITLES
FROM SEAL PRESS

The F-Word: Feminism in Jeopardy by Kristin Rowe-Finkbeiner. $14.95, 1-58005-114-6. An astonishing look at the tenuous state of women's rights and issues in America, this pivotal book also incites women with voting power to change their situations.

Under Her Skin: How Girls Experience Race in America edited by Pooja Makhijani. $15.95, 1-58005-117-0. This diverse collection of personal narratives explores how race shapes, and sometimes shatters, lives—as seen through the fragile lens of childhood.

Secrets and Confidences: The Complicated Truth about Women's Friendships edited by Karen Eng. $14.95, 1-58005-112-X. This frank, funny, and poignant collection acknowledges the complex relationships between girlfriends.

Cinderella's Big Score: Women of the Punk and Indie Underground by Maria Raha. $15.95, 1-58005-116-2. Women not only rock as hard as the boys, but they also test the limits of what is culturally acceptable in this tribute to the women of punk rock.

Without a Net: The Female Experience of Growing Up Working Class edited by Michelle Tea. $14.95, 1-58005-103-0. The first anthology in which women with working-class backgrounds explore how growing up poor impacts identity.

Body Outlaws: Rewriting the Rules of Beauty and Body Image edited by Ophira Edut, foreword by Rebecca Walker. $15.95, 1-58005-108-1. Filled with honesty and humor, this groundbreaking anthology offers stories by women who have chosen to ignore, subvert, or redefine the dominant beauty standard in order to feel at home in their bodies.

Cunt: A Declaration of Independence by Inga Muscio. $14.95, 1-58005-075-1. An ancient title of respect for women, "cunt" long ago veered off the path of honor and now is considered an expletive. Muscio traces this winding road, giving women both the motivation and the tools to claim "cunt" as a positive and powerful force in the lives of all women.

Seal Press publishes many books of fiction and nonfiction by women writers. Please visit our website at www.sealpress.com.